TOP STICK

WITH SOME HELP FROM A GUARDIAN ANGEL

HAROLD A JACOBS

ISBN: 1-4033-5924-5 (e-book)
ISBN: 1-4033-5925-3 (Paperback)

Library of Congress Control Number: 2002093562

This book is printed on acid free paper.

Printed in the United States of America
Bloomington, IN

1stBooks – rev. 12/06/02

1stBooks Library
Bloomington, Indiana

17545 Drayton Hall Way
San Diego CA. 92128
Tel: 858 485-9422
e-mail: jakes43k@aol.com

Printed in the United States of America

This book is dedicated to my wife

Madeline R Jacobs

For her steadfast support and patience in this lengthy effort

& to

Our children, Marla, James and Kerstin

& to

Our eight grandchildren

===============

ABOUT THE AUTHOR

Harold A Jacobs is a retired Air Force Lt Colonel whose entire career was in the field of aviation. Though trained as a single engine pilot in the AAF class of 43-K, he and his entire class were assigned to multi-engine aircraft upon graduation. He first served as an instrument flight instructor, then as a four engine C-54 transport pilot in Casablanca, French Morocco, Cairo, Egypt, Karachi, India, Paris, France, and Rhein-Main Air Base, Frankfurt, Germany. He then flew B-29s and B-50s on long range reconnaissance missions. He also served as a reconnaissance operations officer at Wing and Command Headquarter levels.

In 1955 he was honored to serve on the original U.S. Air Force Academy staff at Lowry Air Force Base, Colorado.

After 21 years active duty with the USAF he retired from the Air Force and then worked two years as an aircraft accident investigator for the National Transportation Safety Board. The next 15 years were spent as an FAA Air Carrier Operations Inspector (check-pilot) in the B-707s and DC-10s at Northwest Orient Airlines, in Minneapolis, Minnesota. His flying experiences were varied and global as he amassed over 15,000 hours of flying time.

He and his wife, Madeline, married 51 years, reside in San Diego, California.

INTRODUCTION

Why write a book? Having written many documents and staff studies as an officer in the Air Force, and as an aircraft accident investigator for the National Transportation Safety Board and all kinds of correspondence while with the Federal Aviation Administration, one would think I would have had enough. When I asked my three children, Marla, Jim and Kerstin, if I had ever told them of the Great Depression and the Big War they learned at an early age to make a hasty retreat. Perhaps someday they will enjoy reading about old Dad's experiences .I started an outline many years ago when I opened an old foot locker and found a treasure chest of material. My mother had saved every letter, newspaper clipping and picture she had received through the years of my military service. I had also saved a huge box of military flight and personnel orders, and like all Air Force pilots, I had my Form V, a record of all my flights from training days to retirement. I had all the material for a book!

In reviewing this treasure trove, nostalgia ran rampant. I quickly realized that nostalgia begets memories, which in turn expands and confirms more and new memories.

However, let's cut to the chase: I had a rather unusual and near fantastic military career. It was not because of heroics on my part, or because of unusual bravery or courage. It was most unusual simply because some great opportunities came down the pike and presented themselves to me. Serendipity, some call it. Being a most inquisitive type, and having a bent for challenge, I would invariably go for it-whenever the opportunity presented itself.

One might say that the title chosen for the book is immodest, too bravado or vain-glorious. It really is not. I was awarded the title, but I must admit that it was my lucky day, or karma descended on me when I was assigned the very finest advanced flying instructor. We were always on the same frequency, and our personalities meshed; thus the award. And that's the way things went, by and large, through the years. Everything kept coming up roses.

My story is a period piece and told with the mindset of a young 21-25 year old pilot. It is factual and true to the best of my ability. As the Brits would say, "There's no duff gen in the book; it's all pukka gen!"(Good stuff) But I think that just maybe, Lindy, when flying the airmail between St Louis and Chicago, may have sprinkled just a dab of lucky dust on me as he flew over our farm in Lacon, Illinois.

FORWARD

As you read Hal Jacobs' account of his wartime service, you will see that he was a standout in flying. His record shows that. But you will get more from his writing than just a wartime flying memoir.

As an author, Hal Jacobs brings us a unique view of a number of aspects of the war that don't appear in other journals—wonderful accounts of cadet hazing in Preflight School in San Antonio, TX, his RAF flight training experiences, vivid descriptions and historical backgrounds of wartime activities which took place in localities unrecognized by most students of World War II. No Omaha Beaches or Iwo Jimas here. And the reader will discover that Americans served in places that were totally unknown to the general public.

Through Hal Jacobs, you will meet these forgotten soldiers in out-of-the-way, even exotic, locales. While there are enough stirring flying adventures in TOP STICK to satisfy any aviation fan, the author gives us a bonus ride through history and cultures of ancient societies, all mixed in with modern warfare.

Grab a seat and hang on for a great reading experience.

Charles A Watry Colonel, USAF, Retired
Carlsbad, California May 2002

TOP STICK
WITH SOME HELP FROM A GUARDIAN ANGEL

CHAPTER I
THE SPARK

I was just a sprig of a lad, a bit under six when Lindy flew the Atlantic, solo, and became the century's first international hero; an instant star. Four to five million people lined New York City streets to welcome the young 25-year-old hero upon his return home. I knew that earlier he surely must have flown over our farm many times flying the mail between St Louis and Chicago as he followed the Illinois River. I was convinced that many of those airplanes I ran outside to spot had to have been Lindy. So let's say that on a scale of from one to ten, I was a very clear ten in my desire to fly, with my eye on the sky and a great big dream in my heart.

My first plane ride would not be made until after I got out of high school. I had every intention of going "up" before that, but my mother always intervened as she thought flying was unsafe. One year I had tentative and somewhat reserved approval from my mother to take a flight. A pilot by the name of Ken Ringle would fly to Lacon, Illinois, my home town, for our Old Settlers' Picnic celebration each August and hop rides in his biplane. He had the helmet, goggles, Army Aviator style jodhpurs and boots, besides many scars on his face and brow. He was a real hero to me. He had crashed many times, I was sure. Well, in 1935 I had saved my pennies, nickels and dimes for the $1.00 ride. However, it was not meant to be. As often happens, well laid plans go amiss. Wiley Post and his very famous passenger, cowboy and columnist Will Rogers, crashed on take-off at Point Barrow, Alaska and both were killed. My parents revered Will Rogers, so his death totally zapped my chances for the plane ride.

The home and buildings of our farm just outside of Lacon were all new and large. We had city water, electricity and even an extra telephone in the barn. The three youngest of seven children were born on this farm and it was a lovely setting for a growing boy.

In about 1925 my Dad, who bred Polled Hereford cattle, attended a stock show in Kansas City with some other stock men from our area. He greatly admired a Hereford bull but felt he could not afford it. He returned home without the bull, however, after arriving home, he felt he had missed a great opportunity. so took the next train back

1

to Kansas City and purchased the bull, Disturber the Fourth. It was his prize bull for several years. Disturber's lady friends reportedly dropped beautiful calves. Through the years my Dad liked to expound upon Disturber's performance in the breeding arena and upon his wonderful progeny, although, I believe, that Disturber nearly killed my Dad, on one of his bad days; the bull's, that is. Disturber, however, was not man enough to save the farm when the big crash of 1929 came and the Depression took off with a vengeance.

In 1930, after the start of the Depression, we moved from the lovely farm to a very small farm on the outskirts of nearby Sparland, Illinois, just across the Illinois River. For us younger three it was the first time we'd experienced no electricity, no running water, no bathroom and we were introduced to the outdoor privy. What a change! I well remember the first night in that house; my mother, who was an unusually courageous woman, broke down and cried as I had never seen her cry before. I am sure there were a host of reasons for that rush of sadness and feeling of being overwhelmed, but lighting the kerosene lamps touched it off. She finally laughed, saying that it was so silly of her to feel bad since she had grown up without electricity and was very used to light by lamps. As young as we were, we knew there was more to it than that. Just as in millions of homes in America at that time, all facets of life seemed to have totally collapsed around families and communities, and the outlook was very bleak indeed. Though I was only in third grade, I remember it well. (One year later we moved to a nearby home and we again had the modern conveniences.)

In retrospect, I cannot imagine how we got along as well as we did. I would chalk it up to faith, hope, and perseverance, especially as embraced by my mother, who was a very religious woman. She practiced in everyday living the concept of brotherly love. For example, when I was a youngster we had "tramps" or "hobos" who came to the back door for handouts, usually asking for a sandwich. I think our house was marked as we had many of them and we noticed that they only hit certain houses. One day a man came and asked for some food. My mother told him that she was not prepared to give him a sandwich; she had no provisions from which to make a sandwich; she had only bread and butter. Nevertheless, she prepared a bread and butter sandwich and a glass of milk; the man was happy with that and went on his way. I think that she could not imagine turning away a beggar and I never saw her refuse one.

Jobs in a small town were very difficult to come by and were short lived. My older brother, Merriman, though a teenager, was a fine mechanic and he worked in a garage. He generously shared his income with the family, which helped immensely. When I was old enough, I got a paper route pedaling the *Peoria Star*. I made a penny on each paper and I had about thirty customers, spread three miles apart. On each Sunday paper I made three cents. Many people would default on paying simply because they didn't have the 25 cents that week. Most were nice folks and I felt I could not cut off their delivery. Being somewhat naive, I felt it was not the Christian thing to do and sometimes I had a hard time paying my paper bill. However, if the lady of the house was baking cookies and I could smell them, I was cagey enough to compliment her on the aroma wafting forth from the kitchen, and I usually received a cookie or two. How could you stop the paper on such a sweet little old lady? But that cookie or two didn't pay my bill.

My first experience with a labor union was at a very tender age. There was a large truck garden farm about six miles south of our small town. It was the Boehle Fruit and Vegetable Farm. Kids in my town could earn "big bucks." Mr. Boehle was from Germany and he believed in the work-ethic principal to the nth degree. He had a large family, and all of his children worked the fields along with the hired help. String beans and strawberries were two large crops that needed fast action and hired hands. Ten or twelve-year-olds worked there, and we could earn almost a dollar a day. One day when about ten of us were working diligently picking green beans while toting our peck baskets, one boy started to complain about how hard we worked and how his back was killing him. He was Pete, from Chicago, spending the summer with relatives. He was older than most of us, perhaps sixteen, and he knew all about unions. He elected himself to be our leader and spokesman and decided we would not be slaves any longer. Most of us agreed with him about the aching back and very sore knees, but were a bit doubtful as to his cock-sureness. His opportunity came when Mr. Boehle drove down to pick up a load of freshly-picked green beans. This brash kid from the Windy City faced up to Mr. Boehle and demanded we get 14 cents a peck for our labor instead of the lowly eight cents a peck. There was no pause, there were no negotiations whatsoever. Mr. Boehle in his best English said, "You little sons-o-bitches get your ass off my land right now, and don't ever come 'round again. I haul these beans to the market in Peoria and only get 15 cents a peck…you are idiots!"

As my little brother Michael and I headed for home, the realization that we had blown a wonderful deal formed in our small brains. When we arrived home, my mother, concerned about our early return home, asked what had happened. We informed her that we had formed a union and had gone on strike and had been fired on the spot. She advised us that what we had done was wrong. She wanted us to return to the Boehle farm and ask Mr. Boehle to take us back; to tell him that we really were not thinking clearly and were sorry. So down the road we go—only six miles,—and approached Mr. Boehle with fear and trepidation. He was a big man and quite gruff. As I was three years older than brother Mike, I naturally was the spokesman. We were probably quite a sight at that point; skinny, straw hat, bare feet, sun-burned to a fare-thee-well, and really scared! After I made my apologetic presentation, Mr. Boehle, who very much needed hired help, simply said, "Ok, you look like you mean it, get your butts out there in the bean field and start pickin'. And I don't want any more trouble out of you!" I'm sure after we took off with our baskets he had himself a good laugh. I don't think there was a mean bone in his body. Our strike had failed. To this day I have never joined a union and have held union leaders in low esteem. Michael and I love to rehash this episode and recall how, on that day, we learned all we ever needed to know about the basics of labor-relations.

My father worked part time on the state highway. He got the job because he was a good Democrat. We had a Democrat for governor; Henry Horner. Henry demanded recompense, and at election time it was mandatory for my dad to kick in twenty dollars or more to help win the election. Twenty dollars was a small fortune, but it had to be "donated" or the job would go to another who would pay it. My father also took care of the village water system and ran for township assessor and won, though there were few Democrats in the township.

Neither job paid a hefty wage. My second eldest brother Peter worked in a filling station part time. If an adult could make one or two dollars a day he considered himself lucky. Many people, including "talking historians" today think that FDR did a miraculous job of turning the Depression around in the thirties. From where I viewed things, he did not quite accomplish that feat. The mid and late thirties were extremely tough on families, due to the Dust Bowl, two extremely hot and dry summers, and a scourge of bugs that decimated the corn fields in several areas of the Midwest. Though we were not officially in the heart of the dust bowl, there were many days when the sky was a yellowish-gray and one could taste the dust in the air.

In the mid-thirties my two older brothers left for Civilian Conservation Corps Camps. My eldest brother's assignment was not a choice one; he went to Mound, Illinois, where there was nothing more exciting than a few Indian burial grounds. My second older brother, was luckier; he went to Oregon and then northern California where he worked in the big timber at building roads. CCC members were paid 30 dollars a month; they were entitled to keep five dollars and their parents received twenty-five dollars. That's the way it was; FDR said so. Of the many programs that were laid-on by the administration to help the unemployed find work during the Depression the 3Cs was one of the best and most productive.

After graduating in the famous "class of '39" (famous because we were the biggest class to ever graduate from our high school, and because we said so) I worked at the state duck shooting grounds on the Illinois River through the duck and goose hunting seasons. Like my brothers, my salary was one dollar per day. I then moved to Starved Rock State Park, Illinois, some 30 miles from home, where I worked as a waitress assistant, i.e. one step above a bus boy. I worked for a wealthy Greek restaurateur. My wage was again one dollar per day but, with board and room. I did earn tips, but ten or twenty cents was a normal tip; not too great. The waitresses pooled ten percent of their total tips for the day and we assistants and bus boys divided it. The job was hard in that we worked from 6:30 a.m. until 10:00 p.m., with a one or two hour break between meals. Mr. Nicholas Spiros, who leased the beautiful lodge, cabins, and large dining room from the State, (all built by the CCC boys), seemed to like my work and offered me the proposition that if I would stay, he'd work me through the various jobs and I would end up, perhaps, in a position of general manager. I definitely knew I wanted to be a pilot. I knew too, I had to attend college for two years to qualify for pilot training, so Mr. Spiros' offer though flattering, was not at all tempting. My plan had been to lay-out of college for a year to earn money to attend. I had done that successfully. I was a frugal guy, but I felt pretty rich when I had a five or ten dollar bill in my pocket. College would change that feeling quickly.

I left for Monmouth College, Monmouth, Illinois, in late August 1940, a no-smoking, no-drinking, no-nonsense Presbyterian school; the same college an older brother, Pete, was attending, and from which my sister Lola had just graduated. It was a fine college that had opened in 1853; it was one of the many colleges in the Midwest Conference, all built mid-century.

At college I worked 44 hours a week as a janitor, elevator operator and as a furnace stoker. Once again my pay was one dollar per day, plus room, but the job was one of the best for a guy at that college.

We three Jacobs kids had scholarships, but we all found it necessary to borrow money. We borrowed from the Methodist Book Concern at two and one-half percent interest. I was very concerned having a loan debt. Being steeped in the financial rigors of the Depression, a debt was to be avoided at all costs. Our mother urged that the loan be paid off in the quickest possible time after we left college, and it was. I paid back during flying school; not much, but $6.00 each month was more than adequate, considering I made only $75 a month. After I won my wings, I paid off the loan within the first year of my becoming a wealthy second lieutenant. Compare this with to-day's scenario where tens of thousand of dead-beat students owe money to the tune of over two billion dollars. And though some have well-paying, professional jobs, they apparently have no intention of paying off their loans, provided the tax-payers pick up the tab.

In retrospect, I cannot imagine how two parents managed to get seven kids through school, including college for four, during the Depression. Many other parents also did it, but I only know the intimate details about our family. Our parents grew up before and at the turn of the twentieth century, starting their working years soon after the end of the Industrial Revolution (1890). They were made of really fine stuff, as were so many of that period. They went through the Great War, The Depression and then World War II; all extremely stressful times. Our parents persevered, endured, and pressed on. All of their offspring seemed to wax strong, became married and raise families, moving on to become solid, successful citizens. We, their children have great admiration for the part they played in promoting and sustaining the American Dream in their own limited sphere. Looking back from our advanced years, we observe that we never suffered, nor were ever hungry. Yes, we wore some hand-me-down clothes, as did our friends, and three of us shared a second-hand bicycle for a while. But what kid didn't endure a few hardships during the thirties. We were, by and large, as neat, clean and respected as the other kids in our community. Some of our friends and class-mates were not so fortunate. Our parents, Michael and Bess, through thick and thin, did us proud. How lucky we seven were to have had them for parents.

America was molded into a great nation by solid citizens like my folks and their generation. In all honesty, I do not agree with Tom Brokaw who wrote the book, The *Finest Generation*, and aimed his accolades at my generation of World War II. I vote for our parents' generation as the very finest generation. They had all the trials and tough roads that my WWII generation had, and then some. They had moved up through their early years with-out electricity, plumbing, or paved roads. They endured their childhood days in the '80s and 90s as many of the huge advances were made in all walks of life. Yes, the land was broken and tilled to some extent, but it was my parents group who rapidly moved things along from the horse and buggy era to the era of John Deere machinery. They mechanized and improved the farms in leaps and bounds, built the rural gravel roads and the paved highways and made the small towns flourish. They worked very hard and struggled through a lengthy period of tough times.

In reflecting about the effects of the depression on my generation, I believe that the Depression was possibly a positive factor in our lives. We had great fun in our youth, but, by age seventeen or eighteen we became quite serious minded. A guy named Adolph

Hilter helped move us in that direction as we listened to him rant on the radio in our school assembly hall in 1938-39.

It was in 1937 and 1938, when Army Air Corps leaders started to clamor loud and clear for a build-up of air power. It was then that I had read an article in either the American or Liberty magazine about the Air Corps Flying Cadet Program. It was a lengthy and complete article with lots of colored pictures of blue and yellow training planes and a depiction of the life of a Flying Cadet at Randolph Field, Texas. Could you believe it? Any red-blooded, healthy young American boy could get into this program and become a second lieutenant with the silver wings of the U.S.Army Air Corps, and it did not cost a dime! In fact the little pamphlet which I mailed for, and still have today, tells that the pay and allowances are: $75 per month pay, in addition to this a one dollar per day ration allowance. Modern barracks are provided to the cadets as well as necessary uniforms, books and flying togs.

In 1938, the Depression had still been in full swing and money was always the prime consideration for any educational pursuit. The Air Corps offer to learn to fly at government expense was totally electrifying and almost unbelievable. I had been an immediate convert. On-the-spot, I formed a single goal. I'd finish high school, get two years of college, with lots of mathematics and sciences, pass the physical and I would be a part of that great Army Air Corps Flying Cadet Adventure! I would become a pilot by taking the same training my idol, Charles Lindbergh, had taken.

In the late summer of 1939, when I worked at Starved Rock State Park Lodge as a bus boy, I went down to a little airstrip in nearby Utica, Illinois, and put down my two dollars for my first plane ride. The airstrip was a small, insignificant clearing of clipped alfalfa. The pilot was nothing like Lindy, my boyhood hero. The plane was a simple J-3 Cub, but when we lifted off of that alfalfa strip I was in heaven. We had defied gravity and were climbing out over the beautiful Illinois River Valley. It was truly a fabulous sight to behold. Never mind the totally nonchalant pilot who walked with me out to the aircraft as though he were going out to gather eggs; I was on cloud nine and all aquiver. It was all that I had expected, plus much more. My resolve to become a pilot had just received a super shot in the arm!

Now this all may sound somewhat fanciful and romanticized. Perhaps it is, to a degree, but not too much so. I was one of those very fortunate young guys who knew, without a doubt, what he wanted to do with his life. There was a myriad of things that I did not know about the life of a career Air Corps Officer, but typically for my youthful age, it did not enter my mind at all. Flying was to be my career and the path was clearly laid out by the U.S. Army Air Corps. I would simply adjust everything else to their program, and all the bits and pieces would quite naturally fall into place. Ah, Youth!

The world scene changed dramatically in 1939. The war clouds gathered, darkened and Hitler, who had built his vast military forces, unleashed them against Poland. The French were totally laid-back and England, particularly Prime Minister Chamberlain, was still dithering and speaking of "Peace in Our Time." Things came unglued at an astounding rate.

The war in Europe did not affect my plans. It simply added purpose to them, and may have made the path somewhat easier. I had entered Monmouth College and embarked on a physics, chemistry and math program. And then a gift appeared from my guardian angel; a government flight program began in 1940 at many colleges across the land. It was called the Civilian Pilot Training Program or CPT. It was a winner. It came about because of the foresight of visionaries like General Hap Arnold. The aim was to get as many young men (and a few women) interested in aviation as soon as possible, in anticipation of the conflict that many foresaw. Any college student, who could pass the flying physical and had five dollars to pay for the physical, could sign up. I had the five dollars, passed the physical in June, 1941, and stayed in Monmouth in my college, money-producing job.

My flight instructor was Leonard Buckler, who had been flying since about 1920. He was a fine instructor; a huge bear of a man with a gentle demeanor. My slim frame gave him ample room in the side-by-side seating in the little Aeronca Super Chief. The powerful sixty-horsepower engine performed just fine for the paces he put me through. My training progressed without a hitch; the plane was new, and we had no maintenance delays. One day, after I had acquired a total of about eight hours of dual training, and had made three or four

9

landings that forenoon, Mr. Buckler stopped after a taxi-back and very causally climbed out and said, "Take her around alone, son, you'll do fine." Quite naturally my heart-beat picked up its pace, my throat became dry and my stomach filled with butterflies.

My solo take-off would be to the east over the city park on what we called the cornstalk runway. The runway was a simple grass strip with corn planted on both sides. In the park that day there was some sort of a celebration and there were loudspeakers playing the hits of the day. Helen O'Connell was singing with the Jimmy Dorsey Band, "Those Cool and Limpid Green Eyes," Bob Eberly joined in. Life was a blast; so great to be alive.

I swung the little bird into the wind and pointed it down the grass strip. I advanced the throttle on the mighty sixty- horsepower Continental engine and the little Aeronca Chief literally shot into the air. I exceeded my pattern altitude by about two or three hundred feet because Mr. Buckler and his 275 pounds were down on the ground. Yipes! I had broken the shackles of mother earth. I had done it alone. I was free!

After three landing and a taxi back, I was congratulated by all who were around the small airport. Helen O'Connell was again singing "Those Cool and Limpid Green Eyes." Even today, when I hear that song, I'm transported back to that time; a cheerful, exuberant, lanky kid, parachute banging on my butt, and the great day of my first solo flight. And, yes, that song will always be a winner for those of us from the "Big Band Days."

The CPT course progressed at a very steady pace. We had practically no weather delays. It was soon time for the check-ride for our private pilot's license. The ride was given by Art Curry, the owner of the flight training school and operator of the airport at Galesburg, Illinois. Of course Mr. Buckler's recommendation for the check ride indicated that he felt we were safe and prepared.

Once again, I took off down the cornstalk runway, as I'd done on my first solo flights, but now with Mr. Curry, a CAA designee examiner aboard. Over the city park he pulled back the throttle and said "forced landing." No sweat, Mr. Buckler had done the same thing several times and western Illinois in July is loaded with ample stubble fields, after the oat and wheat harvest. I continued into the wind and headed for a nearby field. When Mr. Curry knew that I had the landing safely assured, he poured the coal on and I continued the climb-out. At about 1,000 feet he repeated the forced landing. I had no trouble getting set-up for a nice approach to another very adequate field. He then said, "Take me back to the airport and give me a good landing." I did both, and that was it. That's all there was to my check ride; some ten to twelve minutes and fifteen to twenty items that were usually a part of a check ride had been totally omitted. We joked later that the shorter the flight, the less gas burned and the more profit in Art Curry's pocket. But we certainly didn't complain about it. I felt pretty honored; my so-called check ride was the shortest of the group, which probably meant absolutely nothing at all.

With the flying course over, it was a very short time until my sophomore year was to begin. My summer break was gone, but I was very proud of my newly won private pilot's license, acquired in only 64 days and just as I turned twenty years old.

My private pilot's number is 95,916 which is note-worthy today when the numbers are in the millions.

In my second year, I continued with the same scholastic pursuits, was again "rushed" by the ATO fraternity, and I pledged. I was somewhat lukewarm about fraternities, but since I did not live on the campus I felt it would be an opportunity to get better acquainted with some of my classmates. The school was very well represented by national fraternities and sororities. Hell-Week was absolute hell, just as advertised. Nevertheless, I survived and enjoyed the friendship and the social activities, and have long since forgotten and forgiven most of the unpleasant happenings of that very "bad week."

On 7 December 1941, I was out at the frat house. I lived downtown, but usually went to the frat house for the big Sunday dinner and a bit of socializing with my frat brothers. Monmouth College had a strict no drinking policy, so do not assume that this was a wild afternoon as in *Animal House*. We had just finished our big meal of venison (provided by an alumni member) and were up in the main living room area for our annual picture. Right after the photographer had copied our handsome mugs in his big Speed Graphic camera for posterity, one of the guys who lived there went up to his room and turned on the radio. He raced down the stairs

11

screaming, "THE JAPS HAVE BOMBED PEARL HARBOR!!" Of course, everyone who was over six or eight years old at that time can relate to all the details of that tragic day. When I look at that group picture in recent years, I say to myself, "The expressions on our young faces gives no clue, of how the expressions would change a few moments later." Some of those very young men were dead within the year.

The next morning, the entire student body held assembly in the college chapel. We listened intently to the stirring and impassioned words of Franklin Delano Roosevelt as he addressed the U.S. Congress and the American people, saying, "a day that will live in infamy...the American people in their righteous might will win to absolute victory." Few if any of us realized the tremendous, tumultuous tomorrows that from that moment on were to come our way. The President's message, asking for a declaration of war was at 12:30 p.m. Two and one-half hours later the U.S. Senate had approved it unanimously and the House vote was 388-1. FDR signed the Declaration of War at 4:10 p.m. The whole procedure took only three hours and forty-five minutes.

What to do? Many of the patriots ran right down and signed up. I had one semester to finish to complete my required two years to qualify for pilot training. It was a puzzling time for most of us. I went home for Christmas break and discussed it all with my folks and also with some of my friends. My parents, greatly troubled by the war, were basically isolationists and pacifists, a very common mind-set for Midwesterners at that time. However, they were also realists and knew we had a war to fight, and knew they had four sons in a stand-by mode. But my mother just hated to hear me say that I wanted to be a fighter pilot, and couldn't wait to get into combat; so I toned that down somewhat. Slowly, like all parents, they realized that they were going to have to relinquish their offspring to the war effort.

Two close hometown friends, who were also in college, wanted to become flying cadets someday. We had talked of it on many occasions in previous months. The two, Dippy Jury and Don Fleming, had both finished their first two years of college and planned to apply soon. I went back to Monmouth and decided to finish my second year. I also planned to take a secondary flying course at Knox College in the spring semester. This secondary course was also a government-sponsored (CPT) flying course in nearby Galesburg, Illinois. I'd have to hitch-hike.

A short time later, another change threw some doubt into my thinking. The AAF changed the requirements for entering the Aviation Cadet Program. Two years of college were no longer mandatory. One only had to pass a battery of tests. After juggling this whole picture for several days, I decided to stick with my plan to finish the semester. I wanted to have those two years locked in, just in case someone in Washington, D.C. decided to change the rules.

It was a very rough five months. I worked 44 hours per week. Four of us did all the janitor work in a large doctor's office building. We also had to run the elevator. One dentist gave us free dental care. A chiropodist took care of our foot problems. A naturopath got rid of my sinus problems. Four doctor performed tonsillectomies in their office. (Their waste baskets were the pits.) A big argument among us was who was going to get stuck cleaning the spittoons. Yes, cuspidors were still used in 1942. Three doctors were osteopaths. We liked their offices, which we could whip through in short order.

In addition to my job, I carried a full seventeen-hour load at college and also had to hitch-hike to Galesburg, Illinois, some 20 miles, to fly the Waco UPF-7 in the Secondary CPT acrobatic course. In addition we had to attend ground school in the evenings at Knox College.

In looking back on this episode, I don't know how I ever managed to keep it all airborne. Naturally my grades plummeted. There were three other boys who were doing the same thing, but they were "Townies" and lived at home. The flying course was mostly acrobatics and precision rudiments. It was a thrilling course. The aircraft was a big biplane and very similar to the well-known Stearman.

Even with my limited flying experience, I realized that my flight instructor was a real lightweight. I think he suffered from "fear of flying." He seldom went aloft with me after I soloed. He would, however, assure himself that I was reading the manual and that I had a pretty good idea how to do a Split-S, an Immelmann, a Slow-Roll, and a Cuban Eight. He would always caution me to be very careful.

13

When I finished a flight and reported back to my instructor, he would carefully make an entry in his log, just as though he had flown with me. We had all heard of Parker-51 time, and of course it was dubbed P-51 time. Thank God for my very fine Primary instructor. He had taught me well enough so that I managed to stay out of serious trouble in the big biplane. We all finished the 40-hour flying course successfully.

One lovely spring day, a couple of handsome Navy fly-boys visited the college Student Union and handed out leaflets on becoming a Naval Aviation Cadet. Two of my buddies who were in the Secondary CPT program with me were captivated by the Navy pilots. Before long I was swayed too. One was Lester Earp, Wyatt Earp's great-nephew, and the other lad was Mort Pratt. The U.S. Navy had us hooked, and together the three of us decided that flying from the deck of a carrier would be far more glamorous than just off a Solomon Island runway. Also the uniform was snappy and could easily turn a farm boy into quite a cool, and maybe even a handsome, aviator.

In March, we hitch-hiked to St.Louis to sign up as a Navy Aviation Cadet. They both passed their physicals, but I ran into a problem. I was 6'3" and about 149 pounds soaking-wet; somewhat slim (like Charles Lindbergh, of course). The examining Navy physician said, "Hey young fellow, what's going on here? Your pulse is racing like mad, and your blood pressure is sky-high." I said something like, "I'm very nervous and anxious, as I really want to be a Navy pilot. But part of it is my schedule; it's out of sight!" I then very briefly told him my school schedule, my work schedule, and how we had to dash back and forth (via the thumb) to Galesburg for the Secondary flight course. He really listened to me (surprise,) and seemed genuinely interested. Perhaps it reminded him of his days in medical school. He accepted my reasons and finished the examination by saying, "When school is out and you can stop running yourself into the ground, come back and see us, but you must put on three more pounds."

I was crushed. Earp & Mort were "IN" and I had flunked, or was at least delayed. I was really in the dumps as we hitch-hiked the 100 miles back north to Monmouth. My two buddies were on their way to a great Navy Pilot career and I was, well, who knows?

(Les Earp became a Marine Corps pilot and survived the war. Later he and his wife became missionaries in the Philippines. Morton Pratt also survived as a Navy pilot and returned home to his farm in Illinois.)

By the time school was out I had put on the required three pounds, but since my bond with the other two was now broken, I said to myself, "Why go to St Louis? I'll go to Peoria and talk to the Army Air Corps. I did that, at the Aviation Cadet Examining Board #7, the Federal Building in Peoria, Illinois. They liked my mind, my body and my spirit. All of the parts were in sync and working in unison. My pulse and blood pressure passed muster, though I was vibrating with eagerness. All of that physics and math helped me to pass the battery of tests, which I had to take just like the boys who didn't have day-one of college. The examining officer told us that of 100 young men who walk in off the street to apply, no more than six or eight would win their silver wings. I had made it to the launching pad and I was walking on air. Though they could see I was chomping at the bit, they said to me and a very small group of others who had passed the stiff written test, "Go home, and we'll call you!" WOW!

Weeks dragged on, and I was getting highly impatient. 1942 was drawing to a close and, if the Army Air Corps didn't get off its duff and call me to training, the war was going to be over and catch me waiting in the corn country of Illinois. I wanted to be a part of this conflict! Finally, on 6 February 1943, word came, by letter, "Report to 515 So. Franklin Street, Chicago, at 0900 hours on 10 February '43." I had waited a long six months for this!

The day to depart arrived. I was very excited and happy, naturally. My parents were probably happy that the long agonizing wait was over. I know I had been somewhat impatient and hard to live with during the last month or so. But when the day of departure came, I, like most young guys leaving for military training, was treated with great respect and affection. Several of the neighbor ladies for whom I had worked as a kid shoveling snow, mowing lawns, carrying in coal and hauling out ashes, came by and most wanted to assure that I had at least a small copy of the New Testament to keep me on the straight and narrow. My Aunt Tillie gave me a nice sewing kit and someone gave me a money belt, which I seldom used.

15

I was the first of our family to enter the service. It is amazing how some episodes in one's life remain in the memory drum so vividly. My departure for the service is one such instance. As I was about to leave to go to the railroad station, not too far from our home, emotions were running high. My mother, a most loving and caring person, wanted to give me a little gift of sorts. The AAF had instructed me to bring a bare minimum; like a change of shorts and a small shaving kit. My mother hustled around and cut a piece of wool cloth from a pair of old trousers, and said, "Here Buddy (a family nickname), you're going to need a good hard cloth to keep your shoes shined." She was fighting back the tears as she busied herself with this small task. It was of course a simple gesture but symbolic of a very loving Mom. The departure was a most poignant moment in my young life, as our family of nine was very close knit. But then, I was off to win my Silver Wings! That celebrated shoe shine cloth is still in my shoe-shine box today, decades later. It still works great! It will not be retired!

I boarded the 5:45 Rock Island Railroad train, and was in La Salle Street Station in Chicago at 8:30 p.m. My brother Pete met me. I stayed overnight with him, reporting the next morning in a large warehouse-type building in the Loop. At about 1000 hours, after the recruits drifted in, an officer came in, called roll and explained to us what our schedule was to be. We then went upstairs to the 8th floor to a big mess hall and had our first Army chow. It was a very good meal, huge portions and it was heavvveee—The depression was over!

At 1 p.m. (1300 hours) we trooped in our civvies in a somewhat disorganized fashion, through light snow flurries, down Franklin St. to the Dearborn Station. There, approximately four hundred of us boarded a sixteen-car Pullman train, which included two dining cars. I imagine that the vast majority of our gang, like me, had never been in a first class rail car before.

We were not allowed off the train until we were in San Antonio, Texas, even though in many of the small towns in Missouri and Oklahoma there were people at the rail station who wanted to visit with us. The girls in the small crowds wanted to pass their addresses to us through the opened windows. The two or three non-commissioned officers in charge of our movement warned us to discard the addresses. "Don't be taken in by the Fifth Column!"

Yes, we all had berths and it was first class all the way. By nightfall we were leaving the state of Illinois, crossing the Mississippi River at Hannibal, Missouri, Mark Twain's hometown. Tom Sawyer and Huck Finn's stomping grounds were nearby. Tom and Huck had their thrills and adventures, to be sure. Not to be-little Tom and Huck, but I thought to myself, "Wait 'till I strap on that P-51 or P-47; my thrills will make those on that old river raft seem like nothing!" We headed southwest into the Ozarks. "San Antonio Aviation Cadet Center here comes a long trainload of eager fighter pilots!"

CHAPTER II
THE BIG GRINDER TURNS AND SORTS

Our group of would-be pilots/navigators/bombardiers, having departed Chicago just after noon on the 10th of February 1943, arrived in San Antonio in the afternoon of 12 February. The train pulled into Kelly Field, which was just down the hill from the huge Cadet Center. Many referred to the SAN ANTONIO AVIATION CADET CENTER as SAACC or as "The Hill". We were loaded onto personnel carriers and trucks and driven to our squadron area. It was on this drive that we first heard the call, "You'll Be Sow-rree." I was pretty happy and right where I wanted to be. Cadets loved to see newly arrived, civilian-attired basics. It gave them something to hoot & holler about. I'm sure we looked as wide-eyed and apprehensive as any other bunch of new "gadgets."

Within the hour we were in a long hall with several young doctors, where we stripped to our shorts. It was then that I first learned what a short-arm inspection was all about. The guy next to me said that he always thought his arms were the same length and we all laughed. We then turned our head and coughed while the doctor probed digitally. We also learned that the AAF was vitally concerned in knowing how many of the troops had hemorrhoids. Maybe they felt there was an outbreak of hemorrhoids on the troop train. We were greatly amused that after only an hour on the base, the Army Air Forces Docs had determined exactly what each man had in his shorts. Could this have something to do with flying by the seat of your pants?

We were issued a pair of coveralls so that we could get our GI bodies out of the old civvies clothes and into some nice, green GI fatigues. We were also given our blankets and sheets. I was assigned to Squadron 109, Section 7, Army Air Forces Classification Center, SAACC, San Antonio, Texas. Guess what! A GI party the first night; which was: on hands and knees, on the floor, with scrub brushes and brown bar soap. Then we did the windows, of course. Lights out at 2130, a welcomed command.

The next day was spent doing the routine initial things that recruits have done for years and having that behind us we were ready to be put through the serious testing starting Sunday the 14th. We were technically privates and would not be in the category of Aviation Cadets until we were satisfactorily classified as such. The anxiety was starting to mount. I wrote to my folks and said, "Don't spread too much news about me making the pilot category yet, as everything is so uncertain. We'll know all in about one week." The latrine rumors were rampant, and though this was in the days before folks talked about stress, we were loaded with the stuff.

On Sunday we sat taking all kinds of written tests. We had sixteen in all and it was a long day indeed. Some were like IQ tests; others were on reading and mechanical comprehension, mathematics, physics, the ability to interpret technical writing, map reading, etc. Some of the test questions dealt with good old common horse sense. We were not told the results of the tests.

On Monday, the 15th, we took the famous psychomotor tests. These were tests to determine one's reaction times to various lights and sounds, and to determine one's dexterity and coordination. Some were accomplished with dummy flight controls, i.e. stick and rudder, others with round/square pegs and holes. One novel test was a plate with a copper-like spot on it about the size of a quarter. As I recall, the plate moved in an elliptical orbit and it also rotated. The test was to see how well one could keep a pointer on the end of a flexible 8-inch probe, on the quarter-size spot as it turned and rotated in its crazy unpredictable pattern.

The psychomotor test was very innovative and looked upon by the AAF as a very valid and helpful test. The Air Force used the test for many years, and the airlines picked it up later from the AF. Several were still using it in the 1970s. It was said that a good score on the psychomotor would assist greatly in achieving the pilot category. My attendant gave me a slight word of encouragement, but just a dab. This day we also had enough time left over for a cadet clip; all haircuts- off to three-quarters of an inch. Not to worry; all the other "Misters" had the same look, and very few had real long hair to begin with as it was not the style of the day.

On Tuesday, the 16th we were given our complete issue of clothing, and we packed all of our civvies and shipped them home, not to be worn again 'till who knows when. We got 12 pairs of socks, two pairs of fatigues, six shirts, and six pairs of slacks, towels, toothbrushes, a shaving kit, two pair of shoes, a rain-coat, an overcoat, neckties, belt, gas mask, four caps and one hat. Our issue also included olive drab boxer shorts, and a funny styled athletic supporter which I called a Lower Slobbovian designed jock-strap. Also we got undershirts, handkerchiefs and PT shorts. The total issue included more than a regular private would get. Two of the above-mentioned shirts and slacks were a fine cloth, an Aviation Cadet issue and very attractive. Contrary to the old stories, our uniforms were new, and were fit to us carefully. If one didn't look really sharp, we could blame it on the frame in the duds.

On Thursday, the 18th, we started our physical exam. The first course was x-rays, lab tests and inoculations. Then we met the psychiatrist! He asked a lot of questions, some very personal, and this was a new experience for all of us. Among other things, he wanted to try to figure out how badly we wanted to be a pilot/ navigator/ bombardier and why. I believe he was also very interested in weeding out true loners, as his questions drew answers relating to teamwork. We had heard rumbles about this psychiatric interview, and the hot tip was to watch your every word and be very, very honest, as the psychiatrist could be trying to catch you in a lie. Don't take personal offense at the questions and the joke was: they are definitely looking for bed wetters. Although the interview lasted only about forty minutes, it was supposedly a brief encounter that could wash you out. I wrote my folks that ten percent of the cadets got ground duty only (GDO), after their interview. I did not know if this was fact or fiction. It seemed a bit rough, but that was the way it was in the classification process. So, "Mister, Watch How You Answer Those Off-The-Wall Questions." My doctor was a cool one, very young, sober and officious, but I supposed that is what the specs call for in a shrink. After our talk and he had assured himself that I liked girls and other "normal" things, he dismissed me with a terse remark and without an encouraging word. What a confidence-builder! They should have sent that Doc off to Charm School.

We had a young man in our bay by the name of George. He was an absolute wizard with a deck of cards and he had shown us all why we should never gamble with strangers. He had been a professional magician, a protégé of a famous magician and had traveled extensively nationwide in the show. Well George was also a hypnotist, and he told us all how we could calm ourselves down when we went in to take the physical. He hypnotized two or three of us in the barracks that night and I was his first pigeon. I didn't particularly want to be hypnotized, but he had selected me and I did a poor job of begging off. He was a professional and maybe I looked "trancey" to him. He told me later that he preferred intellectual candidates. Ha! I chalked that up to pure malarkey. Well after I was under his hypnotic spell, I'm told he started by having me sing the Star Spangled Banner, so you know without a doubt I was really under his spell! What a song for starters! I could sing, but that is one song which, if you don't start on a proper note, you're in big trouble later on. I should have had a pitch pipe. Major Bowes would have given me the gong. Later, I was told he had me shivering, sweating, and fighting off a swarm of ants that had attacked my entire body. He finished up by telling me I was slowly getting drunk and had me staggering around and bouncing off the bunks. Considering that I'd never been inebriated before, I guess I did that well. He then told me to lie down on a bunk, and instructed me that, when I heard the phrase "Wild Blue Yonder" I would simply, slowly and quietly, rise and join the fun.

Several minutes later, when I heard the phrase, I did just as he said, and I was immediately surrounded by many guys wanting to know what it was like. I was labeled a terrible singer, but given credit for being "a gutsy guy!" The audience was sizeable! I was known!

George, who was very much the youth that we all were, told us very seriously that we had to talk to ourselves when we lay out on that table for the doctor, talk calmly and quietly, tell our hearts to slow down and picture in our minds a very peaceful scene. Would that really work? On Friday the 19th we went to the hospital at Preflight for our main physical examination. We were assigned to one doctor who would give us the entire examination. We had all taken a physical when we signed up for the aviation cadet program, but this physical at Pre-flight was very crucial. It was the physical that would be looked at by the selection boards and all of the numbers had to be just right for one to be accepted into the pilot training category. The majority wanted to be pilots. We were all sweating-out this "six-four" (AAF terminology for a flyer's physical.) I'm sure many of us were following George's admonition to keep calm and think of peaceful meadows. I know I did: about 640 acres of very, very peaceful meadows with butterflies and daisies galore.

My examining physician was an older man, perhaps forty or forty-five, with a pleasant and relaxing demeanor. My physical went well except that the doctor wanted me to have a recheck for my vision in the right eye. The next day, with drops in my eyes, I was apparently still a bit off the mark and he scheduled me for a retake on Monday. Was this the beginning of the end? Back at the barracks I learned that there were all kinds of retakes scheduled for Monday, so misery had company. A lot of guys went to the chapel that Sunday. Most of the retakes were for high pulse and high blood pressure. Would-be pilots and doctors don't mix. They called it the white-coat syndrome. For some it lasts decades! We were doing a splendid job keeping each other revved up. Our oil pressure was high and our props were over-speeding! Guys were saying, "George (the hypnotist), where are you? The cool valleys and green meadows aren't working."

Monday came, and with great apprehension several of us returned to our doctors for the third day. It was our tenth day on active duty. I went through the eye check in a short time, and this wonderful middle-aged doctor told me that I had passed. The big "physical-hurdle" was over. Back at the barracks I learned that most of the retakes had made it through also. It was a happy barracks that night. We had met the six-four and had conquered it; another definite hurdle in the big grinding and sifting process. How many had been helped by our bay-mate George, the magician? By George, we'll never know.

While George was a very able and competent magician and hypnotist, we did not know what a celebrity we had in our midst until we heard that George was going to put on an evening show in one of the large theaters in Preflight. His act had the Flight Surgeon's approval. One other cadet who had been hypnotized by George following my performance under his spell was David, a tall, thin, handsome lad, who was not endowed with a whole lot of muscle. He was well built, but slim (like Charles Lindbergh and me). I had noticed on several occasions where George, had hypnotized David on the spur of the moment. He was preparing his subject for the show in the theater. Dave told me confidentially that he was somewhat uncomfortable with it all. He wanted to know if I was getting the same treatment. I was not. I had been weeded out.

On the night of the show, we, of course, attended. George's performance was totally professional. Most of us had never seen anything better. The one act that really set us back was when he hypnotized David, and had him go through several minor exercises. He then had David turn rigid. With the help of two cadets he laid Dave out flat, with his head on one chair and his heels on another, about six feet apart. There was no support under his long, lean body. Then, one at a time, the two cadets were instructed to stand on David's frame. They did so and he was as solid as a plank. He did not collapse. After that performance I was happy that I had flunked hypnosis with George. David, I'm sure, performed more handsomely in the role of a 2 x 12 plank than I ever would have.

Now that most of the testing was out of the way, we had to sweat-out the notices on the bulletin board. Soon the results of the classification board began appearing, usually one list in the morning and one in the afternoon. Each notice created a "barracks event." After each list appeared there would be much jubilation, but also some terribly dejected boys.

One afternoon, on Wednesday, the 24th a boy from my bay said, "Hey Jake, you're classified!" I asked, "What as?" And he said, "I forget, go look!" I liken that moment with what it must be like to be in front of a firing squad. I tore down the steps and out the door. The bulletin board was not 30 feet a-way. Like in a dream, it seemed I slipped into slow motion. I just had to be on the list under the heading PILOT. My heart was pounding and I was almost afraid to look. This was it!! My whole career!! And it was!!

I was near the top of the list under the word "PILOT." Man! My eyes glistened with a tear or two from the flood of emotion as I double-checked it and then triple-checked the information. A ton of weight left my shoulders. I felt that moment was one of the most decisive forks in the road of my life. I tried to walk away with a cool smile of satisfaction on my face, but I was somewhat choked. I took a short walk.

Soon all the boys were classified. Many had been put in the navigator category; they were supposed to be the brainy bunch. Fewer were put in the bombardier category. Some were rejected for any flying schools and were very quickly transferred to another squadron. Many of them went on to be mechanics, gunners, radio operators or into other technical fields. Many of them, in our opinion were still, truly "cream of the crop" as we were repeatedly told we were, but they had missed the golden ring by only a fraction of a millimeter. It was very sad to see them leave, as we could truly appreciate how devastated they felt. One of our "bay buddies" in my barracks made that exit. One of the guys in the bay said, "There, but for the Grace of God, go I." How true! We all had to agree.

We marched, we drilled, we did the calisthenics things and we ran and we ran and we ran. We ate like horses and I didn't gain a pound. Still slim, like Lindbergh! About this time I had a sore throat and had a tonsillectomy. The young doctor who snipped them out cut a bit too close and I was in the hospital for six days. I knew things were not going too well the first night when the nurse said I was bleeding too much. She ran and got a doctor, a lieutenant. He tried to stop it without success and he ran and got a major. Later, when the major went out and returned with a full colonel I was really starting to worry. Well, things finally got squared away and I got out of the hospital and went back to my squadron. That night I went to a big stage show at the theater. I think it was *HELL'S A POPPIN* with Olson and Johnson; lots of slapstick. I laughed too much, and ended up back in the hospital with more post-op bleeding. I was soon released and was O.K. from then on. I had been very worried that I would miss "Going Across The Road" to Preflight with my class. Though we in our barracks had been together for only five weeks, we were a well-knit group and one hated the thought of splitting away from the gang. It would have been miserable to have dropped back a full class.

All in all, the six weeks in Classification were not bad. The food was excellent; ice cream every noon. I pulled KP only two or three times. We had a strict rule about eating all the food we put on our plate. Gigs were handed out for wasting food, and each demerit or gig was worth one half-hour of marching back and forth "on the ramp" with a wooden rifle. It was humiliating. I speak from experience!

One rule of "fine-dining" was that if a Mister requested "Please pass the bread," and some Dodo helped himself to a slice as it went by, (called "short-stopping") the one asking for the bread had the right to throw all of the bread in the face of the short-stopper. Hearing the rule once was sufficient for a cadet. I never saw the rule put into play.

The anxieties and uncertainties of Basic and Classification were behind us! The big grinder had turned and turned, sifting out pilots, navigators, bombardiers and eliminating about 20% of our "entry-group" as not quite up to the very highest standards, usually because of some very small flaw.

What had we really learned in the six weeks at the Classification Center? Besides the routine basic training we had learned, (a) never volunteer for anything, (b) keep your mouth shut in ranks, (c) yellow GI bar soap is hard on the hands when scrubbing floors the AAF way and also hard on the knees, (d) one can really learn to love calisthenics, as long as they chased off the scorpions and rattlers first, (e) we were all far better runners than we ever thought we were, (f) Taps sends a chill down one's spine, casts a spell over the barracks and makes you just a little bit homesick, (g) the stars at night are big and bright, *Deep In The Heart of Texas,* and lastly, (h) we all needed a guardian angel perched on our shoulder.

Once more we felt the vacuous-queasy feeling in the pit of the stomach of the unknown! But, isn't this what we've been dreaming of for months? We were now ready to get into the meat of the pilot training program. We needed to be militarized, reduced to Dodos, learn to obey and follow, then we could ascend from that low level to the highest position attainable in competition with contemporaries. A new-dawning lay just across the road.

We packed our duffel bags, put them on 6x6 trucks and at 0500 hours they hauled them over to Preflight, about a half mile "across the road." We dressed in our finest uniform, the classy Aviation Cadet shirt and slacks. We shined our shoes to a fare-thee-well. On 22 March, more than 4,000 cadets, classified as pilots, marched across to our new base in the smartest manner we could muster. After only five and one-half weeks there was not the faintest resemblance to that klatch of characters who had straggled down a Chicago street to board the train and head out for San Antonio, Texas.

We knew, of course, that the Upperclassmen were awaiting our arrival like lions on meatless Tuesday. BUT WE LOOKED SHARP, WE WERE PREPPED, AND WE WERE READY TO TAKE ON PREFLIGHT!

CHAPTER III
MAKE A NOISE LIKE A CARROT

The formation of approximately four thousand cadets marching to Preflight on Monday, 22 March 43 was sharp; at least we thought so. We wanted to get off to a nice, safe start with our Uppers (Upperclassmen). Not far from the main gate our formation stopped where flights were separated and assigned to Squadrons. Our flight was separated early, in front of Group Nine. I was assigned to Wing 2, Group 9, Squadron 1, Flt E. Most of the boys in my new flight (barracks) were from the same squadron we'd just left, although few were from my old barracks. However, many of my old buddies were in nearby flights or squadrons. It made little difference as my classmates in the newly formed flight were also a great bunch.

We were well situated on the post; we were only one block from a large mess hall and chapel. We were two blocks from the cadet club, PX and theater. We were right on the southwest corner of the very large parade ground (about the size of five or six football fields) and we were as close to the base cannon as any barracks building on the base. Need I say any more about wake up calls?

We were issued our bedding and assigned our bunks. The alphabet, as usual, determined who would be nearby. My bunk mates were another Jacobs (with red, curly hair), Jacobsen, Jorgenson, Jaklinski, Jakunus, Jazmar, Howard, Howland, Hunt, Humphreys, Honeywell, Jay, Jensen, Jensen and Karas. When somebody called "Hey, Jake," about six cadets responded. We were given some quick briefings by a junior officer on the run. Where were the Uppers? We expected them to be all over us by this time. Seems they had Open Post and were in San Antonio. How lucky!

After evening chow, a few Uppers started to return and we started to get the word like, "When you hear Group Nine, you will immediately hit a brace (rigid attention) and will treat the moment with reverence and the utmost respect. You MISTERS have to realize, and realize quick that Group Nine is far superior to any other group in Preflight. DO YOU MISTERS UNDERSTAND?" "YES SIR!" we all sang in unison. Next was, "What does the Little Bulldog say?" We hadn't the foggiest, but were then instructed that he says:

RRUUUFFF! and "That's What its Going to be Around Here if You Don't SHAPE-UP!!" Obviously in the future, the only part of the rendition would be, "What does the little bulldog say?" and we were to growl in the fiercest, most guttural voice we could muster, "RRUUFFF!" So then we knew two new things: Group Nine was the elite of all groups and the Group Nine bulldog said RRRUUUFFF louder than all other Groups' bulldogs. Soon we were down on the floor doing push-ups, for some very slight mistake. We probably didn't say "Sir" with the proper inflection. We were shown how to make our bunks. It couldn't be the sloppy way we made them in the Classification Center; they had to be tight. A quarter when dropped on the blanket had to bounce 3/4 of the way back to the point from which it was dropped, and it seldom would, or could. If an Upper pinged the blanket at the foot of the bed with his finger it was to send a ripple all the way up the blanket to the white collar. The white collar was an exact six-inch fold of sheet and GI blanket exactly six inches below the top edge of the mattress and bottom sheet. If it were not, the message: "Mister get that ruler and protractor out and get it into your bed-making routine!" If not perfect the bed was torn apart and the bunk's owner was privileged to get "additional training" at making bunks properly. Everything was called "training." Safe!

In short order the main cadre of Upperclassmen roared in from Open Post and they were all over us. We wondered what hit us. Fortunately before they got up a head of steam in their "training session," Tattoo sounded, which meant that the Underclassmen were free to get ready for the sack. Thirty minutes later Taps sounded. We had made it through the first day, almost unscathed. But tomorrow will also be a day in Preflight! YIPES!!

"From the sidewalks and the countryside of every part of the nation, young men come to San Antonio Aviation Cadet Center to learn to be not only pilots but officers as well. In order to instill the importance of strict discipline as a fundamental of good soldiering, everything a cadet does must be executed with exaggerated precision. Cadet life at the San Antonio Aviation Cadet Center is comparable to a college campus camouflaged with war paint - a campus on which men are taught to fight and fly, to command and to obey."

This was the printing at the top of our PX stationery. Above this caption was a beautiful eagle, feet down, ready for a landing. To the left was the full-blown color guard. It was very impressive looking stationery, and we were right proud to write our letters on it, though it was a trifle more expensive. Money was no consideration. We were loaded. We made the $50 per month, the same as a buck private, but got an additional $25 monthly because we were Aviation Cadets, though not doing much flying yet. I was so flush with dough I started paying off my college loans, and took out a $6.00 allotment to buy war bonds, as well.

At 0550 hours the next morning the bugle sounded on the loud speaker system and on the last note, the nearby cannon went off. It was impressive! Needless to say the barracks shook. Another day was almost dawning. An Upperclassman, whom I shall call Miller, and who was a cadet officer, had a room at the end of the building. He shared it with another cadet officer, Mister Nance. The room was one of their bennies or perks. As the bugle sounded, Miller threw the light switch on in the main bay area and immediately berated us because we were "sleeping away the forenoon." He informed us that in the future that light switch must go on before the bugle gets through a dozen notes that all feet must hit the deck, and that all cadets must shout in unison at the top of their voices, "Hooray for Cherriobusko, Indiana," his home town, of course. If our timing was proper, right after the last word, "INDIANA," the cannon would blast and Mr. Miller would be overjoyed. Now this all sounded like a very logical and reasonable request to the average Underclassman, but we soon learned that this man had a fiendish quirk. He had an alarm clock (unheard of) and he would set it for 0549, jump out of bed and be standing at "our light switch" when the bugle sounded. This gave him "I win, you lose," status and license to haze us again and again for being so slow. We lost daily! We conferred and tried to figure how we were going to get around this turkey. Someone even proposed that we take turns getting up real early, say 0530 hours and sleeping against the wall under the light switch as best we could for the twenty minutes. We were all losing a lot of restful sleep anxiously waiting for the bugle to sound. This affected one young chap more than the rest of us, because one night at about 0200 hours he sat bolt upright, in the still of the night, and cut loose with: "Hooray for Cherriobusko, Indiana" at the top of his voice. He woke himself up and all the others in the barracks as well. He leapt from his top bunk and threw on the light switch. Well, that didn't win him any friends, and it also increased the wrath of the Upperclassmen upstairs. We think that soon thereafter some of the Upperclassmen called Mr. Miller aside and told him to cease and desist, or "Cool It, Buster!" They liked to sleep too; however, the morning eulogy continued for the Indiana town, but with less fanfare, and Miller's appetite for hazing abated... just a bit.

The class system worked. It allowed the senior cadets to administer the military training, and at the same time learn something about leadership. The Upperclassmen kept a check on their fellow cadets, and it was their responsibility to see that if one of their classmates crossed the line of reason or propriety he was to be reined in. An Upperclassman was not allowed to touch an Underclassman. He might yell in his face with much gusto, but touching or striking was taboo. I disliked someone yelling orders in my face, two inches from my nose. Everyone I knew had the same strong dislike for this form of hazing. Wracking and bracing a cadet was extreme, but at first was not at all uncommon. When told to hit a brace it meant extremes at the position of attention. Then the "trainer" might slowly walk around the trainee and tell him to "suck in your gut, throw out your chest, pull in your chin, make those shoulder blades click together, stand more erect, eyes forward, drive those arms down, etc." The trainee's eyes might move, and he was then accused of looking around like he wanted to buy the place. He would invariably start to perspire, and then be accused of having feelings of guilt, or maybe he was "unstable?" The more imaginative the trainer, the worse it was on the trainee. Some Uppers were extremely imaginative. One could not allow himself to take anything as a personal insult. One had to be able to cope with this stress or he might find himself in front of a Wing Board and be gone. A Wing Board was a board of senior cadet officers who ruled on the more serious disciplinary problems. They had the power to recommend washout to a board of commissioned officers. Much of the stress-related antics and gymnastics were simply mental games of cat and mouse, and our Upperclassmen really knew the games well! They seemed to know every West Point and

30

Annapolis trick, poem, and song, and, of course, we had to learn them all.

I'm sure this all sounds very sophomoric to someone who has not experienced the delight and dividends of all the special attention in this educational process. Today I look back on it all with great amusement, with no bitterness or rancor. It was without a doubt highly effective. All you had to do was maintain self-control, keep your cool, do as you were told, keep your sense of humor, but not laugh and try not to sweat. Easy? No! Not on your life! And some days it seemed it was next to impossible!

You might ask, why would a fine group of young men go along so readily with such an outlandish program? Why were there not flare-ups and maybe some back-talk and questioning, or even fist fights? Unheard of! The goal we sought and the dream we cherished was a pair of silver wings. Very, very few would jeopardize that esteemed prize. We also realized the "System" dated way back, long before the first airplane ever lifted off of the sand dunes at Kitty Hawk, North Carolina. We wanted a piece of the pie!

Our first full day in Preflight, 23 March, included close order drill, physical training, including calisthenics, and several lectures by officers. At other times, when we were not busy and were in the barracks we were fair game for the Upper-classmen. Needless to say we figured that out in very short order. One soon learned where there were "hiding places." We had to do a lot of memory work, and one needed a certain amount of space to get that done. Much of the memorization was not earth shattering, but taught one to memorize with ease. An example:

Cadet Creed: "My bearing is along a course directed toward the accomplishment of a high mission; that mission being to raise my earthborn self into the blue above, to develop honor, self-discipline, and strength of character in myself, so that when called upon to defend these principals, I will disgrace neither my country, my duty, nor my honor. To this end I will strive diligently, honorably, and hopefully."

When an Upper asked for the cadet creed, he expected it to be rattled off in a very loud crisp voice without a stammer or the slightest hesitation. Amazingly, sometimes he would say, "Well done,

Mister!" and walk away, but not too often. We learned the chain of command for the Preflight School and all the officers' names and ranks in our Wing, and in the other three Wings as well. Our commander was Col. Pearl Roundy. We memorized the Position of a Soldier at Attention, the 12 General Orders, the wing span of a P-39, P-51, P-47, B-17, B-24, B-25, B-26, A-20 and A-26, the temperature at which magnesium burns, that mustard gas smells like garlic or horse-radish, that phosgene gas smells like new-mown hay, and that Adamsite smells like coal smoke. This we learned because we knew we were going to have to recite it all for the Uppers; however, much of it was not totally wasted learning; practically all of it had to do with flying, military operation or warfare.

Nonsensical routines, such as this were routine: Cadet #1: You look like the man. Cadet #2 What man? The man with the power. What power? The power of Hoo-Doo. Who do? You do. Do what? Look like the man, and on and on. Two cadets are nose to nose, rocking fore and aft reciting this ditty until the Uppers are tired laughing.

WE SANG SONGS!! When we fell out for formation and marched off down the street we had to break into a song on the very first step. It was our responsibility to pass the word that the next song was to be:

She wears her silk pajamas in the summer when its hot, She wears her woolen nightie in the winter when its not, And sometimes in the springtime and sometimes in the fall, She jumps right in between the sheets with nothing on at all,

Glory, glory for the springtime and the fall, glory, glory for the springtime and the fall, Glory, glory for the springtime and the fall.

When she jumps right in between the sheets with nothing on at all.

(sung to the tune of the Battle Hymn of the Republic)

We had some bang-up voices among the Underclassmen and we were always more than willing to burst into song. It was a far-cry better to sing than to be hazed; it used up a lot of time, was non-threatening and inflicted no pain. We were very good and we knew it. Our Uppers enjoyed it; but of course, we never heard a word of praise.

32

In the first five or six days we became totally squared away with what we were to do and not do as far as the Uppers were concerned. The main training program, however, included several lectures on military courtesy, the honor system, chemical warfare, movies on medical aspects from VD to aviation physiology and first aid. We quickly became very sharp in close order drill and were getting super-fit in physical training. We had an obstacle course and we had a two cross country courses. After calisthenics in the large group, we usually would split off into a sport of our choice. We ran cross-country every other day. One course was 1 3/4 miles and the second course, two miles, both courses up and down hills, jumping creeks and ditches all the way. The AAF didn't include boxing in the curriculum, as it posed a potential threat to the eyes, and eyes to a pilot are number one. Volleyball was very popular, as was basketball. Tug-o-war was a big competitive effort between flights and squadrons, as were all the track sports. I ran track in college, so entered training for the 440 yard dash. Our track coach was exceptionally sharp. He had been a coach at the University of Texas. He was very strict and demanding, but really knew his stuff.

On Saturday, 27 March, we had our first 4-Wing parade. That included the entire cadet complement in Preflight, approximately 8,000 cadets in class A's, with a fine marching band. In Preflight there were four Wings; each wing had five Groups, and each Group two squadrons. Each squadron had six flights (barracks) and each flight approximately forty cadets. With that many people it took some time to get all the troops on the parade ground. Unfortunately we were always an early Group, so we had to stand at attention or parade rest for 20 or 30 minutes. We then had inspection, and then, happily, from the front would come the call, "Pass In Review!" It was very impressive. I had played in a marching band in high school and in college. We had entered state competitions, but I had never been a part of anything like this before. If you were upright and had a heart beat, every fiber was alive with a tingle as you marched past the reviewing stand. Or, as some of the WW I veterans used to say, "It made you want to go over the top!"

In a parade, you don't get to see it as the officers on the reviewing stand do, but a participant can tell when things are looking sharp and true precision is in full sway. I think the thrill of being in the group that is performing beautifully in rhythm and alignment is much greater than being an observer. Group Nine had won the trophy as the best group in Preflight the week before we arrived, so, naturally, there was a great deal of talk and threats about that. We had to keep that trophy. It was awarded for excellence in drill, academics, and athletics.

After the big 4-Wing parade, I was summoned to the orderly room and told that I had been selected as a Wing II color guard. I was very thrilled. I suppose I was chosen because I was 6'3" tall. I found out very soon that all in the color guard were 6'3" or 6'4". I received a little chevron to sew on each sleeve. Small-town boy makes good! It is amazing how proud I was of that little rinky-dink chevron, and it was a real blast when our Wing got to act as color guard for the big weekly parade. As thousands of cadets marched past the reviewing stands, we of the color guard were out front with the colors. Throughout Preflight training there was one big parade a week. But our Wing Commander liked to schedule one or two extras, usually in connection with retreat. Practice makes perfect, he would say. The evening of our first big parade I wrote a lengthy letter home to my family. It was somewhat tedious trying to explain what this Preflight place was like. After that letter I wrote a quick letter to my buddy Les Earp. By now he was a newly commissioned Marine Corps pilot. "It's real easy to correspond with him. He'd understand every single thing I said," I wrote in my notebook.

On Monday, we'd been in Preflight one week and went into ground school training phase. We were in classrooms for 6-8 hours per day. The training was concentrated and intense. We had very fine teachers. All were officers, commissioned out of colleges where they had been teachers. Subjects were: Physics, Math, Maps & Charts, Aircraft Identification, and Naval Vessel Recognition. Vessel recognition covered 200+ vessels of Japan and the U.S. navies from the perspective of various altitudes up to 30,000 feet. The silhouette of a vessel was flashed on a screen, at first for 2-3 seconds; later the time was reduced to one-fiftieth of a second. We took 50 hours of Morse code. We needed to pass eight words per minute by sound and five words per minute by light (blinker.) If you were capable of taking

10 words per minute by sound, you were excused from future code classes. I was not doing well in Morse code. It went well at first, but then as the speed picked up it seemed that the code was burbling in my ear drum with an echo effect. It seemed to worsen. I was starting to panic. Then suddenly it all cleared away and I was copying the code very well. One day our instructor said that we could be excused from the class by reciting back sentences he would transmit at 10-12 words per minute. I copied the sentences with the rest of the class. "Who can read back the last sentence quickly?" the Lieutenant asked. I raised my hand. "Read the sentence, Mister!" "Cuban girls love horny cadets." was my reply. "You've got it Mister." and I was out of there. No more code classes for me in Preflight School.

It was amazing how much math and physics the AAF could teach you in thirty days. I had taken two years of college math and physics and that seemed to be about what we covered in Pre-flight school without the lab work.

As Underclassmen, one of the most annoying things we were faced with three times a day was the dining hall routine. This would start with the call to "fall out in formation!" When so ordered we would run, not walk, to the street in front of our squadron, and form up automatically in our assigned position. We then did a right face and on the very first step forward, broke into song. The mess hall or dining hall was about two blocks away, so we had to pick short and snappy songs that would bring us very close to the entryway of the dining hall. *I've Got Sixpence,* one of our favorites, was far too long. Hopefully, the timing of our arrival at the mess, and the end of the song, were synchronized flawlessly. That pleased those Upperclassmen. They would then enter the dining hall first, followed by the Lowers. We would stand at attention behind our chair. Each table had twelve cadets with five Uppers sitting across from five Lowers. The table Commandant sat at the end of the table and a Lowerclassman sat at the other (aisle) end. On the command "Take Seats!" we sat at attention on the first four inches of the chair, looked straight ahead, with our chests pushed against the table. This rigid position helped the Lowerclassmen stave off such vices as slouching or getting round shoulders. Oh, yes, and we had nice white table clothes.

Training in good manners included many things one's parents may have forgotten to teach one, such as, "Thou shalt not dive bomb your scrambled eggs." In order to impress one with this rule, we ate a "square meals" for four and one-half weeks. Looking only very briefly at the plate, a cadet hopefully got some food on his fork, brought the fork straight up, always on a true vertical path, till in front of his mouth, and then moved it horizontally into the mouth. The head was not to be moved to accommodate the position of the fork. Needless to say, sometimes there was very little food on the fork and one did not get to eat as much as he'd like. I spent about half of my time as an Underclassman in starvation corner, the location just to the right of Sir Commandant (usually Mr. Nance) who sat in that exalted position. Saddest was the ice cream situation. It was a large brick, like processed cheese. It was cut into 12 slices. Guess the shape and the size of my slice when it came off the plate last. There was one consolation: when I became an Upperclassman, I was a Sir Commandant and my lean eating days were over!

At the aisle end of the table was the "Gunner" and, when a dish became empty, it was his responsibility to raise his hand until a waiter, (slowly) took it and brought it back refilled. Then the gunner would say, "Sirs, a full meat plate has arrived!" It was then passed around the table, and again going to the Uppers first. Because they were eating square meals, most Lowers had not yet managed to maneuver their first helping of meat into a chewing position.

The Commandant also assured that Underclassmen were trained during the meal. If an Underclassman wanted more milk, he was obliged to sing out, "Sirs, does anyone care for the lactiferous substance extracted from a species of the bovine quadruped by a series of intermittent jerks?" PAUSE "Sirs, please pass the lactiferous substance extracted from a species of the bovine quadruped by a series of intermittent jerks!" It was wise to articulate this rendition in a serious and almost plaintive tone. It added feeling to your desire for milk. I was a very big milk drinker, so I vividly remember the words. I could sound plenty plaintive.

If there was any spare time at the end of the meal, it was very appropriate for the Table Commandant to demand some recitation from an Underclassman. This could be something like "Instructions on how one's place setting should appear before departure from the table," i.e., the knife, fork and spoon must be at a 45 degree angle in the upper right hand corner of the plate with the knife closest to the outer rim and the spoon closest to the plate center, and all equip-distant from the other. The cup and glass must be placed just so. Strangely, today I often find that I leave my silverware arranged on my plate just as we were brain-washed to do many years ago. Chalk it up to behavior modification *a la* AAF. No, I never accidentally slipped into the square meal routine again. Never, ever!!

After chow we were excused from the formation in front of the mess hall; we were expected to race to the barracks door to form an honor guard on either side of the outside steps. This enabled the Uppers to enter the building in the style they'd grown accustomed to, and loved. Many of them would race with us, and, since we had to slow down to turn square corners, they often beat us. Bad News! We were obliged to sing a nice song, thus they could enter with music. Some always stayed behind to have their way with us. While in the honor guard formation, the Uppers expected us to come up with clever poems, songs, or "famous-fors" such as, "Mister, what are you famous for today?" You were expected to have dreamed up something original, new, and would please the Uppers exceedingly, so that they could laugh hilariously and slap their knees. One Underclassman, I remember, asked the Upper if he knew the difference between a WAC and a WAVE (females in the military). The response was then, "Well, what is so famous about that?" The Under then said, "May I touch you, Sir?" The Upper replied," Yes." (he should have known better!) The Underclassman then said, "The wave is like this, Sir, making a waving motion with his hand and a WAC is like this," and with that he whacked the Upper real hard with an open palm, and nearly knocked him off his feet.

Another "famous-for" I recall was the cadet who was famous for cutting toilet seats in half. "Well, what is so famous about that?" the Upper asked. "I cut them in half for half-assed Upperclassmen to sit on SIR!!" Of course we thought all of this hilarious, but naturally our laughter only brought us grief in the end. In all probability these "famous-fors" were handed down from class to class, no doubt dating back to General McArthur's great-grandfather. Few were new. We'd scurry around to other flights to find something new to us. Those that were raunchy were often the cleverest.

In most circles, laughter is looked upon as a positive thing. Not so with the Underclassmen. There was hell to pay for "laughing-boys." Now any slight hint of a smile was categorized as laughter, an open invitation for grief. Mister Nance, an Upper, and a Group Cadet Officer with a Sam Browne belt, was one of those handsome guys with a mouth full of sparkling white teeth. Unfortunately, he also had a built-in smile on his face. His cadet officer room was near my bunk, so going and coming he saw me often, always to my chagrin and uneasiness. He had a habit of walking up, and in a very slow drawl and a soft voice (he was from the South) say, "Group Nine!" Naturally I would hit a brace which was mandatory. He would then very slowly walk around me and usually say nothing or, occasionally, say "Sharpen-up that belt buckle" or "Shoe shine is not up to par," but he would always end up in front of me, and in silence, simply smile. After a very short time there was little I could do to keep from smiling when I saw that big grin on his face. It drove me up the wall! His approach was so different from the typical ranting, raving and screaming that went on. He usually departed saying, "Mister, you have just got to learn to maintain control." To his credit Mr. Nance never really embarrassed me or any cadet. He was probably 19 years old, and a fine role model, but it really galled me that I could never win the "no-smile" contest with him.

When he went off to primary, it was a great relief, but I missed his riding me. He had helped me maintain an even keel and taught me to be a sharper cadet. He was a fine example of an Upperclassman, and he also maintained a sense of law and order over some of the more hostile Uppers. Under other circumstances we might have been good friends. Not so Mr. Miller from Indiana. He really bugged me, but in another manner. I was one of his "laughing boys," and I got more than my fair share of attention. Mr. Miller would always start with the same line, "Ah, here's a real Laughing Boy! Now, all gather round, MISTER JACOBS IS GOING TO MAKE A NOISE LIKE A CARROT." Though I would occasionally grunt, squeak or chirp, none fulfilled his crazy requirement and after thirty five days I realized that I still could not make a noise like a carrot. I had learned, however, to smother my smiles with him. Because of his antagonistic personality, I went into a stonewall mode. I used a technique of thinking mean, malicious, revengeful thoughts about this guy so that he was no longer effective in grabbing my mind or attention. He would then turn to other victims who needed more training, and who would provide him some glee and satisfaction by laughing. However, for some strange reason I was the only Mister ordered to make a noise like a carrot. Puzzling!

In our barracks we had an Upper who was a washed out West Point cadet. He was our Wing II Cadet Adjutant, a very exalted position. One of his duties, at the Wing Parade, was to stand up on the reviewing stand with the other officers and read the modified Orders of the Day. At the end he would sound off loudly with his name and title. You must realize he was shouting all this to 8,000 troops not using a microphone. His name was Mouse, I. NMI (no middle initial). We, in our flight knew when Mouse, I. NMI was going to be "ON", so the tension would mount. How were we going to maintain composure when we heard Mighty Mouse roar, "Mouse, I NMI?" Tough! There were snickers all over the place. We of course paid dearly for this when we got back to the barracks. Laughing in ranks was a cardinal sin. Mister Mouse personally didn't bother us too much, he'd just snap at us when he went by. But he left instructions. He always had bigger things to accomplish. We did not know why we had to crack-up at his name, but we did. On these occasions we were like a bunch of high school sophomores; but it did relieve tension and we had lots of that to get rid of.

Halfway through the preflight school, right on schedule, the Upperclassmen left us and went to Primary Flight Training, 22 April. Our association had been a tumultuous, turbulent and noisy affair, to say the least. They had been on us morning, noon and night for 35 days. Did they think they had taught us anything? It was a love/hate relationship, with a lot more of the latter. The love aspect could best be described by, "I will sure love it when they're gone. Three more days of them and I'd go over the edge!" Though we wouldn't want to admit it, we had learned a great deal. There was very strong hazing in our Group 9, but most was tolerable. All points were driven home with vigor and force. They had done their job well. In hindsight, we really had had a fairly good time along the way. When we had conquered the psychological aspect of it all, it wasn't so bad. The Uppers were also young and learning; they made some mistakes, but I'm sure they had also learned from them. Some of the things that went on had little meaningful purpose. But the system worked very effectively and we had survived. Above all we were a close-knit group, bonded together and "tight."

On the last day before their departure, some of the Uppers let down their crew-cut hair and wanted to be friends and "make-up." Some called it turn-about day. One cadet friend said. "I think I'm actually going to miss them, they have dominated my whole life;" then quickly added, "but not for more than two or three minutes." My "big-smile" mentor, coach, role model, Mister Nance departed. I probably thanked him for being fair and level- headed in the midst of bedlam and chaos. Some day I may stop in Cherriobusko, Indiana to see what happened to Mr. Miller, and maybc I should even check out a carrot patch in that Indiana town with a silly name, and learn how to make a noise like a carrot.

The first five weeks at Preflight had been both demanding and rewarding. We had been led to our limits, and now we were to lead others. We emerged from the Underclass status with a deep sense of pride. We moved upstairs in the barracks and became Upperclassmen. Now that Preflight had "got us completely out of puberty" we were more mature and were ready to administer leader-ship and discipline effectively. It was not quite as simple as one might think. We did not have a group meeting or anything like that, but we knew we didn't want anyone acting like a bully, and, "let's cut out some of the extreme chicken—Let's try to get this job done even better than our Upperclassmen did it." And we had to admit that that was going to be one real tough job.

A group of Underclassmen rolled in by mid-morning, but we were in San Antonio on Open Post just like our Uppers had been when we arrived. This was my first and only Open Post while in San Antonio. Before we went on Open Post we had to run two miles. I am sure that was to take the starch out of us. But to us, two miles was a piece of cake and we hardly broke a sweat. We then showered, dressed smartly and dutifully went to the orderly room to "pass muster" and to sign out. Our Tac Officer, Lt. Hunsdorf, was looking his junior fly-boys over carefully to assure that we looked real sharp. On a table by the door of the orderly room was a shoe box filled with condoms and pro-kits. This was a surprise and a revelation rolled into one! Did this mean that the AAF, after all those VD lectures and health films showing ugly things that happen to the promiscuous and careless, was condoning or encouraging sex? We all knew well the big poster of this absolutely beautiful, innocent-looking young girl, with the caption underneath the picture, "But Doc, she sure looked clean!" Most guys looked at the condoms, and then looked around to see who was doing what. The barracks Casanova grabbed a handful, and said, "WOW, free rubbers!"

Well, we went to town, and for every pretty girl, we saw about 500 cadets, 200 young officers, and 500 GI's. So much for the female species. We went to the Alamo and to a park or two. One was Roosevelt Park, where Teddy Roosevelt formed up his famous Rough Riders back in the late 1890's. We ate in a restaurant by the river. There was a Cadet Club on the mezzanine floor of the famous Gunter hotel. It was filled with cadets, all talking about airplanes, flying and combat, about which they knew precious little. I'm sure many readers realize that flying cadets always talked of girls while on the base, and talked of airplanes and flying when in town. The place had atmosphere though, and it was "our very own club" in town. Thirty years later I visited the Gunter Hotel, and of course I made my way up the stairs to the mezzanine to see our old cadet club. It never pays to go back. All was quiet. No young cadets talking of dragons to slay. No loud juke box. No pretty girls ambling around. It was totally dead. Kind of sad and a bit tired looking.

Every young cadet has to have his picture taken in uniform. Mine hangs nearby as I write this in my "I love me room." Not bad! My little rinky-dink chevrons show properly, just as they should! Sometimes when I look at that picture, I can smell the whole scene and atmosphere of Preflight. It is a kind of a *deja vu* thing: pungent odor, hot winds, blowing reddish brown Texas earth and a mixture of hot and cold sweat with much stress, which, believe it or not, had a very definite odor in Preflight.

41

In late afternoon many of us headed back to the base. We had rituals to perform. Our Underclassmen were there awaiting us with doubtful and calamitous looks, somewhat like a deer in the headlights. I'm sure they tried hard to look and be sharp, but we could spot them a country mile away; they had not yet received the Preflight touch. It was our job and responsibility to change that. We talked like they were 10 yrs our junior. Actually, we were an assortment of ages between eighteen and twenty-five, but most about nineteen, twenty or twenty-one. When I remembered the tremendous rush and thrust that our Upperclassman had hit us with, I somehow was not compelled to re-enact it. Before you interpret this to mean that I was a lightweight or soft, I should state that the word had come down from the Preflight Commander that "Hazing Will End." Too many members of our class, while Underclassmen, had been injured in various forms of extreme hazing. Of course this was not the first time a commander had decreed that "hazing must end." I hear it today, fifty-plus years later. Many in our class felt deprived and cheated, since we had gone through a very rough rite of passage, and now were told we must be "good boys and dispense with all the foolishness."

I'm sure that I did my share of "training" of our juniors, when it was necessary and for my own experience. I enjoyed trying to bring a cadet, who obviously needed training, up to a higher level. I enjoyed the humor connected with our methods. Playing mind games had little appeal. I was not a heavyweight Upperclassman. It was just not my nature to scream in another guy's face. Hey, and at last I could forget about carrots.

I attempted to emulate Mr. Nance, who had been highly thought of by our group, and who had been very effective. I was not alone, as several of our group felt likewise and toned down the class system action as commanded. After all, word to do so had come down, from on high and we could possibly jeopardize our own future in the cadet program.

Now that we were Upperclassmen, the Class System had somehow lost its appeal. There were no longer any surprises or anxious moments. But we all worked together to assure our juniors were top rate, that they worked hard, memorized their songs, wingspans, deadly gases and we "taught" many of the same ridiculous, but effective games and "famous-fors" laid on us.

The day of the big "4 Wing" track meet was coming up. Our track coach worked us hard. We had a run-off first in our flight; I had no trouble winning the 440 yard dash. There was a skinny, lightweight lad in another group named Goode. The guys said, "Jake, just wait till you get to the Wing meet, and come up against Cadet Goode! He runs like the wind."

In the squadron meet I also won the 440. Then with more difficulty I won the 440 in our Group, by a lunge and a nose. I was rolling on the ground after the race, feeling certain I would toss my cookies and I gasped frantically for more oxygen. The coach came over and in his Texas drawl, said, "Mister, that was not too bad, but not too good, either. We've just got to get two or three seconds off your time." I said, "Yes, Sir," and threw up. Well, all you 440 men know what words like his sounds like after you've run your fastest-ever 440. Next big event was the Wing II meet and sure enough Mister Goode was there in the finals. We each had a bit of a reputation by then, at least among track guys. We were almost like twins in height, weight & build. We chatted away before the race, acting like the best of buddies, yet each knowing one would lose. It was quite a race.

We two went out fast, ahead of the pack and ran stride for stride all the way round the track. In the last 30 yards, each of us had a very minor surge, but short lived. As we crossed the finish line I was lucky. I had just enough strength for one small burst and beat him by a bead of sweat on my nose. Both of us totally collapsed off the track. Again the coach came by and said, "Now we just got to cut one or two more seconds off that time!" We both sang out a feeble "Yes Sir!"

We'd all heard about the ride in the altitude pressure chamber, and it was now our turn in the can. I believe it was at Brooks AAF, nearby. It was certainly a new experience. We were sealed in a big tank, perhaps 8-10 cadets at one time. We had two or three technicians in the tank with us, and two outside observing and running the controls. The air was evacuated to simulate flight at higher altitudes. We left our oxygen masks off until we were in the vicinity of 15-18,000 feet. We learned the symptoms of being hypoxic. Then we slowly climbed to a higher altitude and one or two volunteers took off their oxygen masks and tried to perform various tasks. They very soon became incapable of doing so. We learned about purple lips and blue fingernails and the insidious feeling of well-being, while headed for a very serious condition. We observed first-hand the giddy performance by some volunteers, without masks on, which was very similar to intoxication.

At 39,000 feet we were pressurized so that our "cabin altitude was approximately 20,000 feet lower than the rarified outside air" An adjoining tank was at the 39,000 foot level. A seal connecting the two tanks was punctured and there was an explosive decompression that simulated what would occur in an airplane flying at 39,000 feet and pressurized to 20,000 feet in the event of a failure in the pressurization. The condensation was thick and our ears cracked and we were all, in a few seconds, up at 39,000 feet. At this time one of my classmates developed very serious symptoms. The technicians knew what to do. After a certain amount of descent, they ushered him into the adjoining chamber, which was there for such emergencies. He was lowered to sea level and taken to the hospital. Later we learned that he would no longer be an aviation cadet. He would get GDO: ground duty only. His aviation career was over before he actually got airborne. It seems the bones in his skull had not grown together quite right during his growing years, and the pressure chamber exercise revealed this. He was O.K. at lower elevations. We all liked the young cadet, even though he was the one who had awakened us all at 0200 hours, and let out a large scream "Hooray for Cherriobusko, Indiana."

The next big event in my Preflight life is familiar to only a few. Major Lane was the Preflight Military Training Officer. He had a big job. We heard that he was a WW I veteran pilot, and we knew he had a wooden foot. He walked with a decided limp, making a heavy thud with each step. He had a decided military bearing, and, to us, he was old, maybe fifty. One day on the ever-demanding and ever-revealing bulletin board, which all cadets checked numerous times a day, was a notice: "The following cadets will report to Major Lane's office at 1300 hours tomorrow." My name was on the list. Good grief, what

44

kind of deep do-do could I be in? There were only about eight or ten cadets in our whole Group whose names were on the list. Nobody had any notion what this was about. The next day we learned. Upon reporting to Major Lane's office we were ushered into a larger adjoining room that had perhaps 50-60 chairs. I went alone; no acquaintance of mine had been on the list. I walked to the front row and joined two other cadets. All the seats were very shortly filled with ordinary looking cadets. Major Lane entered; we all popped-to and waited for his command to "take seats." His message was very brief. He said, "Everything I know about this deal, I am going to pass on to you. I will not entertain any question at the end, as you will know as much as I do. Is that understood?" We all sang "YES, SIR!" in unison "Here is the deal. The RAF has five British Flying Training Schools in the USA. It has been agreed between the RAF and the U.S. Army Air Forces to put 17 USAAF Cadets into each class in their flying training schools. You will train exactly as an RAF cadet, you will march like an RAF cadet and your curriculum will be that of the Royal Air Force. You are to be goodwill ambassadors and will set the very highest example you are capable of, as representatives of the U.S.Army Air Forces. You have all been called in today because you have a fine record here, you have above average grades and you all have previous flying time. The RAF cadets come to the school with a small amount of flight training also. You will have an American officer, who is a pilot, on their staff, but your check rides could also be with RAF pilots. You will have only primary and advanced flight training. It will all be in the Fairchild PT-19 and the North American AT-6. Before you leave here you will go to school every night for 2 hours to learn all we can teach you about RAF airplot navigation, communications and anything else we can, in the short time we have to work with you. Two of the RAF schools in our command are in Oklahoma and one is in Texas. If you wash-out because of ground school, you will move laterally to a USAAF pilot training school and continue your flight training. We know you have the capability of passing all of our ground school courses. If you wash-out for flying, you will drop back one level and go to an AAF pilot training school and continue. In other words you will get a second chance; you have a safety net, a very unusual and unique status. You will be guaranteed a commission as a 2nd Lieutenant when you graduate, and you'll get your silver AAF wings and also RAF pilot wings. Remember, you will be in a Royal Air Force school and they are in charge. It seems to me, one hell of a fine deal, but you must decide, and today. I will be here at this table with Lt. Smith, and you will be called up individually and asked whether or not you wish to volunteer." He took his seat at the table and the lieutenant called up the cadet sitting two to my left. The young man stepped up to the table, smartly clicked his heels, saluted and reported. Major Lane said, "Are you interested?" The poor young man, who had not had more than two minutes to try to digest all this, said, "Er, A—" and Major Lane said, "Dismissed! Next." The cadet to my left got up and reported very properly and when asked the same question he said, "Sir, I would like to ask one question." Major Lane, without batting an eye, said "Dismissed! Next." Well I'd gotten the message; you do not stammer or ask a question. I was next. For CRYIN OUT LOUD why did I ever sit in the front row? I wasn't sure how I felt about it. It sounded great, but I hated the thought of splitting away from the AAF and my buddies. We knew we'd not all be going to the same flight schools. I also didn't have the foggiest how I would like living with the Brits for a long period of seven months. SINGLE ENGINE! Man, that cinched it. I'll get to go to fighters! That one thought about single engine flight training was the deciding factor. I clicked heels and saluted smartly. When Major Lane finished his same question, in my most positive toned voice, I replied, YES, SIR!" He said, "Fine, sign here!" Just like that the vector I would fly in the Air Force was changed. Little did I realize, in that split second decision, the die was no doubt cast for my flying career for many years. Yet. Drat! What have I done? I returned to my flight and told my buddies of my decision. Most of them thought it was great, and some drooled at the thought of guaranteed AT-6 training. Others envied the certain commission and avoiding the blue chip (purple pickle) Flight Officer rank upon graduation. Maybe I was envied, but I sure had my doubts. I got out my little fifteen cent spiral notebook and started getting my buddies' permanent addresses. As far as I knew, I didn't know a single cadet who would show up at the RAF ground school the next evening.

The ever-revealing bulletin board gave me my message the next morning. I was one of the fifty-one selected to go to one of the three RAF schools in the Central Flying Training Command. A wise choice? I was not the least bit sure!

The four wings or "Hill" track meet day arrived. Our coach never letup at trying to get two or three seconds off of our 440 time. Cadet Goode and I represented our Wing in the 440 yard dash and also ran on the same team in the 440 x 4 mile relay. In recent weeks we'd become good friends as we often trained together. We both heard that there were some runners in other Wings who were Big Ten stars. Now we would find out how we stacked up with real talent. We ran the race, a very tight race, but neither of us won. Cadet Goode beat me by a split second, as I had beaten him in our Wing race. Our finish was very fine. If my memory serves me well, we were 3rd and 4th with about 12 entries. We also ran together in the relay, and won first in that. It was really a great day, and the biggest track affair of my life. With the point system for all competitive events, our wing came in first. We took a beautiful trophy back for our Wing. Colonel Pearl Roundy was happy. In a way we felt a great victory. As the coach departed he told Goode and me to keep working; someday we might really amount to something, but we had to shave off a few more seconds. I'm sure we smiled, and I'm sure we said," Yes, Sir," or "Thank you, Sir." Man, didn't he know we were destined to be pilots? But you know, that coach sensed something; fifty years later one of those two cadets would still be running in 5K and 10K road races, still trying to shave off a few seconds, and improve his personal best time in the "over sixty-five" and then the "over seventy year-old age group." I located Lt. Goode's son in 1996 and learned that Lt. Goode was KIA in the China-Burma-India Theater in 1944. His son was born after he left for over-seas and so he never knew his father.

Anyone who went through the San Antonio Aviation Cadet Center will remember the music played on the loudspeaker system. It was the same speaker used for reveille, chow, retreat, tattoo, taps and the other official calls throughout the day. During open periods, the latest big band-era hits were played. Even today, when many of the top-ten tunes of 1942-43 are played, many of the feelings of frustration and turmoil of Preflight are brought back. There were some very great hits about that time, and most of us knew who was playing, who was singing and could readily distinguish between Glenn Miller, T.D., B.G., Artie Shaw, Jimmy Dorsey, Lionel Hampton, The Count, The Duke, and many more. A recording of Harry James playing *The Mole* brings back the most vivid memories of Preflight, these many years later.

Speaking of music, our Aviation Cadet Club in Preflight had a GI Big Band including many former players in the famous big bands. They played for dances 2-3 nights of the week. We, who were in the RAF night courses, seldom got to go to the club. I pulled guard duty twice in the club, with my white gloves, and it seemed to be well filled with cadets dancing with local girls from San Antonio. One of the main jobs as a guard was to assure that guys did not smoke cigarettes while on the dance floor. Girls were usually with an escort, and they came and returned to town with the escort. As I recall there was about one young damsel for every six cadets. I think that I could have handled those odds as I loved to dance and, though having been a "country boy," I thought I cut a pretty mean rug.

The training for the RAF Flying School continued almost up to the final day in Preflight. Although we were getting only a cursory or broad-brush education, we learned quite a bit, and when we arrived at Flight School and got in the classroom, we appreciated the fact that we'd had the exposure.

On 23 May, the day before our scheduled departure from Preflight, we had a parade. After the parade our Wing Commander had all the graduating class in his wing gather around the reviewing stand in a loose, unorganized group. He gave us a going-away pep talk. He was making a strong point about how we were going to have to really concentrate in flying school. Concentration was paramount. Suddenly, he pointed to a cadet who had his handkerchief out, sort of dusting off his belt buckle. I believe the Colonel decided to use the cadet as an example, but he rather lost it. He asked his adjutant to go down and get the cadet's name, and the name of the flying school to which he was to go. The young cadet really had not committed any great crime. He was absolutely thunderstruck. I was standing almost next to him, and I will never forget the ashen expression on his sun-tanned face. I'm sure he felt doomed.

The Colonel did not stop there. He told us that this young man could not possibly make it through flying school, because he could not concentrate. He also said, "I will follow this cadet's progress, and mark my word, he will not make it!" A pall of despair washed over all of us. We thought the Colonel was being cruel. I did not know the cadet, but I felt the Colonel had just wrongfully dashed all hope for my new buddy's flying career. (At this time we were all bonded together as comrades in arms from our jointly shared misery.) This should have been a moment of great elation, the high point of our ten weeks in Preflight School. It wasn't. I learned many years later that the young man had, in fact, been "tagged" by name and was informed at each school that he would receive special observation and tracked. He did, however, win his wings successfully and graduated on schedule from Lubbock AAF, as a Second Lieutenant. Colonel Pearl Roundy proved to be wrong, and I was glad, as were all his buddies and classmates.

In my little fifteen-cent notebook I had listed most of the names and addresses of my classmates in our flight. I have sixteen names. One cadet washed out due to the pressure chamber incident mentioned above. With myself included, I tracked 16 who went to flight school. Eight washed out and did not get their pilots wings. That is 50%, higher than the routine 35-45%. I was told that one washout, a friend of mine, when he found out he washed, was so depressed he attempted suicide. Two graduates went to Troop Carrier, one to the Air Transport Command, two are unknown to me, and three went to fighters. Cadet Jacobson, who was one of the three who went to fighters, was killed in a P-47 in the 8th Air Force, shortly after the D-Day invasion. Eddie Jay survived the war in fighters and flew into a mountain in a T-6 soon after the war, while in the Reserves. The third fighter pilot, Phil Karas, retired as a Colonel, USAF. Lee Jacobs, my bunk-mate stayed in the service, but succumbed to melanoma, years later, while a Major on active duty. Thus three of the sixteen were career Air Force: Jacobs, Jacobs and Karas.

I feel a sense of humility when I look at these statistics and I think that all of us who were lucky enough to survive these kinds of odds have to ask, "What did I do to deserve such a tremendous gift off of the Christmas tree?" Yes, we worked hard, very hard, but so did those who got the thumbs-down on a check ride, or were swept away by the grim reaper, or who found out his skull did not properly suture as a youth.

On 24 May we were to depart for Flying School and I had been selected to go to Miami, Oklahoma, with sixteen other YANKS (a term that we Yanks used for the next 7 months). We did not leave San Antonio as scheduled, as there were some heavy floods in southeastern Oklahoma and the trains could not go through. All my Preflight buddies departed, going to three or four different schools. It was a jubilant parting. We were really too wound up and elated about the future to feel any sadness. "Hey, see 'ya later, guy!"

I believe it is fitting to insert a good word for the officers and the non-commissioned officers who ran the San Antonio Aviation Cadet Preflight School. The Commander was Col. Walter Storrie. As I look back on the tremendous task involved, it seems to me that those gentlemen must have had extraordinary talents to keep that huge school running like clockwork. The only schedule screw-up that I recall was when we all worked so hard one Sunday picking up rocks and pulling weeds for the arrival of the First Lady, Mrs. Eleanor Roosevelt. She didn't show! Maybe it wasn't Eleanor's fault. She was known for running a hectic schedule all over the world. Our one famous visitor in Preflight was a no-show, and our parade ground was neat, clean and immaculate, but still plain dirt. We generally admired Mrs. Roosevelt because we knew that she had taken a few flying lessons. It was also said, probably by her in *My Day*, that she took Yoga and could stand on her head. Those odd things fascinate and win points from the younger crowd.

During our time at Preflight we did have an honored official in the reviewing stand during one of our parades. He was Secretary of War, Robert P. Patterson. It was noted in our week-ly Preflight newspaper, "The Talespinner," that he stood at attention while 8,000 cadets passed in review. I'm sure he was the only one on the reviewing stand who was at attention, but we chalked it up to his appreciation for our special talents, great precision, trim physiques and handsome faces. We would have readily settled for "parade rest."

On 25 May, I have an entry in my so-called journal saying that after breakfast I went back to bed and slept for two hours. That is no doubt the most unbelievable entry in the book. On the 26th I helped with getting the new Underclassmen squared away. Very few cadets got to welcome two new underclass groups. That meant very little to me; I was very anxious to get out of there and on my way to Primary.

On 27 May, with 30 minutes notice we left good old Pre-flight at 1115 hours and were on the train and departed Kelly Field at 1200 noon. Again we were very, very lucky. We had first class accommodations, each of us sharing a private compartment with a fellow cadet. It really made one feel guilty, as the average train rider during the war felt most fortunate if he was lucky to find a seat. Many stood up on very lengthy trips. We were, however, able to cope with these guilt feelings, all the way to MIAMI, OKLAHOMA.

On our departure from Classification Center to go to Preflight, we felt that we had made it through the big grinder, and survived all the cutting. It was really a tremendous high to have made the pilot category. In departure from Preflight, it was also a great moment of elation, but different. We had been "militarized," and had enjoyed the spirit of great camaraderie few of us had known before. No doubt we were at least a year or two older in maturity, and the training helped shape our lives far into the future. Through all the crazy antics, hoopla and hazing, we had learned a tremendous amount about the military, about ourselves, and about our relationship with one another. We had learned about leadership and had been enriched in academics. Maybe, even our table manners had improved. And in the every day skirmishes with the Upperclassmen, and keeping up with all their wishes and desires, we found that we had memorized an amazing amount of information, both useful and useless, but we had also learned how to memorize. We were in fine physical condition, and having worn shorts the last six weeks, we were brown as a berry. I personally had learned to run the 440 race correctly and victoriously; that was a significant plus to me.

It should be noted that the average cadet seldom saw an officer, except in the classroom. The prodigious amount of military training was done by the cadets, themselves - Uppers training Lowers and then those Lowers becoming Uppers and training the follow-on class. An age-old practice; highly effective and successful.

So, lean and mean were we! Ready to move on to the flying challenge! Ready to prove it too could be tackled and conquered. Good thing, two days later we were up in the blue Oklahoma skies in the Mighty Fairchild PT-19.

CHAPTER IV
BLIMEY MATES, WE'VE ARRIVED!

Seventeen of us departed Preflight school in one Pullman car. I never once looked back. We were totally pumped-up and wanted to get on with the big-time, into the Wild Blue Yonder! On our train ride north, I soon recognized the names of some of the towns we passed through. We were going back up the same tracks I'd come to San Antonio on, just 105 days earlier. I could not help but reflect on what a difference those three-and-one- half months had made in my life. Awesome, is a good word to describe it. Several huge hurdles had been cleared successfully, and I felt like everything was comin' up roses.

In Tulsa, we got off the train for a two-hour break. It was the first time that we were free to go and do as we pleased since the day we entered the San Antonio Aviation Cadet Center. (San Antonio open post doesn't count, as it was a city filled with thousands of cadets and GI's.) An eerie feeling came over me. I was totally free, out of the monastery-like environment, unrestrained, but momentarily uncertain. Could I really negotiate a stroll through the streets of Tulsa without someone counting cadence and barking an order for my every step? Sure I could, this is ridiculous! The doubt vanished quickly and two of us headed down the street with a lusty stride. We were young, laughing, eager-beavers, full of P & V, and our cadet uniforms were sharp and neat. We seemed like a magnet to the folks of Tulsa; everyone was our friend. We were being introduced to the great friendly spirit that Americans had for their servicemen during WW II. It also seemed as if the young ladies of town had heard the claxon sound; and in short order several were circling and closing in, waving and whistling from their cars. Honest! It was very obvious they wanted to meet and be met. Another cadet and I were easy "pick-ups" for two girls in a convertible. Mine was a real knock-out and she had the car. My buddy's was a bit plump, but pretty. They gave us a quick tour of Tulsa. We gave them our names, addresses and the promise to come back to Tulsa some weekend. I think we probably used up their one month's gas ration, but we did promise.

Back on the north-bound train, we passed through Ardmore, Will Rogers' home town. I reflected on Will Rogers and his un-timely death with Wiley Post on 15 Aug 1935, an accident that put the kibosh on my first plane ride when I was a kid. An hour later our train pulled into Miami, Oklahoma, located in the extreme northeast corner of the state. The date was 28 May 1943 and the time was 1530 hrs.

A bus awaited our arrival. With the driver was an American cadet, Harold Spurlock. He smiled, seemed relaxed and acted non-threatening. How could an Upperclassman be so nonchalant and relaxed picking up seventeen "DoDos" fresh from Preflight? We braced ourselves, and he laughed heartily. "Relax, you guys," said the Hollywood-handsome cadet. "We have no class- system here, but you are going to have to study a lot harder to learn all the RAF stuff they throw at you. This is a Spartan School of Aeronautics and now that I've almost finished, I really feel lucky to have been assigned here for my flight training." "What are the Brits like? Are they regular guys, easy to live with?" we asked. "Not to worry, guys, you'll get along fine, just take it slow and easy at first, and you will enjoy the comradeship with them. They are neat guys, much like us. The flight instructors are tops, as are the town folks. The food is terrific. Don't get me wrong, they're really going to work your butts off; the ground school is tough for us Yanks! Now, let's get out to the base!"

We made a short drive to the north edge of town, on U.S. Route 66. Situated right on Route 66, we came to what appeared to be a beautifully manicured and landscaped campus grounds. Holy Cow, could this be our flight training school? It was, with white gleaming buildings, flagstone sidewalks and lots of green grass. We learned that all ground and lawn maintenance was done by contract workers. Great, no more picking up rocks and cigarette butts, or pulling weeds. That fact alone made our day. A beautiful German shepherd police dog trotted over to inspect us. We learned he was the cadets' mascot and his name was Pete. He was an immediate friend and would guard and protect us for the duration of our stay in Miami.

We were quickly divided into four groups with four Yanks going into each flight. Our flight would be our linchpin until we finished the course. I was in Blenheim Flight. We four Yanks were shown our assigned barracks and our bunks. We were systematically mixed in

54

with the RAF boys, which was fine with us and, naturally, we were not consulted. I just happened to have a Yank bunkmate, Larry Maniex from Bay City, Michigan. Though the seventeen of us had attended night classes together in Preflight, at that time we were commingled with the Yanks who were destined to be assigned to two other RAF schools in Ponca City, Oklahoma and Terrell, Texas. It was not until we boarded the train to head off to flight school that we knew which sixteen other Yanks we would be grouped with. Thus we were not yet really well acquainted, except during the train ride north.

The flying school campus consisted of a barracks block for each of the three classes in attendance at any one time. In addition there was a cafeteria, a dispensary, a ground school class room block, a combination gymnasium/chapel and a two story administration building which also housed a PX, lounge and post office. This permanent structure was built by the WPA, Roosevelt's Works Project Administration, in the 1930's as a luxury hotel/service stop for folks driving down the great U.S. Route 66. The lounge was a fine place for a coke, a frozen Snicker bar and time enough to relax with a recording of Benny Goodman's famous *Sing Sing Sing* or T.D.'s *Boogie Woogie*. It seemed the Brits were mesmerized by those two songs. But we all liked them, though the 78 RPM records were very well worn.

The municipal flying field with its hangars and crew room was just a five-minute walk across the 40 acre athletic field. Our auxiliary flying fields were several miles away and consisted of large grass fields with small wooden structures in the center. In the evening, when all of the birds were back on the flight line at the main field, the training planes formed long lines, several deep, of beautiful blue and yellow PT-19s and shiny AT-6s with brightly painted colored cowlings; large numbers were painted on the cowling and fuselage to discourage buzzing by a cadet, who, in a weak moment, might yield to temptation.

Our barracks were new, only about two or three months old. The base had recently completed an expansion program to accommodate more students. The barracks were white colonial structures, one story, but with a large vaulted ceiling which helped to siphon off the summer heat. Each barracks block consisted of two large dormitories divided by a recreation room. We still saw lots of lumber in the ceiling and walls, but large knotty pine lockers were situated in such a way so as to divide the large wing into bays. We had nice, heavy, double-deck bunks and ample space for all of our gear. It was several cuts above anything we'd had before.

The RAF boys, who were in the barracks when we arrived, were very mannerly and respectful in introducing themselves. Some seemed reserved and almost shy. We were no doubt presenting ourselves with the same demeanor and bearing. Once the ice-breaking formalities were over, everyone loosened up and started to act more unconstrained and natural. We quickly learned that their speech and accent varied considerably. The Cockneys were probably the hardest to understand. We were told that the definition of a Cockney was anyone born within the sound of Beau Bells. That enlightened us very little. Of course we had to ask them often to repeat what they had just said. This created much laughter and joshing between the guys from the various regions with the mis-understood boy getting razzed by others who thought they spoke with an accent more easily understood by the Yanks.

We noticed immediately that the Brits were all dressed in woolen uniforms. Now, Oklahoma on the first of June can be hotter than a cook stove lid, and it was. They were very uncomfortable. There had been a goof-up somewhere and their summer issue was not yet available. It seemed like they were living in the shower. Any chance they got, they stripped off those woolens and jumped in the shower. We could not blame them; we were itching and scratching just watching them swelter in those 100% coarse woolens. They confessed that the showers were a true luxury with bags and bags of hot water and no restrictions on how much could be used. It was all so heavenly. Bit by bit we realized what a tremendous switch there was from the conditions in embattled Britain where such a simple thing as hot water for a shower was something very special. We sympathized and laughed with them and hoped too for their khakis to arrive, and they did.

We had no more than stowed most of our gear and belongings when we were told to fall out in formation. Squadron Leader Adderly, the school exec (probably World War I vintage) gave us a short talk. He told us we were going to have a "spot of parade" (drill), and we did. At this point we Yanks didn't have the foggiest as to how to drill in a British manner, having never been trained in the art. We had been told that we would have to drill and salute in the RAF manner, but here we were going off the high board without any practice.

In the AAF, Aviation Cadets drilled that when marching you swing your arms no more than six inches forward and three inches to the rear. The RAF swing their arms forward to the shoulder-high position. Swinging the arms to that height tends to throw one's body off balance, unless you make certain compensations such as shifting your pelvis forward, pointing your toes out at an angle, and bending your knees somewhat outwardly. We learned the technique eventually, but did not know the tricks three hours after getting off the train. The Commanding Officer, Wing Commander Roxborough, observed our first parade. He felt obliged to give a short speech. He told us, in the King's English that the parade was simply deplorable and that in the future we were going to have to "put our backs into the effort." I'm sure his comments were justified. When we heard "By the left, quick march" and "Right wheel" it was for the very first time. He did not single out the USAAF cadets, but we knew we had contributed mightily to the deplorable show. We Yanks thought that, considering everything, we had made a bloody good effort, though a bit shabby in spots. We also learned from the short speech by our RAF Wing Commander that he spoke and sounded exactly like Winston Churchill. We had the feeling that maybe he even practiced from time to time to sound like Winnie, as the resemblance was unmistakable, and very good. He was an excellent and very articulate speaker. Would he be as pugnacious, stubborn and persistent as Winnie? He proved to be a fine commander; however, he and I probably exchanged no more than six or eight words between May and December. However, he did say some very nice words to me at our graduation ceremony.

The RAF boys of our #16 Course, the 16th group to enter flight training at Miami, had arrived two days before us. We were late due to flood waters in Southeastern Oklahoma. We were at this new location no more than 3-4 hours and we learned that the A & M College in Miami was throwing a dance to welcome us that same evening. The town folks wanted to welcome the new class, and the young damsels wanted to size us up, perhaps even as future husbands. Before I give the wrong impression here, I would like to make it clear that the people of Miami and the surrounding towns were truly magnificent with their friendship and hospitality. They were indeed the most kind and hospitable folks on the Great Plains.

The dance was very nice. A good-sized juke box blared out the latest jump tunes. Many of the parents accompanied their daughters. Parents and chaperones brought the girls around and proper introductions were made. We learned real quick that when you asked a girl to dance, she would then take you around after the set and have you meet her parents and friends and maybe an aunt or uncle. They were very genuine in this, and almost too much so. Sometimes I felt that I had just become engaged. The parents would politely and graciously mention that some day they would invite us to Sunday dinner. I was a passable dancer and liked to dance so I met a lot of people. As the evening wore on, I began to feel that I was already getting involved; seriously targeted by maybe two or three girls. WHOA! My mind was in the blue, and early the next morning we were to be up in that blue in the challenging primary trainer, the PT-19. There would be plenty of time for social activities after we get things under control with the airplane.

Naturally, the RAF lads were more popular than us Yanks. We were just as handsome, virile, charming and winning as they, but they were different. We were like the run-of-the-mill boy in the college, though there were very few boys in the school; they were off to war, so the boy/girl ratio was very favorable for those of us at # 3 British Flying Training School.

Early the next morning, a Saturday, we were in a school bus, on a dirt road, headed west across the range land, some eight miles to an auxiliary aerodrome for our first flight. They were not wasting any time. The bus stopped at the ice factory to pick up a block of ice for the water cooler at the crew room. My RAF flying partner was Jimmy James, a Welshman. Jimmy had a very quick and sharp mind, a dry sense of humor, though caustic at times. We got along very well and became good friends. In later years, as I became acquainted with Richard Burton (on screen only), I felt as though I knew the actor as there were so many similarities in the way Jimmy & Richard spoke.

Our flight instructor was Richard Weibley, a young, stoic civilian, an American from Pennsylvania, who impressed us as being all business. He wasted little time with pleasantries and started down the long list of things that we must do in the next 70 hours of flight training. We realized without a shadow of doubt that this man deserved our full attention and respect. Our future was in the palm of his hand. Next to God and country, he was number one in our lives. Each instructor had four students. While Jimmy and I were at the flight line and flying, his other two students: John Foster & Robert Foster, both RAF students, were in ground school back at the main base. In the afternoon we two went to class and the two Fosters would fly. However, before lunch we would take 45-50 minutes of calisthenics and PT, shower quickly, don khakis, run to the mess hall, then off to the class rooms for about four hours.

Our aircraft was a Fairchild PT-19, a rugged, low-wing monoplane which was constructed with plywood wings and a very sturdy center wing box that could stand the brutal landings imposed upon it. The landing gear was wide-spread and cadet-friendly. The inverted Ranger engine was hard-working, highly reliable, and well matched to the airframe for the job. It was unsurpassed as a primary trainer in the WWII era. It was easy to fly, quite stable when left alone, yet with good maneuverability for doing acrobatics. It made fairly good landings if one would just let it do its job, with just an occasional assist and soft touch. It had open cockpits and all cadets had finely chiseled wind-swept features at the end of the course. The high tech gossport tube allowed the instructor to scream through a rubber/metal tube and tell us what a stupid dunderhead we were that day. Note that this was not a two-way communication system. Any back-talk was lost in the air. If feeling rankled, the flight instructor could hold the funnel shaped-mouthpiece in the slip stream and really get the cadet's attention. Such a dastardly act was certain to dislodge any ear wax, or maybe even an ear drum. Our instructor never resorted to this, though I'm sure he often gave it serious thought. There was also a rear view mirror that forewarned the instructor of airsickness. He looked for that pale green shade which invariably appeared before the cookies flew. Flying cookies were not good for a cadet's career progression.

Jimmy James had a real problem with airsickness, and it never seemed to slacken. Since the cadet was in the rear cock-pit, early in the course, the threat was not great for the instructor. Let's remember that General Chuck Yeager also was plagued with this same problem, as were thousands of trainees. Few liked to admit it. Most toughed it out and hoped to survive.

On our first flight Mr. Weibley, emphasized the importance of logging flight time from the time you applied full throttle until the time you touched the line for parking the plane after landing. I suppose the strong emphasis on this subject had to do with the contractor's reimbursement for flight hours. Our first flight was 44 minutes. Mr. Weibley showed me the general flying areas and key villages and topography with which to orient myself. Our flying area had some advantages and some disadvantages. Grand Lakes to the east was a huge recreational lake/reservoir which could be spotted for many miles. Not more than five miles from our base were two huge chat piles from the large lead and zinc mines in nearby Quapaw. The flip side of those advantages was that the land to the west looked like Oklahoma at the time of the Great Land Rush: open range land covered with grazing Herefords and Angus beef cattle. This corner of Oklahoma did not have the east/west, north/south sectional line lay-out that is so predominant in the Midwest. As we flew around the area, Mr. Weibley let me have the controls and fly the aircraft. Never once did he refer to the fact that I had flight time prior to Miami, Oklahoma. I was also privileged to follow through on the landing.

Our schedule called for flying six days a week with ten flight hours a week, including an occasional "down" day due to weather. The first goal was to solo. Though nice for us, to be sure, it would be more so for the instructor, who, at the beginning, was burdened with flying dual sessions daily with all four of his students.

Instructors, much like all other groups of people, come in various shapes, sizes and with a wide range of personalities. Our instructor was quite short and quite plump. I was 6'3" and slim, like Lindbergh, so we were like Mutt and Jeff when walking to the aircraft. His personality seemed to vary from day to day, probably due to the amount of stress and strain we placed on him. He was not a talker, nor did he joke or make small talk. He would not be labeled an easy-going, amiable and calm instructor. He banged my knees hard with the stick more than once and I very highly resented it; highly, but quietly. My personality and make-up did not cotton to this method at all. I was really puzzled by this action as on each occasion he had no reason for slamming my legs, at least in my "cadet-mind." If I had made a grievous error or dumb move, I'd understand why. I pondered on this later at night, but was still in the dark about the mystery. Professionally he met all the standards, I'm sure. He told us, and I felt he was sincere, that he was very interested in having all four of his students finish the Primary course successfully. (I know of one case where one instructor washed-out all four of his students. The instructor was an RAF officer; the four students were AAF cadets in our 43-K class).

We four missed the amiable, more relaxed association some instructors provided for their up-tight students. However, all in all we felt that Mr. Weibley was working hard to teach us what we had to learn, and he was paid very well to do just that.

At the beginning of the RAF training program in the U.S., three different types of aircraft were flown in the RAF schools: the PT-19, the BT-13, and the AT-6. This was similar to the USAAF schools. The RAF commanders did not like the BT-13 and in a few months got rid of them. After that decision, British Flying Training School (BFTS) cadets went straight from the Fairchild PT-19 to the North American AT-6. This presented no great problems, although I'm sure that our ground-loop rate was a bit higher than it would have been if we had progressed at a slower pace using the BT-13.

Yank cadets had at least 70 hours of flight time in order to be selected to go to an RAF school. Most RAF cadets had 12 hours or more in a Tiger Moth prior to Miami. There was little doubt in our mind that the AAF wanted us to perform well while training with the RAF pilots. And we did! However it was no cake-walk for us Yanks. I know that two of my Yank classmates were put up on elimination rides with the Wing Commander. There may have been more; none would have been inclined to volunteer such information. Both did O.K. and completed the course. Before the start of the BFTS in the

USA, the Army Air Corps had provided flight training for the RAF in the Army Air Corps' Southeast Flying Training Command schools. This was called the "Arnold Scheme." The RAF students were commingled and trained with the U.S. cadets. The washout rate for the RAF cadets in the U.S. schools was considered unacceptable to the British high command, including Winston Churchill, and that, in part, is why they wanted to have a flight training program under their control and supervision, unimpeded by what they thought to be an overly rigid and exacting military system.

While we Yanks were in the British Flying Training School, we knew nothing of the history or the struggle that the RAF had gone through to get their own flight training program. I mention this to point out that an RAF school commander would not feel compelled in any way to assure that a US cadet was treated with any special leniency, as some might imagine.

The #3 BFTS military training program was run on the cadet system, very much like our Preflight School at San Antonio Aviation Cadet Center, with cadet officers responsible for the day-to-day military training and discipline. There were no RAF staff personnel living on the base; in fact there were very few RAF personnel at the school. There was a Commanding Officer, an Administrative Officer, two pilot instructors, one navigational instructor, one NCO/ signals instructor, one NCO/ armament and one NCO/ physical training. In addition, there was one USAAF liaison officer (pilot) for the AAF cadets and a USAAF flight surgeon for all personnel.

Unlike the USAAF schools, the RAF-trained Primary Cadets underwent night flying. It was a particularly thrilling and hairy situation at the auxiliary fields where the runway lighting was provided by a string of gooseneck flare pots. Of course some flare pots were accidentally knocked over by swerving and somewhat wayward aircraft on takeoff and landing, which made the picture confusing and a bit more dicey. Other than the flare pots, the area was pitch black. One cadet, I'll call Jerry, was so confused one black night that he commenced his take-off roll 90-degrees to the runway. Fortunately, a fence stopped him before he got up to high speed. The practice of flying both left and right hand patterns, particularly at night added extra spice to our night life. On one occasion I narrowly avoided a mid-air on base leg, while turning final. It was a situation fraught with hazards; each PT-19 was belly-up to the merging belly of another PT-19 coming around from the other pattern, vying for the same final approach center-line. Many of us neophytes wondered about the wisdom of this. But ours was not to reason why, and, luckily, no one ever had a collision using this procedure. We always presumed that The Great White Father of the Great Plains was looking down on Northeast Oklahoma protecting the foolish youth who wanted to be birdmen, even in the pitch-black of night.

In addition to attempting a night take-off 90 degrees to the runway, Jerry was a lad who seemed to have more than his share of misfortunes. One black night he apparently landed long and ran off the end of the grass runway. He proceeded considerably farther in the pitch black, coming to rest against a wire fence. A couple of instructors jumped in a vehicle and went out to evaluate the circumstances. They noted that the flaps were retracted and asked Jerry, "Why are your flaps retracted?" Jerry was always one jump ahead of any interrogator, and he replied, "Oh, I always retract my flaps just before I turn off the active runway." For those non-pilots; without flaps the landing speed is faster, the landing roll is longer and the plane-eating fence is more likely to snare a PT-19. Jerry also had the flap retraction procedure somewhat wrong; they were to be retracted only after turning off the runway. He survived a check-ride but really took a razzing later with his buddies back in the barracks. We all knew he had landed without extending his flaps.

The first solo was every cadet's greatest thrill. It usually took place at the auxiliary field. After a cadet soloed at our school he was not thrown in a horse water tank or sprayed with Coca Cola. He simply walked extra tall and tried to appear extra cool. Soon after the solo, and not as exciting, was a progress check ride. These check rides resulted in some wash-outs, a devastating experience for the doomed cadet. The eliminated cadet seemed to vanish into thin air; a practice that may have been prudent, but was intensely disliked. No good-bye or, "I'll see you around Matey!" They were simply…Just Gone. . After eight hours of dual instruction, a cadet sensed that the solo date was nearing and he became nervous and edgy. At six hours and seventeen minutes, in a very matter of fact manner, Mr. Weibley, after two or three landings one morning, told me to take it around alone for three circuits and bumps. I was excited and eager, of course; my day had arrived. It was a great day to solo. Though most of us had soloed before, this solo was very meaningful as it was one enroute for and "to" the silver wings.

I took off to the southwest and climbed out to pattern altitude. I cleared myself for the turn, then turned cross-wind and then downwind. There was a lot of activity in the traffic pattern that morning and the pattern size was quite extended. Coming abeam the field on downwind, I checked the "T" to assure that traffic was still to the southwest. It was. I was not aware that within a minute or less the "T" would be moved to indicate that the traffic was going to change so that take-offs and landings would be to the southeast. There were others who did not see the change as well, including the solo cadet in front of me. He continued his approach and landed long to the southwest. Just after he passed the stage house in the center of the field on his landing roll he collided with a PT-19 that was about to lift-off the southeast grass runway. There was a deluge of plywood. As I landed, I observed PT-19 parts flying through the air along with a lot of the Sooner State red earth and dust whirling about. More importantly, I observed Mr. Weibley running and waving his arms frantically as I swerved to stay away from the debris. I received a royal reaming for not being more vigilant, although he admitted later that the "T" should not have been changed as the wind was light and there were too many new solos in the pattern. The two who collided and splintered their aircraft miraculously walked away with only a few scratches. I made two more solo landings, got on the bus and rode down the dusty road feeling very uncool. It was not one of my finer days in cadets. Someone once said, "God takes care of fools, drunks, and green kids learning to fly." Yes, I would guess He does, and one never, ever forgets his first solo in the AAF, glorious or otherwise.

After solo we moved into another phase with solo time and dual time about equally divided. On 19 June with 25 hours of flight time I was given my first progress check ride consisting of take-offs and landings, stalls, turns, spins and a forced landing. It lasted 35 minutes and I passed. Another hurdle (none were little) jumped successfully. We then advanced into more acrobatics and instrument training (hood time). We had gone through all of the normal rudiments a student gets early-on, such as "S" turns across the road, figure eights around two trees or cross- roads, and rectangular patterns to learn to compensate for the wind effect on each leg of the rectangle. Later we moved into chandelles and lazy eights and then into rolls, loops, Cuban eights, split S's and Immelmans. The RAF cut back on the time spent on some of these maneuvers in order to add some time for instrument training and night flying. Spins and forced landings were prevalent. We were most fortunate with forced landings as there were so many choices due to the number of large stubble fields and pastures. One could hardly miss in his attempt to put it down safely. An instructor could always offer the opinion that, "Another field right over there would have been a better choice." "Yes, sir, you are right, Sir."

All four of us under Mr. Weibley's tutelage were progressing satisfactorily. Jimmy James still got airsick, and when I flew after he landed I often helped him clean his breakfast or lunch off the airplane. We tried to do it very quickly and quietly so that the dispatcher or instructor wouldn't notice. I don't think we fooled them once. There was a milk pail filled with water and a big brush for such work, and it is hard to scurry around a flight line with a pail of water and a big brush without being noticed. I wanted to see Jimmy make it through the course, but I didn't see how he could if he continued to throw-up so often. What surprised me most was how he managed to get himself airsick when he flew solo. I said to him a time or two, "Dammit, James, don't wring yourself out so much!" He often didn't up-chuck until he was about to land. I found this a bit annoying as I had to climb into an aromatic airplane. Maybe it was the heat and rough air at the lower altitudes. I expressed nothing but sympathy for him as I, like all honest cadets, had come close to airsickness a time or two, but just happened to luck-out.

Most instructors had considerable empathy for the British cadets, as they knew, without asking, that they were somewhat homesick, worried about family and loved ones and some had been through some very rough times. While riding the bus to the auxiliary field we would sing and sing. Strange, but cadets sang like birds all the time, particularly when a bit nervous and under pressure. One morning on the ride down the dusty road to the auxiliary field, we were singing

"Oh, What a Beautiful Morning," from the Broadway hit, *Oklahoma*. We verified so many of the words in the melodies, "there's a bright golden haze on the meadow" and the "corn is as high as an elephant's eye." It seemed to us that they had written that music just for us. The musical had opened on Broadway in March, just a few weeks before we arrived in Oklahoma. An RAF friend of mine, sitting nearby in the bus, became quite choked up and attempted to hide the fact that he was sobbing. It was a long time later that I learned that his home had been bombed and his entire family had been killed. The event was terribly traumatic for him, but he went on to win his wings and lived to produce a family of several children and grand-children.

Flying from an auxiliary field that had both right and left-hand circuits for a single runway resulted in some unusual features. If cadets, after taking off in a left hand pattern, forgot and landed in a right hand pattern, it meant a period of standing at attention by the large wooden tee. All pilots looked at the "T" before each take-off and before each landing and, of course any errant pilot was spotted. In the barracks that night there was sure to be a razzing session with "Who was that standing at attention by the T today?"

John Foster, one of our four, pulled a real boo-boo one day. Mr. Weibley insisted that we always check the obvious when the engine quit. When given a simulated forced landing, John checked the magneto switch, as he had been instructed. Somehow, he thought he viewed the switch OFF, when it wasn't. So, he reached forward and changed the position of the switch (to off) and, since he was concentrating on getting into a specific field, he paid no attention to what the engine was doing. When most of the altitude was gone, Mr. Weibley jammed the throttle forward and the response was nil. He followed his own advice and checked the switch and just in time got the engine back to life. Unfortunately they went through the top of some live oaks trees in the process leaving some tell-tale evidence still clinging to the sturdy PT-19 when they landed. Mr. Weibley tensed.

A short time later, I was on a dual flight with him. He gave me a long set of instructions before take off. They read something like this, "Take off and break out of the pattern. Fly on a heading of 120 degrees for one minute while climbing to 2000 feet, level, do a 90-

degree turn to the right, climb to 2500 feet, do a 180-degree turn to the left, while climbing 500 feet, do a 360-degree level turn, then turn and fly straight south." We took off and I did as he had instructed. How much I got exactly as given, I don't know, but I felt I had nailed it and I was on the correct heading and altitude. I flew on. Mr. Weibley gripped the stick and slammed it back and forth against my legs. ["OUCH!"] He then said, "Are you going to sit here on this one heading, like a bump on a log, wasting gas? Give me a steep 360 to the right and to the left, and make them good." "Yes, Sir. I'm sorry I did not understand, Sir." I felt humiliated, and very angry. It served absolutely no purpose, except maybe to see if he could get me rattled. (I felt like doing a couple of snap rolls and a "split S" or two in retaliation.) I guess we were getting to him and it was his way of trying to shape us up. Since we were getting little or no feed-back from him, we'd go back to our barracks and stew, worry and wonder.

Our flying training had begun on Saturday, 29 May. Two weeks later almost everyone had soloed. Low flying (dual) had been added to our syllabus and we also had started instrument flying in the blue and yellow Link Trainer. On 15 June I got my first solo flying from the front seat. It was nice flying up front. On 19 June I received my first ride under the hood (instrument time) in the PT-19. By the end of June we were starting cross country flights and the next week we started night flying. Things were advancing at a very rapid pace and right on schedule.

The 19th of July found me in the air with Mr. Yakachek getting my final instrument check ride. On landing, I went right back up again with Mr. Bredengerd for my final check ride. It lasted 49 minutes and I passed it successfully, a most happy day. I still had six hours to fly, and, except for two very short rides with Mr. Weibley, all were solo. I concentrated on aerobatics, which I loved to do, while flying solo. I concluded, that Mr. Weibley was not too fond of aerobatics, although he was very comfortable with spins, and we did plenty of those.

I finished the PT-19 course on 23 July by spending one hour in the link trainer. My total USAAF flying time was 70:14 hrs. I logged 28:06 dual and 35:44 solo. Plus the above dual and solo I logged five hours of hood time in the PT-19, which was of course dual. I had flown 06:24 hrs of night time. And in the blue and yellow peril (Link) I had logged 05:30 hours.

Richard Weibley had kept his word and had shepherded us through to a successful completion of our Primary course, though he had not cured Jimmy James of parking his lunch in the cockpit. At a party at the end of the course, when Jimmy had a snort or two of bathtub gin smuggled in from Arkansas, he confronted our instructor with the question, "Sir, why did you feel you had to bash our legs with that g—damned joy-stick?" Dick Weibley was straight-faced and straight-forward. He put the blame on the flight commander, who, according to him, encouraged his instructors to "rough it up with those cadets if they get the least bit complacent or cocky." I guess this meant, slap their knees and legs with the stick. So then, we knew; the punishment was from the Spartan School Of Aeronautics top echelon with maybe a bit from the RAF Commander as well.

Jimmy James survived pilot training but did not survive the war. He, along with approximately 50-60 percent of our RAF classmates, perished in air combat or training flights. No one seems to be able to put the whole story together, but our #16 course at #3 BFTS seems to have been one of the most devastated of all the classes, including the very early classes. Some have theorized that many were killed in C-47 troop carriers or as towed glider pilots in the early days after D-Day. Robert Foster, one of our foursome, also was killed. I had the pleasure of meeting again with John Foster in 1982. He had just sold his pub and was setting up a small shop of health food and vitamins in a small village very close to Stonehenge. I corresponded with Mr. Weibley several times in the early 80's and was about to meet him at a Miami reunion, but he suffered a massive stroke and did not survive. I did meet his very pretty and charming wife, and was surprised to learn that Mr. Weibley was much younger than we all assumed. One naturally felt that an instructor was five to 10 years older, but that was just in our little "cadet-minds."

In one of my letters to Dick Weibley, I asked if he was aware of Jimmy James airsickness through the entire course and he said, "Sure, we knew, and we really had to admire you two guys working together trying to get away by hiding it. In other times we'd no doubt have washed Jimmy for his continued airsickness, but the RAF did not want to lose a man who was flying well; they just could not afford it." Dick Weibley seemed very pleased that I wrote to him and sincerely tried to apologize for what he felt was his somewhat ineptness at "personal relationship." I assured him that all was not only forgiven, but was forgotten, and that no cadet felt that his primary instructor had been through a "charm 101 course."

Thus ended the hot two months at the auxiliary field, with the chunk of ice on the school bus, and singing while bumping across the dusty rangeland road to the stage house in the big square grass field. No one had been injured or killed and we were all totally thrilled and jubilant, like a bunch of kids. We were also very anxious to get on with the next step and into that dream-machine, the North American AT-6. Some said it was a big, heavy aluminum ship that turned gasoline into speed and noise. Most of us cadets felt it was might-near sacred.

Foster, J. James, J. Foster, R. Jacobs, H.

Flight Instructor Ned Darr

Millikin, E. Swider, R. Jacobs, H. Inman, D.

Mister: Keep Your Eye and Mind on That Dream

Jake between two Brits Lead Blenheim Flt as they engage in a "Spot of Drill"

CHAPTER V
YANK CADETS-IN AN RAF FLYING TRAINING SCHOOL?

Let's examine a bit of history leading up to the story of the RAF training in the USA, and specifically to that of the # 3 BFTS at Miami, Oklahoma.

In the late 1930's the vision of General Henry H. (Hap) Arnold and a few fine officers of his vintage, played a very important part in the history of the Army Air Corps flight training programs and the RAF flight training program as well. They foresaw that a war was a very strong possibility and that the USA must prepare without delay. They knew their flying forces had some equipment inferior to that being built in other countries and that their capacity to train pilots was very limited: only 300-500 per year at Randolph Field, San Antonio, Texas.

Acting on his own initiative, and without approval by higher authority, Hap Arnold sent telegrams to eight private flying school operators, including Captain Max Balfour, of Spartan School of Aeronautics, in Tulsa, Oklahoma, He requested that they meet with him in Washington, D.C. The purpose of the meeting was to discuss the creation of civilian contract training schools for cadets in the Primary Phase of the Army Air Corps pilot training program.

According to General Arnold's plan, the civilian operators of the schools would supply the instructors, mechanics, office staff, avgas, barracks and food. The Air Corps would supply the cadets, the aircraft, the medical staff and would pay the operators on a contractual basis, that is, if Congress agreed. A goal of 2,400 pilots a year was established. Since Hap Arnold was acting without congressional authorization for these schools, no immediate government money was available for the private operators with which to start up their training facilities.

Anticipating that congress would approve contract funding, these men were enticed by the persuasive General Arnold to go out and hock their homes and borrow money in order to finance their schools. Congress eventually did authorize the contract schools and the funding for them by a two-vote margin in the House of

Representatives. An interesting aside here is that the #4 BFTS in Mesa Arizona, called Falcon Field, was operated by Southwest Airways and was highly financed by Hollywood movie stars. Some of the notable stockholders in the venture were Jimmy Stewart, Cary Grant, Henry Fonda, Hoagy Carmichael, Ginger Rogers, Daryl F. Zanuck and Dorothy McGuire.

This program grew rapidly, with many new contractors across the country joining the program as fast as the cadets and training planes could be put in the pipeline. The 2,400 pilots per year increased to 12,000, then to 30,000. In 1945 110,000 pilots were trained. Civilian contract schools employed civilian pilots. They were paid approximately $400 per month, which was a fine salary in the early 40s. The Basic and Advanced Flight Schools were operated by the U.S. Army Air Corps with military staffs and AAC flight instructors. Thus Preflight, Basic and Advanced were in a total military environment. This is only a broad-brush picture of the development of the U.S. Army Air Corps Pilot Training program before the huge build-up of the Army Air Forces program during World War II.

To enfold the RAF training program into this mix, we go to the story about the early RAF flight training in the USA. Early in 1941 President Franklin D Roosevelt offered "facilities" to Mr. Churchill, in order to train British aircrews in the USA. In April, 1941 this was approved and things moved so swiftly that training actually got underway in June of 1941. At this point the U.S. was not yet in the war. The complete scheme was in three parts:

First was the Arnold Scheme, under which the British cadets would be sent to US Army Air Corps schools and mixed with classes of American cadets. Some 7,800 RAF cadets entered training in the United States Army Air Corps between 6 June 1941 and February 1943, with the last cadets graduating with their American wings and diploma in February 1943. During the period between Jan '42 and well into 1943 several hundred RAF graduates were commissioned and then served a tour of duty with the USAAF as flying instructors. They served in many of the states including the West Coast Training Command.

Harold A Jacobs

All Primary flight training for the RAF was given by civilian instructors at Lakeland, Florida; Albany, Georgia; Tuscaloosa, Alabama; and Camden in South Carolina Basic Flight Training was received in the Vultee BT-13, with American military instructors at Cochran Field, Georgia and Gunter Field, Alabama.

Advanced Flying Training, also with AAF Instructors was accomplished at Craig Field, Maxwell Field and Napier Field in Alabama, and Moody and Turner Fields in Georgia. Aerial gunnery training was accomplished at Eglin Field, Florida.

The second part was the Tower Scheme, a much smaller operation, with British personnel sent to the US Navy flying schools for flight training.

The third program was The 'BFTS' Scheme, under which six civilian operated flying schools were set up, using all civilian instructors for the entire flight training course. These schools were designated BFTSs for "British Flying Training Schools." Things came together so rapidly, with all of the six schools' permanent location unfinished, that the training was commenced at temporary locations. The six schools, temporary locations and permanent bases are as follows:

SCHOOL NO.	COMMENCED AT	PERMANENT
No 1 BFTS	Love Fld. Dallas, Texas	Terrell, Texas
No 2 BFTS	Glendale, Calif.	Lancaster Calif.
No 3 BFTS	Tulsa, Oklahoma	Miami, Oklahoma
No 4 BFTS	Phoenix, Arizona	Mesa, Arizona
No 5 BFTS	Arcadia, Florida	Clewiston, Florida
No 6 BFTS	Albany, Georgia	Ponca City, Okla

There was actually a No. 7 BFTS at Sweetwater, Texas, which opened in 1942, but trained only one class in primary, and then was taken over for the WASPS (Women Air Service Pilots) training program.

As the BFTS program gained momentum, the Arnold Scheme and the Tower Scheme where RAF Cadets were trained at USAAF and Navy Air Force schools, were phased out. British Flying Training Schools numbers 1, 3, 4, and 5 were in operation from June 1941 to

August 1945. School number 2 closed at the end of 1942 and school No.6 closed in June of 1944.

It is interesting to note that when the go-ahead was given to provide lend-lease for the BFTS scheme, it took very little time for things to get started. Pearl Harbor was bombed on 7 December 1941; at that time the BFTS Schools had been in existence for only about six months. The U.S. entered the war the day after the bombing of Pearl Harbor. Very soon thereafter, the USAAF requested the flying schools used by the RAF be returned to them in order to increase their AAF pilot output. The AAF had a global war to fight, almost immediately, and they, likewise, needed pilots desperately. After some high level negotiations it was agreed that the BFTSs could continue, but they would have to include a small number of American cadets in each class. Thus the answer to the oft-asked question, "What were you USA cadets doing in a Royal Air Force Flying School?"

How did Miami, Oklahoma acquire a Spartan Aeronautics Flight School? Harry Berkey was the secretary of the Miami, Oklahoma Chamber of Commerce and he learned that the US Air Army Air Corps was contracting schools for training military pilots. When he pursued the matter he found that the quota was already filled. This did not slow Mr. Berkey. He went first to a British government office in St Louis where the British were recruiting ferry pilots to fly American-manufactured planes to England. They suggested he go to the British embassy in Washington, D.C. Mr. Berkey had both vision and tenacity. He could foresee the day when the British would have to train their pilots in the USA. He prepared an elaborate, leather-bound proposal which depicted NE Oklahoma the ideal spot for a pilot training school. The ambassador and Lord Halifax were intrigued, but said that nothing could be considered until, and only if, the Lend-Lease legislation was approved. Lend-Lease passed in March of 1941. Lord Halifax contacted Captain Balfour of the Spartan School of Aeronautics at Tulsa and asked that he establish one of the RAF training schools, and told him of the visit by Mr. Berkey.

Captain Balfour traveled north to Miami and was given a complete briefing. The city fathers felt very optimistic and were confident that their city would be chosen for the school. To their dismay, Captain Balfour informed them that he had selected Ponca City, Oklahoma. Harry Berkey refused to throw in the towel. He requested one more meeting in Tulsa. The Captain agreed, but said it must be both early and brief, as he had to fly to Washington, D.C. that same day. Harry Berkey took a Miami business man, one H.B. Cobban, with him and drove to Tulsa at the crack of dawn. Mr. Cobban had charisma and charm, and he and Captain Balfour hit it off from the very start.

The departure to Washington, D.C. was delayed. The three men had lunch together. Captain Balfour said. "Harry, I didn't know you had such a man as H.B. Cobban up there in Miami. For two cents I would cancel Ponca City and put the new school in Miami." Mr. Cobban reached into his pocket, found two pennies and tossed them on the table. Captain Balfour picked up the pennies, put them in his pocket, and that is how some two thousand of us came to know that there was a Miami in Oklahoma as well as in Florida.

One of the points that American authorities insisted on as part of the arrangement for setting up the schools was that the conditions in the schools should be at the same standard as those found in the USAAF training schools. This, the British government accepted, albeit reluctantly, because of the extra cost. The RAF cadets were most grateful and were most appreciative of the very high quality of the living conditions, especially the food. And the food was certainly outstanding, cooked by Miami housewives in the good old-fashioned way: lots of cream, butter and sweets. We loved it all, ate like horses, thrived, and gained not a pound.

Thus came about, the unusual situation of American cadets being trained on a British program in America, by American instructors, under the command of an RAF Wing Commander. It was an unmatched experience for both the British and American cadets. This was the first opportunity, in most cases, for them to meet young men of their own age from another country. Most of what each group knew of the other was only what they had learned from the movies and newsreels. Consider that these young men were commingled for about seven months in every aspect of their day-to-day activities. Both nationalities settled down very well and mixed together without any problems, much to the surprise of the authorities, who felt that there might be friction. Believe me, it was the pot of gold at the end of the rainbow that kept things absolutely shipshape! The WINGS, that prize at the end of the struggle kept each cadet on his very best behavior throughout the courses.

In my personal experience I found the Brits a very gregarious group, full of life, full of fun and exuberance. They were a very easy bunch of guys to live and associate with. It was a very enjoyable relationship once we convinced them that the B-17 and the B-24 were superior to the Lancaster and the Halifax bombers. Actually, none of us had any first-hand experience with any of the planes, but if you gotta wrangle a bit, and we did, best go at it arguing about the merits of flying machines.

One hundred seventeen American Cadets graduated from the #3 BFTS at Miami, Oklahoma. They were from the Aviation Cadet Classes 43E, 43G, 43I, 43K, 44B, 44D and 44F. The first "Yank" class graduated in May '43 and the last Yank class in Jun '44. According to the official Royal Air Force Records at Kew, England, 2124 RAF cadets and 117 USAAF cadets started in the training program at Miami, Oklahoma. 1493 pilots graduated and were awarded their coveted wings. Of these, 116 were USAAF, one was a civilian and 1376 were RAF. Sixty-five percent of the RAF students completed the course satisfactorily. Although the above figures do not reflect washouts of Yank cadets, I have been assured by some Yank cadets, from other RAF schools, that some of their classmates did in fact get washed out. Unfortunately the RAF records at Kew do not reveal any detail on this subject.

My best estimate is that approximately 575 USAAF cadets graduated from all of the British Flying Training Schools in the USA. No Yanks attended the #2 BFTS, as it was closed before the assignment of Yanks into the British Flying Training Schools, nor did any Yanks attend the # 7 BFTS at Sweetwater, Texas.

CHAPTER VI
TOP STICK!

Primary flight training was wrapped up by the 29 July and the class was free to go on leave; ten days off. This was a real bonus for the Yank cadets; the AAF normally granted no leaves, except for emergencies during the pilot training program as there was always a move to make for the cadets from one phase to the next: Primary, Basic, and Advanced. In the RAF schools there were no moves, thus some of that time saved could be given to all cadets, and it afforded the RAF boys the opportunity to see the USA. The Brits scattered like eagles to the four winds, and a great many headed for California and to Hollywood. Most hitch-hiked and made fabulous time, often receiving free meals from the driver who picked them up on the roadside. Some were happy with shorter trips such as to Denver, Chicago or even Kansas City. A few accompanied a Yank back to his home town. I did not take a RAF-ite home on leave with me as I was from a small town and I felt that, frankly, it would be a real bore for the guy, compared with Hollywood or Chicago.

I caught a train to Kansas City and a bus to St Louis. I could not find any connection to northwest Illinois, so I simply hit the road and hitch-hiked. It was totally safe in those days, and I was experienced in thumbing from my college days. It was great to be home to see my folks and some of my siblings, but very few of my high school friends were about; most were in the service. After a nice visit with family, relatives and neighbors, I became anxious to get back to the flight school; strange, but the place drew me like a magnet. I knew that I still had two- thirds of the flight training to complete, no doubt the hardest part. I was chompin' at the bit to get it underway and finished.

Everyone in our class got back to the post on time. Two of the RAF guys just barely made it, or, shall we say, were a wee bit tardy. They were returning from California and got a rather deluxe ride headed for Texas. They knew that Texas was just to the south of Oklahoma but didn't bother to give Texas geography too much thought until they got to San Antonio. There, they felt it was time to head north to Miami, Oklahoma. They had less than a day to cover approximately 800 miles. Recall that during the war folks drove slowly due to gas rationing. The roads were two-lane and speed was a luxury. Sometime in the dark of night, probably just before the crack of dawn, they crawled over the fence and slipped in to their bunks. What a trip!

Upon returning there were many tales to tell and yarns to spin, and lots of hilarious laughter. We Yanks laughed the hardest hearing about the Brits exploits and their interpretation of things they saw and did. It was a wonderful opportunity for them to travel, and most had done so on an extremely small allowance. Jimmy James had asked if I'd loan him $20. That was a sizeable sum, even to a relatively high-paid Yank cadet. I did so, certain he'd never have the ability to repay me, at least while in flying school. Their salary was very meager, just enough to buy sundries, cover their laundry bill, maybe an occasional movie, a coke for 5 cents, and a hamburger for 15 cents, (with two thin slices of dill pickle on the side).

On 9 August, the two Fosters and I, plus a new RAF cadet named George Grigg met our instructor. Jimmy James had been moved to a different group. We were very fortunate to draw an instructor who was highly experienced, Ned R. Darr. Mr. Darr was a handsome, personable man who turned out to be the ideal instructor: one every cadet prayed he would draw. He could easily have qualified to act with John Wayne in a thrilling movie about flying. We all liked him very much right from the start. The flight schedule called for us to log 130 hours of flight time by 1 December which was only 115 days away, including our one day off each week- maybe. Our plane was the North American AT-6.

With Mr. Darr as the man in control of our destiny, all seemed bright in our small orb. But for cadets learning to fly, big things could occur on any given day that would change our destinies. Our flying would be from the main aerodrome, just a short walk from our living area. A single north/south blacktop runway had fine approach and departure areas at each end. A cemetery on the south side of the field caused some comment early-on, but after several jokes, it went unnoticed, at least until November. At the beginning of the course we went over to the flight line after evening chow, sat in the cockpit of the AT-6 and got the "touch and feel" of the array of instruments, levers and controls. We were trying to get the jump on everything we were going to need to learn by heart. We also wanted to get comfortable with the big beautiful bird and rid ourselves of being awe-struck by its size and powerful appearance. We practiced the blindfold test, which was to touch and identify all cockpit controls, and to recount the routine with another class-mate.

The AT-6 was, and still is today, a very fine aircraft. Some said it was the toughest of planes to land consistently well. We heard that some P-51 pilots said they should have checked out in the Mustang first to prepare them to land the AT-6. The "Six", some said, had little feet, meaning; a narrow landing gear. North American Aviation, the manufacturer of some of the finest planes for the Second World War, engineered, built, and flew the AT-6 in a 120-day period. Yes, that is 120 days. This occurred in 1938 and the planes were first delivered to the British Royal Air Force, as the Harvard. It was also flown extensively by the U.S. Army Air Forces, the U.S. Navy, and the Canadian, Australian, Swedish and Spanish Air Forces. Two hundred of them still fly today in the South African Air Force. More than 15,000 AT-6s were built in the U.S.A. and approximately 5,000 more were built under license in Australia, Canada and Sweden. It has been estimated that more pilots have trained in the "Six" than any other airplane ever built.

My first flight in the "Six" with Mr. Darr lasted only 31 minutes. We did level turns, climbing and descending turns, steep turns and spins! Wow! No time wasted that day. The next day we added stalls, forced landings and some more spinning. It was very apparent that Mr. Darr was born to fly; he was so smooth, so easy with the controls, everything seemed totally effortless to him. His feathers never ruffled, and he always spoke in a composed, un-troubled voice. On the next flight, which was almost an hour, we started on aerobatics. What a beautiful, powerful bird, in all attitudes, including inverted flight!

The next three days was spent on circuits, landings, go-arounds, overshoots and forced landings. On 17 August after 19 minutes of dual, the familiar words, "MISTER Jacobs, it's time to solo!" I did, and it was again the thrill of a lifetime, a prime moment for each of us who loved to fly and were very comfortable with the plane. At solo, I had six hours of dual, which was the minimum necessary for solo. Three days later we added low flying. The RAF took lazy eight, onpylon eight and chandelle time and spent it on low flying, formation flying and heavier aerobatics, the same as they did in Primary. Because of this, the rumor mill had it that we would be going to combat in the Douglas A-26 when we graduated. The A-26 was a new, very fast, beautiful Douglas twin that could fly as fast as most fighters. We who had our hearts set on fighter-type aircraft assumed that the A-26 was really not acceptable.

By the end of August we were right on the school's flying schedule. All was going well with Mr. Darr and his four aces. At this time I had also logged six hours in the advanced link trainer program, which was also right on the published schedule.

The aircraft maintenance at #3 BFTS was accomplished primarily by women. It appeared they did all the same jobs that the few men who were there did. Very few of the work-force in the aircraft maintenance section were certified aircraft mechanics; usually only the shift chief held a certificate. We considered the maintenance of our aircraft to be outstanding. Seldom did we abort a training mission, and I don't recall any forced landing by guys in our class. As I recall, the maintenance work was done regularly on a swing shift in addition to the regular day shift. The dispatchers were men, but the administrative workers who kept our flight log records were women. All of the parachute riggers were female. You might say that without the fairer sex, the clockwork of our flight line would have folded. Such was true all across the USA during the war, so what we saw at the Spartan School of Aeronautics was really commonplace.

The sporting events at our flight school were a bit odd, to say the least. None of us Yanks played soccer, rugby, or cricket. None of the Brits knew anything about baseball, football or basketball. We tried cricket; what a blast! We were total failures and what's more, we thought the game was really off-the-wall. Not one of us had an interest in pursuing it. Some of us tried soccer, but we were not good at running and kicking a ball with the two feet we needed for running. And batting the ball with one's head seemed pretty dumb. The Brits, of course, were so much better than we were so it was their game all the way. We couldn't hope to get any skill in a few short months. We threw in the towel on that sport without delay. The Brits tried baseball (softball) and some of them hung in with the sport and tried to get good at it. Football was out except for a quick pick-up game of touch football occasionally. Basketball was different. Several Brits got very interested in the game. Our gym was also our chapel; it was not regulation size. There were no out-of-bound lines so, when a player bumped the wall, he was considered out of bounds. Bit by bit we didn't bother to slow down to take the out-of-bounds toss and our game of basketball disintegrated into what we called Texas basketball. It was sort of a free-for-all, with most of the rules altered and only the two baskets and the ball remaining to tell an observer that the game was, in fact, some kind of basketball. I played basketball as my preferred team sport. Several of the RAF-ites were surprisingly good at it.

Track, at which I had excelled in Preflight school, was a disappointment. I was consistently beaten by a Brit named Iniff. He had a heavy build, was barrel chested, legs like a draft horse and looked like a football lineman. He was very powerful, but certainly did not appear to be built for running. But, when he took off on a 440 race he ran like a deer. In a 220 race he was a gazelle. In the mile run he always came in first. I was not used to being beaten so consistently, but I learned to accept second place while at Miami. "Oh where was my Preflight coach when I needed him?"

On 1 September we started cross-country flying, including map reading and pin-pointing. On 7 September we started instrument training in the aircraft and the Link trainer time continued at about one to three hours per week. On 9 September I had my first dual formation flight in the AT-6 and it was a great thrill. Mr. Darr liked to tuck it in real close in formation and he enjoyed formation flying as much as I did.

Our next thrill was a dual low level cross country. This was flown over the range land to the west of Miami, and at 200 feet. We planned a 90-minute trip with our instructor and laid it out on the map. That evening we memorized the headings and the times between check points. We also memorized anything depicted on the map that would be of help. The turning points were usually a very small town, a grain elevator or an intersection of a railroad and a stream or a road. The instructor referred to the map and the flight plan and we referred to our memory drum and navigation prowess (no map at all).   This exercise was more difficult than it may sound. At a very low level the check points appeared suddenly and any mistake was quickly compounded and magnified as the flight progressed. When we returned from the flight I was exhausted. but felt I had done a passable job. Mr. Darr, with a twinkle in his eye said, "*incidentally*, Mister Jacobs that was a fine job." I said, "No Sir, *accidentally*, that was a fine job." We had a good chuckle at that silly little joke. It helped to relieve the stress that built so readily in the training program.

Formation flying, instrument flying (hood time) continued and on 22 September we started night flying. After two hours of night dual I was given the clearance for a night solo. Another step up the ladder and another thrill indeed. On 28 September I had another low level cross country at 200 feet, again memorizing the flight plan. After returning from that flight I had my first solo formation. We were approaching the halfway point in our Advanced flight training. A couple of weeks later I had my first check ride with an RAF Flight Lieutenant. It was a formation check ride, and all seemed to go well. After we landed, Flt. Lt. Gartshore asked, "Did your instructor teach you to fly formation that tight?" I told him that Mr. Darr and I flew formation, just as I had with him. He said, "You were really close, but you seem to have no fear, and you did a bang-up job, but you jolly-well had my pucker string working overtime!" Later, I was one elated cadet when I learned that Flt. Lt. Gartshore had given me an "above average" grade on formation work. Mr.Darr was teaching us well.

Some days are much better than others. Things were going along quite smoothly when I had a Link trainer period with a cross-country planned. "Honorable Cadet Never Has A Bad Day!" was an in-house funny. This day was to violate that quip. I planned and double-checked my cross-country. The X-C form was secured to my leg clip board and I was anxious to get this trip behind me. I cranked up the blue and yellow Peril, the instructor closed the lid and I blasted off into the blue; though, in the Link it was always black: night time. I climbed out on course to Okmulgee, Oklahoma, and was leveling off at the prescribed altitude when I felt a large jolt. In my preoccupation and reverie I thought I was actually in the air, and momentarily thought I had hit another airplane or maybe a goose. A second or two later I realized where I was; no sweat, not to fear. Then came a heavy slap on the lid of the trainer and it was opened. There stood a tall RAF Flight Lieutenant looking me squarely in the eye and with his prominent mustache twitching somewhat, sternly demanded that I dismount. I climbed out of the trainer and sensed that I had committed some kind of a cardinal sin. He was very provoked and a bit profane. He asked if I had ever been to West Texas. "No Sir, I haven't, I've never been west of San Antonio." "You were headed for west Texas, Mister, and west Texas is a dangerous place to be when you think you are somewhere else; there is nothing there but bags and bags of 'sweet bugger-all' (a very favorite RAF expression). You were not flying your compass heading. I think you were totally bollixed and maybe flying your ground speed as your heading and you were headed for El Paso." He didn't stop, but continued to let me have it with both barrels. I sensed from his remarks that he was not particularly fond of Yank cadets, and notably the one he was scrutinizing at that moment. He spoke of an immediate check ride. I wilted, as I could see the red ink tracing on the plastic sheet and it revealed an improper course. Yes, I was guilty as sin! He stormed out the door muttering some rather unsavory and tasteless comments about things to come.

My Link instructor was quite calm and composed about it all and told me to jump back in and finish the trip. He positioned the tracking device properly on the plastic sheet and I flew the cross-country flawlessly, of course, with that dire threat on my mind with every turn of the prop (whoops-no prop). To the best of my knowledge nothing ever came of my "reckless ways" on that "bad day" in the Link, high in the skies over Oklahoma. From that day on, I was painstakingly cautious to high-light my flight plan in heavier colors, and to assure I flew the compass heading. At the end of the training course my Link Flying grade was *High Average*. I had to chuckle. Now, I must apologize to all west Texans for the Flight Lieutenant's remark that west Texas was nothing but bags and bags of sweet bugger-all. He could get himself shot for saying those words west of the Pecos.

Soon thereafter we started air-to-ground gunnery. The class, two ahead of ours had an air-to-ground gunnery accident. The student was solo and he got fixation on the target and flew his AT-6 right into the ground-positioned bulls-eye. The plane was demolished and the RAF cadet was patched up in a hospital over the next seven to eight months and then finished the course. The cadet was a student of Mr. Darr, my instructor; thus Mr. Darr was very thorough in his briefing and included a very strong admonition about fixation on the target. After the accident the school did alter the procedure somewhat. They placed a chalk line on the ground about 100-200 yards before the big wooden bulls-eye. As the student crossed over the chalked line in a dive, he was obliged to pull up abruptly so as to avoid coming too close to the target. It took a bit of the fun and realism out of the attack, as one tended to be more concerned with the chalk line than with the target.

Next came some night instrument time and working the radio range at Neosho, Missouri. We had considerable experience with this in the Link trainer prior to the real thing in the air. When we worked the radio range we were always dual; sometimes the man in the front seat was my flying partner, George. Sometimes we reversed roles; he in the back under the hood with me in the front. We flew the radio range on day flights also, and to the man under the hood it made little difference. He was always somewhat in the dark, sun or moon!

In late October we had a high level solo cross-country at night; some flew at ten, some at eleven and some at twelve thousand feet. We wondered about flying this high without oxygen, particularly at night. The triangle flown was north into Kansas. It was a gorgeous night with clear skies and a full moon. All went well with all those who flew that night, except for one RAF pilot, Wally Elliot. He did not return. Soon a call came from a county sheriff telling of a wreckage in the middle of a state highway, with no known survivors. It was Wally's aircraft and the wreckage revealed that he was in the cockpit at the time of the crash.

Everyone liked Wally. He was a kind and gentle man and somewhat shy. He was in my flight and I knew him quite well. Wally was older than most all cadets, as he was 29; most of us were 19 to 22 years old. In our naiveté we thought the probable cause of the accident may have been the fact that Wally was simply too old to be flying these hotter airplanes. Of course that was absurd. We buried Wally in the city cemetery very near our flight school. It was a military funeral and all cadets in our class were in the funeral parade;

a very slow march was the way the Brits did it, with a pause after each step. It was very moving and very nicely carried out.

Wally is one of 15 RAF cadets buried in a single line in that cemetery. For years and years a local Miami lady, Mrs. Hill, cared for each of those grave sites, placing flowers on each grave on each Memorial Day. Her husband helped, but it was Mrs. Hill who was totally devoted to "her boys." She is, today, with her husband, buried in that single line with "her 15 boys." A plaque honors her with a message on it from Queen Elizabeth II.

At each #3BFTS reunion in Miami, a solemn ceremony is held at the grave sites, and we who are there and were Wally's class-mates, assure that a wreath is placed on his grave. Today an RAF officer who is on temporary duty with the USAF at Tinker AFB, Oklahoma City, assures that each grave is properly cared for and he personally goes to the Memorial Day services. When he rotates back to the UK, his replacement does the same. The Royal Air Force knows how to take care of its own.

Wally's grossly mangled and smashed AT-6 was placed on the flight line near the point where all cadets approaching to fly would see it. It was meant as shock treatment and it certainly was to us who knew him and enjoyed his friendship. The wreckage still had human tissue imbedded in the cylinder flanges and blood stains were very evident throughout the wreckage, even though the wreckage had been washed down. We did not appreciate this repugnant flying safety lesson at all, but of course we said nothing. We felt it was grossly improper and insulting. But that's the way it was; flying safety messages had to be jolting.

A new phase that started at the end of October was Air-to- Air Gunnery. We used cameras only. Live ammo was out of the question, even in the sparsely settled rangeland of Oklahoma. We started with dual and then had some solo sessions. It usually started as a formation flight, then one plane broke away and made passes at the target plane. This took good coordination, and Mr. Darr, again taught me very well. After some periods and some filming, he proudly announced that my film was being used as a "how to do it" sort of thing. At that moment I knew I was destined to go to fighters upon completion of the course. It was so nice to dream. The guy cutting the orders with our graduation day assignment would never once look at my air to air gunnery film. A fat chance!

One day on a dual flight Mr. Darr apparently concluded we could goof around some. In inverted flight he asked me to center the ball. Of course that was impossible as its concave only when right side up. He then said, "Let's see how this thing climbs to 15,000 and let me know if you are feeling real woozy, and I'll do the same." We did, and I felt how sloppy and sluggish the controls were getting, and also I was feeling flushed and sluggish myself. Then he suggested we see how many turns we could do in a spin. Down we came and rolled out after about sixteen complete turns. Except for plugged ears and the close terrain, I thought it was great. Mr. Darr said, "Let's just keep that little exercise to ourselves, okay?" Sure thing, it was fantastic!

As we went from phase to phase, we continued to spend a certain amount of time doing the basics, aerobatics, steep turns, spins, circuits and bumps (landings), and flying under the hood. When we were dual we got a goodly number of forced landings. The end of our flight training was drawing near as we worked our way through November but we still had our overnight cross country yet to complete. We hoped we would get to fly to El Paso. But the Wing Commander thought it best to fly north where there was heavier population and, in the event of a forced landing a student would not be way out in the middle of those bags and bags of sweet-bugger-all... which is very dangerous, you know, particularly in the winter months!

We left on 9 November and I flew with Don Inman, a Yank cadet, from Miami to Oklahoma City (El Reno) then north to Wichita, Kansas, where we landed. I was navigator on that leg. Then we swapped seats and I was pilot with RAF Cadet Jameson as my navigator and we flew from Wichita to Lincoln, Nebraska. We stayed overnight at the Army Air Field in tar paper shacks and nearly froze to death. It made us appreciate the fine billets we had back in Miami. The next morning after breakfast we flew from Lincoln to Chillicothe, Missouri, and then on to Des Moines, Iowa, where we landed. I navigated for Charles on that leg. He was not the best pilot in the RAF, and while flying in formation on that leg we came within inches of hitting another aircraft broadside in a totally foolhardy maneuver. The other plane's prop missed my skull by a few inches. Charles broke every rule in the book. He simply explained it away by saying, "I have no idea why I did that totally stupid maneuver." I found it quite unsettling, since we were so close to winning our wings, and I'm sure there were several other reasons why I wanted to live a few more years.

The next leg was from Des Moines back home to Miami. I was pilot and Don Henderson was my navigator in the back seat. Don was a solid troop, a good pilot, and we still correspond today. Thus ended our "grand tour" of Oklahoma, Kansas, Nebraska, Iowa, and Missouri. It was on this trip that we learned that it is better to have a three-hour bladder and two hours of gas than vice-versa. It was a fun trip and we got our first exposure to snow and ice on the runways and taxi-ways at Lincoln Army Air Field.

We got more and more solo hours as the course drew to a close. Coffeyville, Kansas, an AAF Basic flying school, was not too far to the north of us and at Independence, Kansas there was another AAF Basic school just to the west of Coffeyville. Our practice areas were tantalizingly close to these two schools. Their BT-13s and BT-14s were no match for our AT-6s. When one (not saying who, of course) saw these slower, gear-welded-down basic trainers, the temptation to engage in something verboten was very great. Most of us satisfied our egos by cobbing the engine and racing by them at twice their speed. We were too close to the WINGS to do anything stupid, though it would have been nice to have done a roll around them. The boys flying those aircraft in the early portion of our AT-6 training were our 43-K classmates from Preflight school in San Antonio, and our so-called Basic training was in AT-6s. We often wondered if some were old buddies. Years later, we learned that many were.

On 12 November I got my Wings final instrument check ride with a Spartan Flight Commander, Mr. Fichter. It was 45 minutes and I passed. On 17 November I flew again with Flt. Lt. Gartchore on my Wings final general check ride. It was only 46 minutes and it went fine. On 22 November I flew with Jay Daffendol, another Spartan Flight Commander and received my Wings cross-country check. It lasted 2 hours. I passed! Could it really be? I had finished all of the check rides satisfactorily. I had about six more hours to log to finish my total hours and most of that was solo. My final flight at Miami was on 26 November and I practiced aerobatics, and as always, circuits and bumps. I finished all air training with 200 flight hours in the USAAF. Now to those wretched written exams.

Our ground school training was very thorough and the instructors were excellent. All were Spartan civilian employees except our armament instructor. He was an RAF Sergeant and was a Cockney and was very difficult to understand. He murdered the king's English, but got his messages across to his students. In my notes I wrote down a phrase that caused some snickering: in speaking about a machine gun that we were obliged to study, he said, "When the pin fires, the bullet nips smartly up the barrel, hotly pursued by the residential (residual) gases." When there was talking between students, his expression was "Po us hup chaps." Shades of Casey Stengel!

We learned to disassemble a .30-caliber machine gun and, we hoped, put it back together in the allotted time. Why we had to learn that, we never quite understood. We had a somewhat archaic bombsight and worked problems on paper. Our U.S. Norden bombsight was, of course, top-secret, and only bombardiers were taught to use it. Our three biggest courses were Navigation, Meteorology and Theory of Flight/Aerodynamics. The Navigation was the most difficult as it was all done as a navigator does it, on a map, plotting everything out using pencil, ruler, compass, and protractor.

The final Wings Exams were really tough. We studied far into the night to bone up on some of the subjects. The finals were comprehensives, carried a lion's share of the final grade and covered all material received from day one. When I saw the problems on the Navigation written test, my gyros tumbled. It was a kind of problem we had never worked before in that it put us over the target (Berlin), the navigator was dead, and all data up to that point was supposedly lost. Get out a new map and get us home! It was a toughie, and I thought it was a bit extreme, but who was I to question the RAF? Get with it man! When we got over the channel we had to descend and do a square search for a downed crew. All of the square search had to be plotted out as well. On top of all this there was a time limit for completing the test. I busted the thing wide open. Several others did too. We had a retake, but even if the repeated test grade was perfect, the final grade for Navigation would be 70. Fair enough! We had the same rule in Preflight School in San Antonio. I got a 70 in Navigation. We all managed to finish all the writtens with a passing grade and the high pressure had ended. It was a heavenly feeling. Now, on to the party and the Wings parade.

We Yanks went to Camp Crowder in Joplin, Missouri, some 30 miles northeast of Miami, to purchase our officer uniforms. We had a one-time sum for that, and as I recall the $250 bought all we needed, including the forest green blouse, the pink trousers, green trousers, and a nice trench coat and caps. We also bought new summer uniforms from that fund. No doubt it paid also for socks, shoes, ties, and maybe even new underwear and maybe a hankie (RAF term) or two.

Our new Flighter caps were immediately given the fifty-mission crush treatment. This, as I recall, was very simple. You took this nice new cap which had a leather bill on it, you removed the grommet and wrapped the cap in a damp bath towel, put it under the mattress and slept on it. The next morning you let it dry out, you banged it against the bunk a few times, you jumped on it a few times and you had yourself a fifty-mission Flighter that made you look like you'd spent ten months in combat in North Africa. This really boggled the minds of the Brits, as did many of our other antics.

Our graduation party was in the mess hall. Oklahoma was a dry state, and our county and city were even drier. But there seemed to be booze from somewhere. Most of it was Arkansas White Lightnin. There seemed to be an ample supply, brought in by town officials who loved to be invited to attend each graduation party. We were all quite amused at the reason given for having a "dry state." The story was that the Indian population was prone to drink heavily and go off the deep end; thus, the white man had to protect them from self-destructing. From my observation some of the movers and shakers from the town, and of course a "few" cadets needed the same protection. Never mind, the booze flowed. It was a fine party, but mostly stag and mostly eating, drinking, talking and naturally some singing. I remember we had tremendous steaks, big enough to choke a Great Dane. I would guess that one of the city fathers provided those huge steaks. No girls, so no dancing. The tales got more bodacious as the night went on. Our instructors were there, of course. The party was the social climax for our class. The next morning we got to sleep in; a very rare luxury.

One of my most vivid recollections of the final two weeks before our Wings parade was the fatigue. I imagine every cadet felt just about the same. We never seemed to get enough sleep and it seemed as though the energy was slowly fading and being drained out of every fiber of our youthful bodies. We felt old.

It was Saturday, 4 December 1943. The day for the Wings parade really, finally, arrived! The whole scene is seared for-evermore in my memory drum because it was my dream come true. We had been so vulnerable throughout the course, from start to finish; a thousand opportunities to washout had visited each of us, but somehow, someway we had deflected them one by one. We were young, full of life and full of folly and so naive about so many things which we, of course, felt totally cocksure of. We had persevered, we had survived, and we all agreed that we had been very, very lucky.

The weather was great, the temperature suitable for those beautiful pinks and greens without need of a trench coat. We wore no rank on our new officers uniform, as our commissions to Second Lieutenant had not yet arrived. The band played and we paraded on the flight line tarmac with a hint of gunk in the air. The AT-6s were all precisely aligned and lustrous in the sun. Pete, our mascot, with his usual non-regulation air, trotted alongside the formation. We knew he would miss us. This was the last day we seventeen Yank Cadets would have to march RAF style. We could return to our AAF way which was much more comfortable. After we passed in review we turned and came back to form in front of the reviewing stand, where the officials and guests were gathered. Our RAF Wing Commander gave a short, inspiring speech, and, as always, sounding like Winston Churchill. AAF Brigadier General Hornsby also delivered a very nice appropriate message. His words hardly penetrated my mind. I was in a daze.

First we were all pinned with RAF wings; on the left side. Then we seventeen Yanks formed up in front of the class formation and General Hornsby came down the line and presented each of us our: SILVER WINGS- WE WERE IN!!!

Emotions ran high; those long, arduous months, loaded with doubts, excitement and trepidation, were at an end—the end of our beginning chapter and the start of a whole new life. We were all on cloud nine, right there on the black tarmac which we had crossed so many times before, carrying our parachutes out to fly the Six.

Then RAF Cadet Jeff Hanson and I were called forward and given special recognition for the number one spots in the course. Jeff was recognized for scholastic achievements and I was recognized for the highest flying grades. The award for Jeff was no surprise; for me it was a surprise, and maybe, even for my flight instructor. At no time during my cadet days did I envision receiving the "top stick" award. My aim was to complete the course successfully. On receiving the declaration of the award, I choked, but quickly recovered.

After we broke ranks, my very proud mother and my sister Lola, pinned those beautiful silver wings on the left side where they belonged, and moved the RAF wings to the right side of my blouse. I said, "Hey, Mom, Hey Lola, how about that? How lucky can a guy get? Not only wings and Second Lieutenant's bars but TOP STICK, Wowee!" She smiled proudly, but I'm sure her mind was on concerns about my future flying and where I'd be going and if I'd get that long dreamed-of fighter plane. Perhaps she offered up a quick prayer that I'd be flying cargo.

Two hours later the RAF boys were on buses headed for the train station a mile away. We Yanks were there to bid them goodbye. Excitement filled the air, the whistle blew, some steam was released from the giant locomotive and the train rolled north and disappeared. For a moment we felt sadness, but then had to blink a few times and say, "Just like that, the Brits are gone!" But, there was so much excitement, and so much to do, those feelings quickly passed.

Finally a word of thanks and praise for our Ned Darr who coached his four fledglings through the program successfully and did it in a way that we truly appreciated. He was a talented pilot and flew an airplane in such a classy way. It was easy to absorb his talents and feel good about each phase as we progressed through it. We were truly fortunate to have had "the very best" of the many fine Spartan Aeronautics instructors. Ned flew professionally until age eighty. We corresponded and visited on the phone many times until his passing in year 2000. I am the sole survivor of the five of us. Two were lost in the war. Ned told me I was the only AAF cadet he instructed at the #3 British Flying Training School.

On 8 December our commissions arrived and we all pinned on our gold bars and did our final packing. The tortuous, wonderful, fantastic and totally unique experience had wound down.

SILVER WINGS!! Top Stick!! What a Deal! What a Life!!

Second Lt. Jacobs receives a handshake and congratulations from AAF Brigadier General Hornsby. Wing Commander Roxborough, #3 BFTS School Commanding Officer, looks on.

CHAPTER VII
BERRY, BIVUOAC AND BASIE

On 8 December the high waters in southeast Oklahoma subsided, the trains got through and our orders arrived. Our AAF commander called us in and presented our orders. The orders stated that we would be discharged as Aviation Cadets for the convenience of the government, commissioned as 2nd Lieutenants and ordered to aerial duty as pilots. All was accomplished on a very few thin sheets of recycled paper. We had heard rumblings that some of the previous USAAF graduates from the RAF schools had been assigned to the Air Transport Command.

I was absolutely certain that that just could not happen to this "hot pilot". What a travesty of justice that would be. But it happened for sure. All seventeen of us received identical orders; we were given travel time, about one week's leave and ordered to report to Berry Field, Nashville, Tennessee for further processing. My reporting date was 19 December. The very popular song, *I'll Be Home for Christmas* was probably not yet on the Hit Parade.

To say that I was disappointed is an understatement. The abbreviated leave and the reporting just before Christmas was not the big downer that the assignment was. I was taught as a youth that a real man will do what has to be done regardless of personal wishes and will do it to the very best of his ability. The AAF got that same message across to all of us, though in somewhat different terms. There was a big war raging and we knew we were the luckiest guys on earth to have finished the very demanding pilot training program successfully. We also fully realized there were tens of thousands of young guys who would be very happy to trade places with us. So with dogged resolve, but with deep disappointment we turned to doing our final packing and headed for the train station.

Before we left our immaculate flight training campus we were instructed to swing by the Flight Surgeon's office and have some of the latest exotic medicine that would stave off all the bad germs in vogue. I believe the pills were sulfa, and the size of the them was befitting a race horse. I took the pills and gathered all my gear, including all the heavy sheepskin lined flight boots, pants, jackets, helmet, etc, and joined other classmates and headed for the train station. The big pills were kicking in and I felt very woozy and tipsy. Other passengers probably said under their breaths, "Look at those young Lieutenants, half tanked, and it is not even noon yet!" As with our departure from the Classification Center and Preflight School, we never looked back. We had the whole world in a jug, and everything lay out in front of us. It was ours to have, and by and large we felt ready, eager and able.

I had traveled in high style ever since reporting in at the Chicago Loop in February. What a rude awakening! We who were headed to Kansas City for connections, climbed into a passenger car that appeared to be de-mothballed, and thrust back into its first duty since the Civil War. I recall the seats were wooden and wicker, and each seat had some small foot rests that looked like the kind you see at a shoeshine stand. Fortunately K.C. was only a two to three hour ride. From there I caught a Santa Fe connection to Chillicothe, Illinois. I will never forget what a difficult time I had getting my A-3 bag and my B-4 bag, plus other bags from one train to another. I was either too scotch to pay a porter to assist me, or maybe none was available. It seems everyone else was struggling like I was. Such were the conditions in a train or bus station during the war.

I arrived home, and was warmly greeted by the hometown folks. I was the second local small-town boy who had successfully made it through the big grinder to win pilot wings. My mother was very discreet in her comments about my being assigned to transport aircraft as she knew full well that I had my heart set on fighters, but I felt that her prayers had no doubt been answered. Both of my parents felt that flying was a very risky profession. The leave went swiftly and I was off to catch a train to Chicago, then south to Cincinnati and Nashville. I was ready to enter the real world in the Army Air Forces. I was ready, but subdued, and not at all satisfied with the picture formed in my mind about the future.

Another aggravation was that we had to spend some time in the Ferry Command in the states in order to build up some experience before shipping overseas as a transport pilot. We really didn't know too much about being a ferry pilot. We thought of ferry pilots not only as "fairy-pilots" but those who had not been trained in the military:

Service Pilots- they wore an "S" on their wings. We were ill-informed, very naïve, but most of all Muy Macho. Most of us wanted to see action, in fighters or even in bombers and without delay. Keep in mind, we were trained in single-engine to be fighter pilots and all else was repugnant. It is this kind of "youthful logic" that makes young men good warriors. With a bit more maturity and sagacity we'd have been very happy to be going to transports.

Our stint at Berry AAF in Nashville was approximately one month. We joked that they had sent us down there to learn how to fill out a per diem voucher. We also got our flying time in for December and January and we were trained very well with the .45- caliber pistol. When we had a light day we went out on an eight or ten mile hike. The band was always there to meet us as we arrived back at the base and we'd march to the parade ground where we would stand retreat. Another day was done. Sometimes the hike and the band would lift our spirits to a higher level.

Though it was mid-winter we went off on a bivouac for about six or eight days. Of course it snowed and rained most days and it was not enjoyable. The benefits were questionable, at least in the minds of a bunch of young second lieutenants. We learned how to pitch tents and make camp in the Tennessee mud, but we who had been Boy Scouts already had that skill.

One lucky encounter was with a Personal Affairs Officer. He was a very personable Captain and had been an insurance salesman before joining the AAF. He encouraged us to convert our straight $10,000 term GI policy into Twenty-Pay-Life. Doing so increased my payments from $6.60 per month to $20.20 per month, a very hefty increase. After twenty years my policy was paid in full, and since then I have received a most handsome annual dividend; the latest approximately $650.00. Simple math will tell one that meeting that sharp Personal Affairs Officer was one of our better days at Berry AAF. The dividends have far exceeded the amount of the premiums I paid. It pays to keep breathing.

It was during our brief stay in Nashville that we saw General George C. Marshall, the Chief of Staff of the U.S.Army. I have no idea what he was doing at that rather insignificant Army Air Field, but I saw him in a long line of GI's at our consolated mess hall. He did not go to the head of the line, and enter as would be befitting his rank and position. Instead, he waited in line like the rest and talked with the GI's around him in the same line. We were in the same line, but too far behind him to be noticed or questioned.

The day before Christmas there were several invitations on the bulletin board in the officers' club, for officers to join local families for Christmas dinner. Larry Maniex and I accepted one and went together. The family was a local prominent family and the head of the house was, as I recall, a U.S. congressman. There were about eighteen or twenty around a beautifully set table and two or three servants served the meal. The lady of the house had a very heavy southern accent and she very often told us northern birdmen what we were being served. She usually started the statement by saying, "Now this dish is peculiar to the Ole South". Larry and I, today refer to that statement and get a chuckle out of it. The meal was fine and we expressed our thanks and made our egress at the earliest convenient and properly polite moment…back to our tar paper shack at Berry Field.

On another occasion a notice was posted for handsome young junior fly-boys to attend a "tea" at Ward Belmont Girl's School. A couple of us felt that we just might meet those qualifications, and submitted our bid and attended. Everything at this tea was ultra proper. First we were introduced to several of the young ladies, then we sort of paired-up, were served tea and took seats in a large lounge. Small biscuits or cookies were also served. We made small talk. The girl that I seemed to have connected with, was without a doubt the beauty queen of the school. (My guardian angel had just flown by!) She was from Coffeyville, Kansas, not far from Miami, Oklahoma, so we had that geography in common. There were several chaperones in the room and the surveillance was very heavy. I made a date to see her the next week-end. I thought perhaps we could take in a movie. No problem with that, but an eagle-eyed chaperon would go to the movie with us. On receiving this news, we both decided to sit in the lounge and visit, again under the eagle eye of a stern-looking matron, and again drinking tea. I thought to myself, "the temptation to sin must be really rampant around this school." That was the end of that brief courtship, as I transferred soon thereafter, though I did receive several letters from "Joan, in her Tower of London," but then it all slowly fizzled. Apparently absence did not make the heart grow fonder.

Another episode at Nashville was attending a Count Basie dance. Three or four of us envisioned ourselves as authorities on Big Bands. I had seen and danced to many of the big bands, but never Count Basie. He was playing at the Armory. We were not fully aware of the "colored situation" in Nashville. When we got there and went to the window to pay our entry fee, the lady looked at us with puzzlement, and politely asked us if we knew that the dance was for people "of color." We rather ignorantly said that we just wanted to watch, and listen to the Count. She talked to another person beside her and they "lowed-as-how" we were in uniform; we could come in, but suggested we sit in the balcony. Thus I got to hear the great Count Basie Band, just tapping my fingers and my feet. There was real jiving and jitter-bugging on the floor below by perhaps one to two thousand fans. We enjoyed it all and were glad we went. The Count played for perhaps 50 more years, but I never had another chance to hear him, or to jump to his very unique sounds. By mid-January the AAF/Air Transport Command/Ferry Division had decided where each of us should be assigned. We seventeen from Miami were still together. Fifty percent of our original group was to go to Newcastle AAF, Wilmington, Delaware. Two were to go to Kansas City and the rest to west coast bases. I was to go to Newcastle along with several of my best friends, so things were looking good. Berry AAF had been just a staging area and we would not miss the rather poor accommodations or the shortage of aircraft, or the hanging in limbo, but after all, it was a repple depple (replacement depot).

Once again we bid farewell to a base, packed our gear and boarded a train for Washington, D.C. and nearby Wilmington Delaware. I managed to turn in all my heavy winter flying gear so that I did not have to lug it to the new station. The supply officer assured me that I would receive "like new issue" when I needed it. I did keep my beloved A-2 leather flight jacket and my white nylon scarf made by the ladies in the parachute rigging shop in Miami, Oklahoma. Cheers, Berry AAF in January, 1942

CHAPTER VIII
THE MAGNIFICENT MARAUDER (B-26)

On our train ride from Nashville to Wilmington there was an episode in the dining car I remember vividly. Four of us classmates were at a table for dinner and one of the four at the table was a classmate I did not know well. Joe was from the deep South and had never been north of the Mason-Dixon Line. In addition, he had apparently been raised in a very segregated community.

All of the waiters were black, which was quite routine in those days. Our waiter was changing linen on the table across the aisle. He hurriedly placed a lot of silverware on our table, while he changed the white cloth, and then he picked it up and placed it on the table he was going to set up. Normally in those days the pace was hectic in the dining car as many people were waiting in line to eat. Our southern classmate became very excited about the noise the waiter made moving the silverware around. He addressed the waiter in a very patronizing and commanding way, almost as though they were in the cotton field back on the plantation.

The overstressed black waiter was obviously not from the south side of the Mason-Dixon Line and he politely told Joe to go pedal his papers. Joe became so incensed and distraught he was choking on his words. In a violent Huff he left the dining car. All of the other diners around us were very happy to see him go and almost cheered for the waiter. We were very surprised at this affair and somewhat embarrassed. A couple of the guys who knew Joe well were jolted by his actions, but of course none of us had been raised in his surroundings. I saw very little of Joe at our next duty station, but I imagined that he was not a happy Southerner "way up north in Delaware." I believe he was assigned to India some weeks after our arrival. It all made me wonder how Joe managed to get by that psychiatrist in the screening process at the Cadet Classification Center.

About midday we rolled into Washington, D.C. where we had to make connection. The railroad depot was quite close to the U.S. Capitol building, so Bob Harris, Russ Polan and I spent as much time as we could sightseeing. During our stay in Nashville my friendship grew with Russ Polan and Bob Harris, classmates from other flights at Miami. Both men were star athletes in college; Russ in basketball in Wisconsin and Bob, who was from the University of Michigan, held the record in pole vaulting in the Big Ten. Our close association would last for many years.

We arrived at Newcastle AAF, Wilmington, Delaware and cleared onto the base. We were assigned to various squadrons and very quickly got the lay of the land. Our base was close to Baltimore, Maryland, where the Martin Marauder, B-26 was manufactured. Naturally, that was one of the most common aircraft for the pilots at our base to fly and ferry. It was a fine aircraft, but had a somewhat soiled reputation, as it was a bit unforgiving. Some pilots were spooked just walking past it on the flight line. Today, one could say that Glenn L. Martin had really pushed the envelope when he designed and built the B-26 Marauder, a beautiful medium bomber.

There were several political snafus involved in the aircraft's birth and growth and they adversely affected the normal flow in the development of the aircraft. Senator Harry Truman conducted extensive hearings on the problems of the Marauder, and I believe the senate committee recommended that the development of the aircraft be totally scrapped. The AAF knew it could be a great airplane if the politicians and the faint of heart would just step aside. The aircraft went on to have one of the most spectacular combat records and one of the highest survival rates in World War II. It was deployed worldwide in almost every theater of operation.

When I checked into my squadron's operation office, the Ops Officer, very up-front, said, "Lt. Jacobs, what route do you want to take, single engine or multi-engine"? I quickly piped up with "Single engine!" Without batting an eye, he said, "Well, let's see, we often have P-47's going through the base. Get the books and a questionnaire to fill out and get to work so you can fly the P-47." It was music to my ears. "And, oh yes, you'll need a blindfold test in the cockpit, so get in the cockpit and memorize everything for a blind-feel test."

While I was working my way through the process I was quickly scheduled to some transition training in the UC-78 and the Lockheed C-60. We ferried some PT-26's to Long Island from the Fairchild plant in Hagerstown, Md. Later, on a ferry flight, we flew some AT-6s (Harvards) from Montreal to the Long Island area and it was on this trip that I learned that things in New York State work differently than in any other part of the coun-try. Two or three of us stayed overnight in Albany, New York, in a downtown hotel. While checking out I found that I did not have enough cash to pay my bill. I took out my check book and started to write a check. The man behind the counter said, "What are you doing, writing a check for your bill?" I replied in the affirmative. He laughed and said he didn't take any personal checks, and that I had to pay in cash. I asked to see the manager, and was ushered into his office. The manager said, "My God, soldier boy, do you really think you can pay your bill with a personal check?" (I was not only an officer and a gentleman; I was a 2ND LIEUTENANT, WITH WINGS TOO!) I said, "Sure, why not?" I was laughed out of the room. Fortunately, the other two pilots had a few dollars to help me pay my bill, and it kept me out of jail. Credit cards had not yet been invented.

I soon learned that when one was not scheduled for a ferry flight, he was hustled off to ground school to learn all about another aircraft, or another engine, or another propeller or turret. Before I got everything in shape to check out in the P-47 (the JUG) I was sent on a trip to deliver a B-26. On return, another trip in a B-26, and then another and another. I really liked the aircraft. It was hefty, lusty, stable and fast. It had the feel of a fine aircraft and was the heaviest and biggest ship I'd flown. I always flew as copilot as I had had no transition training and was, in comparison, a low time pilot. Some of the pilots I flew with were not really comfortable with the aircraft. Some were non-militarily trained pilots and a step-up to the B-26 was a colossal leap for them. Their shortcomings were readily discernable. One or two I flew with gave me serious doubts about their airmanship, their knowledge of aerodynamics, and of the aircraft in general. One pilot I made a short delivery with left the wing flaps at the 15-degree position in climb and cruise. I reminded him that he still had flaps out. Piqued that a skinny young shave-tail would tell him how to fly, he told me "the flaps were down because we had a good tailwind, and that we'd get a boost by leaving them extended somewhat." Now I did not have an aeronautical engineering degree, but I knew he was dead wrong. I made sure I never got near that guy again. (For non-aviators, flaps do not help the aircraft fly, but only assist it to fly at a lower speed, such as on a take-off or a landing. A tailwind is not in the equation at all. The standard operating procedure is to retract the flaps after the speed builds up so as to fly with a clean configuration; aerodynamically clean and efficient.)

"The B-26 had a higher wing loading than other bombers and the take-off and landing speeds were higher than our fighters' speeds at that time. It was the first medium bomber to go into combat in the Southwest Pacific, out of Australia in April 1942. Few people know that the B-26 fought as a torpedo bomber in the Battle of Midway. General Jimmy Doolittle used three groups of Marauders in the North African campaign very effectively operating at 10,000 to 12,000 feet, utilizing the Norden bombsight. Eight Marauder combat groups went to England in 1943 and 1944. The groups flew against targets in occupied Belgium, Holland and France. They were also used extensively against the V-1 flying bomb launching sites. The Marauders led the bombing of signifycant strong points on the beaches of Normandy on D-Day. Though the B-26 groups had rent great destruction on the Lufftwaffe and the Wermacht, they and their crews were always overshadowed by the long-range "heavies" of the Mighty 8th Air Force. Most U.S. civilians knew the B-25 Billy Mitchell bomber because of the Doolittle raid on Tokyo. Those who did know something of the magnificent Marauder knew only about its early soiled reputation and the various derogatory terms like: The Widow Maker, Flying Coffin, and the Flying Prostitute (no visible means of support). The Marauder crewmembers chafed under the heading, "they also flew." They formed a B-26 Marauder Historical Society, which has a tremendous archive including 500,000 photos, and documents and also a new hanger just for the B-26. They are located in the fine Pima Air Museum, third largest in the U.S. in Tucson, Arizona."

Finally, all was set for my solo in the Jug. I had finished everything and I was prepared. I got my parachute and headed for the ramp where the bird was to be parked. It was in the air, but was scheduled to be down shortly. When it landed and was refueled it was all mine to shoot landings. When the pilot came in and landed, he went by me at what I thought was a pretty rapid clip. In his effort to stop, he braked hard, raised the tail, and ticked the prop on the runway. An engine and prop change were mandatory. Scrub Jacobs' Jug flight!

"Forget the Jug for the time being," said the Ops Officer, "but hey, would you like to check out in an A-25 (Curtiss Hell-diver, SB2C) it is almost identical to the Jug. It has two seats so you can get some dual transition." I said "Yes, Sir, I sure would. Where are the manuals and the questionnaire?" And that is how I got checked out in the Helldiver instead of the Jug. I was on the go with so many deliveries I never got another chance at the P-47. I never did receive the suggested dual instructions in the Helldiver, but did get dual in a somewhat similar dive bomber, the A-24, Douglas Dauntless, which the Navy called the SBD. It was the dive bomber that played a very major role for the U.S. Navy in the Battle of Midway in 1942. It was a beauty to fly and a real cream puff to land. To this day, I declare that the A-24 was one of the loveliest flying planes I ever flew.

One morning when I walked into Ops, the Capt said, "Lt. Jacobs, there is an A-25 probably sitting under two feet of snow in Manchester, New Hampshire. Go up there and ferry it to Bruning AAF, Nebraska, ASAP. I dressed on the warm side and caught a train to New Hampshire. He was right, the plane was buried in the snow, and, yes, it was about two feet deep on the ramp. Maintenance men helped me get all of the snow off and I went into base operations to check the weather, select a route of flight and file a clearance. I did not have an instrument ticket at that time so was constrained to fly VFR (visual flight rules.) While in operations, a Staff Sergeant came up to me with a doubtful expression on his face and in his voice. He scanned my skinny frame and youthful appearance and asked, "Sir, can I hitch a ride with you to Buffalo." I said, "Sure, do you have a parachute?" He assured me he would have one in minutes. We then tromped out through the deep snow to climb aboard. I probably had no more than four or five hours in the aircraft, and had never managed any huge, single-engine aircraft in so much snow. Under my breath I thought, "Does this young fellow have any idea what a novice he is going aloft with?"

We got to Buffalo, mostly by map reading, the old fashioned tried and true way. The plane had a radio compass in it, but I could not get it to work because it had a push button control on it so that control of the radio could be switched from the front seat to the backseat and vice versa. The function of this simple little push button had never been explained to me, and the very valuable piece of navigational equipment sat there unused. We landed in light snow, on a snow-covered runway. I think I heard the Sergeant breathe a great sigh of relief. All was fine until I turned off at the far end of the runway. I failed to unlock the tail wheel and the tail wheel tire blew out. The aircraft was built at that same field so they had plenty of Helldiver spare parts and the next morning I was on my way. On the ramp at Buffalo, the home of Curtiss, the refueling man said to me, "Curtiss knows how to build great airplanes, but they sure don't know how to put them together!" The fact that he had to work the nozzle for the refueling hose through some control cables prompted his remark. The aircraft seemed to have an extra little gas tank anywhere one would fit.

My next leg was to South Bend, Indiana. I spent the night in South Bend because of bad weather to the west. I learned a lesson on take-off the next morning. In my cockpit check before take-off, I checked the electric prop in Manual, Decrease and Increase mode, but failed to place the switch in Auto mode at the completion of the check. On take-off I went right over the golden dome at Notre Dame. As my speed increased the propeller RPM naturally increased, since it was set in the "fixed" position. As the prop screamed louder and louder, I came to my senses, realized the error and then did a dumb thing. I threw the prop control switch into Auto. The prop did what it was designed to do, but in its attempt to get to normal and out of that abnormally high speed, it went right through normal and far too low. Luckily no cylinders left their mounts. It then tried to compensate, and increased again but over-shot normal, with a secondary roar, and then finally settled down and normalized. The students at Notre Dame probably bailed out of their class-rooms en masse. What they heard was a screaming banshee, a big drop-off followed by another roar. "Another one of those wild AAF pilots trying to get some girl's attention!" was probably the talk of the campus. I said to myself, "If they know the aircraft, maybe they'll blame it on the Navy."

I found Bruning AAF, Nebraska out on the plains, and felt at home, since it looked a lot like Oklahoma and Kansas. The ramp was loaded with Jugs. It seemed to me there were hundreds there, and wasn't it a shame that I couldn't get to fly just one, once.

I sold my Helldiver, caught a bus to Omaha and a flight back to Delaware. I never had another chance to fly the Hell-diver. In many ways it was an odd bird. There were bags of restrictions on flying it. It was designed primarily to be pointed down at an enemy vessel, unload the stores and pull up. It could take tremendous positive "G" forces, but one would not dare do snap-rolls, spins, slow-rolls, or pull negative G's; so said the pilot manual.

Back at Newcastle AAF I went on several B-26 deliveries to Nassau, where we delivered the planes to the British. Then I was put on orders to deliver one to the U.K. via the South Atlantic. We were to leave the states from Morrison AAF, West Palm Beach. There were three B-26s and we were to fly together, if all went well.

Take-off morning arrived. We were up very early, pre-flighted the aircraft, and had everything shipshape for departure. The aircraft was combat ready, had several hundred pounds of parts aboard and a full bomb bay fuel tank. We taxied out in the number two position. The number one aircraft took off and at about 300-400 feet we noticed smoke from his left engine. He slowly climbed straight ahead and then turned crosswind, and then downwind. He never got above 600-800 feet. On downwind he angled in toward us and had his nose 'way too high. His speed was decreasing. We yelled, "Drop your bomb-bay tank!" But of course our words never left our cockpit. His aircraft dropped a wing and headed for the sugar beet field below, only some 400-500 yards from us. So ended the life of that crew and that aircraft. We were shook. We had eaten breakfast with them an hour before. We were ordered back to Newcastle AAF as our ship numbers were close together and in sequence. An investigation would be made for the cause of the accident, primarily to rule out sabotage. Unfortunately, I was never again on orders to deliver a B-26 to the UK.

Shortly after this tragic event, my guardian angel arranged for me to fly with 1/Lt Dave Bolton. Dave was a returned combat pilot from the North African campaign. He knew the B-26 better than a young kid knows his Model A Ford and he had not the slightest fear of the aircraft. He tossed off all wild stories as simply latrine rumors. It did not take me long to figure out that this is my kinda guy and the pilot I want to latch on to. All the rest of my flying at that base was with Dave. Fortunately he was also checked out to deliver B-24's, so with those two very popular airplanes, when we completed a delivery, we didn't have to go far to pick up another aircraft to deliver. We rapidly crisscrossed the USA and I saw all kinds of new airports, air bases and aircraft plants. The great benefit from this association was that I learned so much. Dave continually taught me vast amounts of detail and made me appreciate that flying multi-engine aircraft could, in fact, be challenging and even enjoyable. I was shedding my "hot rock" attitude and was "growing up," one might say. (You single-engine pilots can keep that last remark under your crushed Flighter.)

In late May the word was out that Newcastle AAF was to immediately become an FTM (foreign transport mission base.) The base was to be outfitted with C-54s which were coming off the assembly line at ORD, Orchard Place, Illinois (today we know it as O'Hare Field.) All pilots and aircraft not slated for FTM duties would be transferred. The C-54's would be flying various routes across the Atlantic.

Several of us Miami graduates wanted to hang together and we made our requests known to the powers that be. Our wishes were granted. We would be reassigned to Romulus, Michigan. Russ Polan, Bob Harris, Gene Millikin, Larry Maniex and I would remain together. John Peterson had been transferred to the Central African Division, the only classmate to be assigned there, and a couple of others went to the west coast. By this time we had lost our first classmate; John Postempsky had "bought the farm" in an accident in Kansas City when an engine failed on his Douglas A-26 attack bomber shortly after lift-off.

Russ Polan had invested in an old Plymouth and he was able to get gasoline stamps to provide just enough gas to our next station. We had a short delay en-route. I rode with Russ as far as Northern Illinois and went home for a very brief leave. The Pennsylvania Turnpike was our route of choice. We motored down that famous highway at about forty-five or fifty miles an hour trying to get the most mileage out of each precious gallon of gas. He knew he'd have to scrounge some gas while home.

Hello Romulus AAF, several eager second lieutenants are headed your way.

CHAPTER IX
TALL AND SLIM, JUST LIKE LINDY

I was home on "D-Day," which bothered me a lot. It was almost 24 months since I had signed up for the Aviation Cadet program, and I was still in the States. The war raged across the world and I wanted to be a part of the conflict. Here I was headed for another Ferrying Group Base in Michigan.

I probably had not given too much thought as to what kind of aircraft the pilots at Romulus would ferry. I'm sure that my move to Romulus had more to do with what my buddies wanted to do than with my flying goals. I quickly learned that the huge Ford plant at Willow Run was nearby, and Henry Ford was cranking out B-24 Liberators faster than any other plant in the U.S.; and at a lower price. I had flown several B-24s all over the country with Lt. Bolton. I had grown to like the "Big Slab" and felt very comfortable in the bird, so I welcomed the assignment to Romulus AAF. I was gradually accepting the fact that my flying career was taking on a much more mundane scenario than I'd ever imagined.

None of us had received our instrument card in flight school and had not attended an instrument flying school since graduation. We had received considerable instrument training under the hood and in the link trainer in the cadet program, but were not officially instrument-flying qualified. My Miami buddies and I were assigned to the Ferry Division Instrument school, which just happened to be at Romulus AAF. Bob Harris and I decided that we would really show our eager-beaver attitude by taking several extra hours in the Link Trainer. Some would consider us odd, but we were both single and had the time to get "in the box and sweat-out the problems." My instructor was a very personable, handsome young Staff Sergeant named Peters. Before the course was over I learned that his sister was a movie star, Jean Peters and, as I recall, she later married Howard Hughes. Sgt. Peters, of course, did not tell me this. He was a fine instructor and a real professional in his specialty. He may have had much more to do with my future than I ever realized at that time.

We Miami Grads all signed in to the ground school at the same time and in a few days started our flight training. Bob and I continued to get extra Link Trainer time, and Sgt. Peters kept challenging me and pushing me into more difficult things. As we progressed in the course, my flight instructor suggested that I might be tagged as an instructor if I kept displaying such talent. I immediately told him that I wanted to be a sharp instrument pilot, but I definitely did not want to stay in the instrument school as an instructor. A week or ten days later I passed my instrument check ride and was then called into the Major Bieberbach's office. The Major was a very positive and definite man. In no uncertain terms he told me that I had been tapped as an instructor and that I had no choice in the matter. I could expect to stay there for nine additional months. The next day, disgruntled and somewhat dejected I started Instrument Instructors Training.

Three of us from Miami had been tapped as instructors, each by a different instructor. We attended the instructor training together. As we completed the training and were preparing to start our duties as instructors, Bob and I were called into the Major's office again and told that we would be the two new flight commanders in the school. We were very surprised, as the flight commanders we were replacing were first lieutenants. Bob Harris and I would not only be instructors, but the final check pilots for each student, in charge of the flight training program and in charge of all the instructors; We then learned that our fine performance in the Link, and our eagerness to learn all that we could and get as much time in the sweat box as we could, was a big factor in his selection of us as flight commanders. Thank you, Sgt. Peters!

So our nine-month tour began with operating the two flights that conducted all of the instrument flight training. It was a hefty step up. We each had about eight to ten flight instructors working for us. We handled the scheduling of the flying and usually gave the final check rides. We each had very good second lieutenants working for us, all very much the same vintage, which greatly simplified things. We all loved to fly and vied to check out in additional aircraft and build up our flying time. We worked six days a week and frequently on Sunday. Often, in the afternoon, after flying all morning we would get in our favorite airplane and fly off to another AAF, have a cup of coffee and return back to Romulus. There were few restrictions on such activity, as part of our job was to increase our flying time,

experience and prowess in the various flying machines Our
instrument school had several airplanes assigned. In Addition, we had
use of some aircraft on the nearby ferry ramp, if needed, or if we
wanted to fly something bigger and faster. Our assigned airplanes
were the BT-13, AT-6, A-24 (Dauntless Dive-bomber,) UC-78, and
the Beechcraft C-45. We all got checked out in the B-25, as they were
plentiful on the ferry ramp. They wanted us to ferry them to Montreal
any time we could fit a trip into the schedule. It only took a half day
to do that, and there was always transport back to Romulus in the very
late evening.

I soon learned that I could get a B-24 check-out, since I had a fair
amount of B-24 co-pilot time. So I started going to B-24 ground
school every chance I got. I did this while working my regular shift in
the instrument school. A rigorous schedule like mine was not at all
uncommon during the war and was going on all across America.
After a few local training flights and a couple of ferry flights to
Alabama with an instructor, I was qualified to fly left seat in the B-24.
With this qualification I could also go to the Willow Run Ford plant
and pick up brand new airplanes to use them in our instrument
training program. I had an ulterior motive. I wanted to build up my
four-engine time so I could go overseas as a four-engine transport
pilot. When I had a student who was a returned combat pilot or a
heavy aircraft ferry pilot, I would usually use a B-24 for training or
for an instrument check-ride. This sounds excessive in this day and
age and very wasteful, but actually a B-24 used less total fuel than a
jet fighter uses today. And using the aircraft locally was advantageous
in one respect; it gave the ship a couple of shake- down flights before
going overseas.

I saw the name "Charles" on the chalk board, one day while at the
Willow Run Plant flight operations counter. The information on the
board indicated that Charles was on a local test flight. I asked the
operations clerk if that was Charles Lindbergh. He kind of winked at
me and said, "Maybe it is, but then again, maybe it isn't." I later
learned that that was the name put on the board when Lindy, my
boyhood hero, was flying local test hops. We oft-times had to wait
around after "buying" a new B-24 before the aircraft was ready, so we
stood around on the ramp or just inside the hanger where they rolled

them out for delivery. I thought perhaps one day I would see him, but it never happened, at least not until later. (But I had seen Lindy speak in the coliseum in St Louis at a very famous "America First" rally in 1940, when Dippy Jury and I hitch-hiked down to visit Don Fleming who was in medical school there. That was a bit of luck to be sure. All we knew then was that Lindy was our hero and did not factor in the tremendous political uproar that would ensue.)

On another occasion when I was standing by the big hanger doors waiting patiently for my B-24, I started up a conversation with a man who was perhaps 70-75 years of age. I asked what he thought of that big silver bomber which we were both looking at. He said, "Don't know a thing about them, and really don't think I ever will." He had a merry twinkle in his eye, and a Southern drawl. I asked him what he did in the plant and he told me that when it was time for the plane to go outside, he went over and pushed that there button and the big doors opened. I jokingly asked if he also got to close the doors, and he said, "No, that guy 'way over there does that. The union won't allow the same man to close the doors that opens them." I asked if he got bored and he said, "Sure do; one day I got a broom and started doing some sweeping, but the union wouldn't hear to that." I said, "Good luck, and I'll see you here again someday." He said, "Hey Lieutenant, if there's any thing you'd like to know about a wheel- barrow, I'm an authority on them things. It's good for a man to get on the working end of those things every now and then." So there!

In September, Bob Harris and Russ Polan got promoted to First Lieutenant. I did not. It was more or less routine for a Second Lieutenant to get promoted in nine months if he were doing above-average work and had no marks against him. I learned that I had been marked down on an effectiveness report while at Newcastle AAF because I did not salute a Major in the entryway at the Officers Mess. I did not salute him because we were under a big over-hanging marquee and that, technically, made me correct. The Major, I learned, was a lawyer. So naturally, being technically correct had very little bearing on the subject. He was incensed and wanted to flaunt his position and rank for two or three junior officers with him. He asked for my name, called my Squadron Commander and had my report down-graded. He had just been called in from the reserves, so I heard, and probably was not up on the fine points taught to us. I recall the other officers with him seemed rather disturbed by his churlish manner in the encounter, but that helped little. Major Bieberbach called me in and said that I was to continue in the job as Flight Commander even though I was outranked by some who worked for me. He said he was going to correct things ASAP, and he did. I was promoted three months later on 11 Dec 44, almost a year to the day of my appointment as a Second Lieutenant.

One snowy day when it was not good enough for local training, a call came from the tower via our squawk-box. The voice said, "Hey guys, if you want to see General Hap Arnold, run down the ramp to Operations right now." Russ Polan and I took off and were out the door immediately. Sure enough, a shiny B-25 taxied up near the front door. The hatch opened and down stepped Hap Arnold, our AAF boss. He had no sooner scrambled out from under the fuselage when a long, black limo drove up to within a few feet of him. The driver opened the limo door and out stepped the frail, elderly Henry Ford in a long, heavy overcoat and a hat. That was understandable; it was cold, windy and snowing. They greeted one another with a handshake. The two men talked for perhaps four or five minutes, then shook hands again and Henry re-entered his limo and Hap Arnold entered his B-25. The engines cranked as the hatch closed and the plane was rolling immediately. Henry Ford's limo was gone within the same minute. That is how business was done, and how great things were accomplished during WWII. Russ and I did not have the foggiest what was said, though we had the curious audacity to stand quite close by. I'd bet it was a very substantial agreement dealing with B-24 production, and done, no doubt, without paperwork.

In late November '44 I got permission from the Major to ferry a B-24 overseas. Since I had not been overseas yet, except to Nassau, I flew with another first pilot, 1/Lt Kermit E Wurl. We took turns flying the legs enroute. Technically, he was giving me a foreign flight route check. Apparently, the South Atlantic route which was the shortest way, was overcrowded with twin- engine aircraft, so we were sent on the northern route. Our destination was Bangalore, near the southern tip of India.

Normally, to fly to India, one would not head north to Labrador, Greenland and Iceland. Our first leg was from Mitchell AAF, Long Island to Bangor, Maine on the 28th of November and on to Goose Bay, Labrador, on the 29th of November. We landed in very heavy snowfall. About 200 four-engine bombers landed at Goose Bay that same day. The snow storm raged on and the air field was totally clobbered and forced to close down. The snow removal equipment worked 'round the clock, but it was a losing battle. The barracks we were in was one floor and the building was totally covered with snow, except for the doorway. We dug trenches in the snow to some of the windows as we feared we might suffocate.

The base commander was most concerned. He wanted us out of there. Two hundred crews meant about 2,000 live bodies consuming rations three times a day and he did not have the provisions for so many transient airmen hanging around for days on end. The bulk of his food was shipped in by boat in the summer and the bay was frozen solid for about six months of the winter. After five days the snow stopped and we crewmembers were alerted for departure. We were slated to fly, not to Greenland, but to Iceland, which suited us fine. It was farther, but the airport at Keflavick was far superior to the one at Blui West 1, (BW1) Greenland. Our navigator, 2nd Lt. John C. Lawrence was in the hospital and feeling very raunchy. The night before we were to leave we felt we would be given a substitute navigator, which was not our preference at all. But the Flight Surgeon discharged John from the hospital with a most un-professional comment, "You are good enough to make the flight and besides the tail winds are unusually favorable, and we have to get you guys out of here before another blizzard hits."

The next morning we were given a new briefing and an afternoon reporting time at base operations, and an estimated departure time. Obviously with a great number of planes departing, they had to be systematically spaced and stacked for proper separation and for air traffic control. When we arrived at our B-24 we saw the great amount of snow that had to be removed before we could leave. Another crew from Romulus, who we knew somewhat, as the pilot had gone through our instrument school, was parked next to us. His crew had been out on the ramp for about two hours, cleaning snow off of their bomber. They were not doing a good job of snow removal, but the pilot blithely stated that a lot of the snow would blow off as he made his take-off roll. We doubted it, but said, "Good luck, hope you make it!" He taxied out, his props causing huge cloud of snow which showered us. About 15 minutes later we saw his B-24 rotating for liftoff, just prior to passing us. His nose gear came off the runway and retracted, but his main gear did not. The big heavy bird did not want to fly with all that crud on the wing. He was soon going to run out of runway. He cut the power and braked to a stop, with his nose wheel still retracted and his tail high in the air. He was lucky he stayed on the centerline as there were huge walls of snow on each side of the runway. All of the crew members climbed out and scrambled up on the wing and started brushing off the snow that had failed to blow off the wing. They used their gloved hands, attempting to sweep away the evidence, you might say. If it had not been so stupid and pathetic it would have been a hilarious sight. The pilot had guessed wrong, put the crewmembers life in jeopardy and damaged a bomber. Additionally, he closed the only active runway for several hours, which delayed the departure of perhaps 20 or 30 crews, who had to be rescheduled to depart the next day, including our crew.

That evening, still at Goose Bay, we briefed for a departure the following day. Our call sign was ENDWAY WILLIAM. Many of us were now scheduled to fly non-stop, straight across the Atlantic to Valley, Wales. The briefings were very thorough and complete. We had gone through the briefings for BW1, then Keflavik, Iceland, and now Valley, Wales. We would get our assigned altitudes later. We prayed for a lower altitude, as they told us that some would have to fly far higher than ten thousand feet, making it essential to use oxygen masks for the entire trip. The next A.M., we found out that Lady Luck was not in our corner. We drew 15,000 feet and a mid-afternoon departure. Our navigator was still feeling very puny and Lieutenant Wurl was very edgy. I was thrilled and excited. I imagined I felt a lot like Charles Lindbergh before his departure across the Atlantic. Ah, Youth!

We departed on schedule with a maximum-gross-weight take- off. We had two bomb bay tanks full and all wing tanks topped off. Our aircraft had all turrets and guns installed and, as always, various extra parts stowed for delivery as part of the aircraft inventory. We had started this trip on 28 November and now it was 5 December and of course the sun was very weak and low at that northern latitude.

It was a night take-off and almost the entire flight was made in darkness or in that twilight condition of the higher latitudes in winter time. We climbed on course into the night sky to 15,000 feet and immediately noticed air coming in from the canvas seal wrapping around the nose turret. It was due to a tear, and was in front of the pilots' positions. We knew it would be a very cold night indeed. We had heavy sheep-skin-lined leather pants, boots, jackets, gloves and helmets. Strange how that cold could work through all that leather and fur lining. We had electric suites, but, as I recall, we had a problem with some electrical arcing. So we made only minimum use of them, fearing an electrical fire.

John, our navigator, got the chills and a fever. He was shaking like a dog. We had lots of blankets on board so we placed them on the floor in his compartment directly behind us, covered him up with several more, and still he shook. He instructed us to simply follow his flight plan. We were on instruments most of the time, so celestial navigation was not possible, although good Loran was available. We flew the flight plan and trusted our shaky Nav's basic training.

Later we got heavy icing on both the wing and the propellers, and though we knocked it off the wings with the deicing boots, and off of the props with deicing fluid, it built back up repeatedly. We called for permission to descend and got it. When we got below about 6-8000 feet we were below and clear of the clouds, and we got the ice totally off. At that lower altitude we could view the raging, icy North Atlantic. I marveled at Lindbergh's courage sitting in his little monoplane, looking at that ocean for over 12 hours from the very low level that he flew. We had three more engines turning for us.

We then were cleared back to 15,000 feet to suffer through the rest of the trip in the frigid air. We commented that at least we were not being shot at by Germans. We made landfall over Ireland quite close to our expected time of arrival and right on course. The radio compass helped the last 150 miles or so. We had been warned about enemy submarines, that, if learning of a big movement like ours, would surface and broadcast a false signal in an attempt to cause pilots to steer off course and exhausting their fuel.

After an 11:00 hour flight we landed at Valley, Wales, an RAF Base on 6 December. We were given a very small Quonset hut to sleep in. It was cold and damp. They gave us a few lumps of coal to burn in a tiny stove to take the chill off of the room. We knew it was inadequate, and we started scurrying around the area looking for anything that might burn: twigs, paper, card- board, anything. We found next to nothing; the area had been combed for the same fuel, no doubt, countless times before. We ate some K rations and went to sleep. John, the navigator was not well, but wanted to get out of Wales and down to Marrakech where he knew he would thaw out. Lieutenant Wurl was also coming down with something bad after the long exposure to cold air from the nose-turret leak.

We slept through the afternoon and all night and left early 8 December, one day later, for French Morocco. On this leg of our journey we had to fly well to the west of the French, Spanish and Portuguese coasts, to avoid enemy interception. We landed in Marrakech and though it was December it was W-A-R-M, and oh so nice. Lt. Wurl was feeling very sick and went to the hospital. John felt much better. This was a most interesting stop as it was my first exposure to North Africa, a totally different world. Though we did not go into the town, we observed much of the local color on the base. We also saw many German POW's working on the base, especially in the mess hall as waiters, and in our transient quarters as orderlies or house-boys. Our flight from Valley to Marrakech was 8 hours and 15 minutes.

Early the next morning we took off and flew about 1,000 miles to Tunis. Captain Orville S. Rae, the base operations officer, replaced Lt Wurl, who was too sick to continue the mission. In Tunis, we stayed in an AAF hotel right down town on the main, very wide, boulevard. The architecture in the city was heavily influenced by the French and it was a very attractive Mediterranean seaport city. We went into the officers' mess in the hotel to eat our evening dinner. When we entered the large dining room, with an adjacent bar we saw a young Lieutenant playing the piano. He was very good. John, our navigator immediately went over and stood by the piano, as did I. The pianist and John started talking like old buddies. Both men were navigators and both were Jewish. It was news to me that John was an accomplished pianist. There was another piano over in the corner of the bar and we pulled it over next to the one the lieutenant was playing. John sat down at his piano and miracles happened. These two guys who had never seen each other before played for almost an hour on two pianos, side by side, just as though they had rehearsed it all for weeks. They played classical, semi-classical, popular and jazz. No sheet music in front of either, and they brought down the house. I thought they were better than George and Ira Gershwin, or Ferrante and Teischer. Things were looking up, and I was starting to enjoy North Africa. (It was well that I had this feeling. I would later spend three years of my life in Casablanca, Tripoli and Cairo.)

On take-off out of Tunis the next day for Cairo, Captain Rae circled the ancient Carthage area and showed us that the Romans had indeed dealt Carthage a death blow by knocking down every building and then spreading salt all over the entire area. Through history this has been known as a Carthaginian Peace. It was much worse than Unconditional Surrender. Remember, it was Hannibal, the Carthaginian, who whopped the Romans with his elephant brigade. But the Romans had the last word a bit later, and made the destruction very, very permanent. No more Carthage, except in the history books.

The flight from Tunis to Cairo was very, very interesting historically, though not particularly scenic. Below us lay the desert battlegrounds of the largest tank battles ever fought by man. Rommel was gone now, and so was Monty, but the scars of those maneuvering vehicles of all types were etched into the land for years to come. We flew east along the north shore of Libya, over the bay of Sidra, abeam Tripoli and Misarata (very famous for fine woolen rugs,) and over Benghazi and Tobruk, both towns very heavily damaged from bombing and shelling.

The British had taken Benghazi from Rommel on Christmas Day, 1941; a month later Rommel had recaptured Benghazi and held it almost a year. In November '42 Monty recaptured the city. Mile after mile of wreckage from the to-and-fro battling by two great armored units; twisted guns, broken and smashed planes, trucks and tanks were laid out between Benghazi and Tobruk as though in preparation for the making of a super Cecil B. De Mille movie.

The B-24 Liberators of the IXth Bomber Command were located in Benghazi a year-and-a-half earlier, and it was from this base that the Libs made their long twelve-hour foray into Romania to strike the Ploesti oil refineries. One early raid was at very low level; 50 to 100 feet over the target and just above the buildings and smoke stacks. Our AAF losses were tremendous; as high as 25%. The Ploesti missions are said by some wartime historians to have been the pivotal point in the war with Hitler. The bombings literally cut off a huge oil supply which, though it often returned to life, eventually diminished to a meager output and stalled the great German mechanized panzers. Little did we know but right at the time of our flight in 1944, in the Luxembourg area, the last great push was forming up against the Allies, and fuel would be a most critical factor. Yes, as we now know, the Germans thrust in the Ardennes faltered; they ran out of gas.

Our next stop was Cairo. Capt. Rae had been there many times as he flew the North African routes routinely. Our flight time to Cairo from Tunis was 6:45 hours, all daylight. He descended over the area of the Pyramids and the Sphinx which were just to the west of the city. The inspiring Nile River dominated the scene with the lush growth along banks stretching back in some cases eight to ten miles. Pedal-powered irrigation pumps did the job; pedaled by young men and old alike, all with very strong legs, they moved an amazing amount of water from the river outward through the sandy soil, making hundreds of thousands of acres tillable and very productive. .

We landed at the huge John Payne AAF about fifteen miles from the city center. This was the largest aerodrome in the Middle East and the hub of the Air Transport Command in North and Central Africa, southern Europe and the Near East. It was, at that time one of the busiest airports in the world, with a take-off or landing every fifth minute. It was the funnel for all the traffic between theaters of Europe, Asia and the Far East. Captain Rae said we would take the day off in Cairo, so that we "tourists" could see some of the sights. Our one-day tour of the city with Capt. Rae was very enjoyable. Cairo is unlike any other place. It has a flavor of both the East and West. We spent the day as sightseers. John and I took a camel ride at the

Pyramids and then went up into a chamber room of the one pyramid that was open for visitors at that time. It was a climb up a rickety ladder at about a forty-five degree slope. The air was foul and the guide did not provide much in the way of light, but when we got to the big burial room he lit strips of magnesium so that for short intervals we could see very well what he had been talking about in the dark. For dinner we went to the famous Shepherds Hotel and enjoyed a fine meal. The hotel was one of the top ten in the world. It was said that it had some of the flavor of the Plaza in NYC, some of the Claridge of London and some of the Ritz in Paris. It had a most colorful large dining room. The white-frock coated, tarboosh-hatted waiters made a scene most unique. Unfortunately the hotel was destroyed by fire in a riot in the late 40s or early 50s.

After our dinner, Capt. Rae took us to a famous night spot that supposedly had the best belly dancers in the Arab world. We accepted this as the unvarnished truth. We were indoctrinated in all the fine points and movements of the belly dancers' forte. Worthy of note is that these dancers did not necessarily look like Betty Grable, but were more buxom and older. But I'm sure Betty Grable would have given a lot to be able to make all her pivot points propel in all of those alien moves. The music they danced to was entrancing; almost hypnotic. But enough about this. You have to see it; I do not have the words to fully describe the scene.

The next morning we departed for Abadan, Iran, which is located at the top of the Persian Gulf and on the joined Tigris/ Euphrates Rivers, very close to Kuwait. The air route from Cairo to Abadan is above the area known as the Fertile Crescent, with Egypt as the western anchor. On departure from Cairo, even before we got to cruising altitude, we crossed the Suez Canal. It was built in 1859-1869 by the French. Napoleon had speculated on such a canal, but abandoned the idea when one of his engineers reported that the high level of the Red Sea would flood the Mediterranean Shores. (Why do you suppose that engineers would assume that the Red Sea would be at a higher elevation than sea level?)

A few minutes later we passed over Gaza. Soon the Mediterranean was far behind us as we approached Bethlehem, a small village that had led a charmed life and had been spared by every invader. Not so

Jerusalem, which was five miles or so off to our left. The next point of interest was the mouth of the Jordan River where it empties into the Dead Sea, under which lies, legend says, the cities of Sodom and Gomorrah. The Dead Sea surface is 1,300 feet below sea level.

A bit short of two hours after take-off we were abreast Mt. Nebo, which was as far as Moses got after 40 years of wandering. A bit farther we were abeam Philadelphia, now Amman, Jordan, and then we were out over the flat Syrian Desert. Below was the straight line of the Trans-Jordan pipeline which could be followed like a railroad track. Next we passed over the salty Lake Habbaniya, where a British airfield was located and where our Air Transport Command had an air station for re-fueling our short-range aircraft. We could make out Baghdad on the Tigris River in the distance.

The region we next crossed spawned man's most persuasive beliefs. It is where the wheel was invented and also where were charted the constellations of the Zodiac. We crossed Mesopotamia ("between the rivers"), the eastern abutment of the Fertile Crescent. From here we turned southeast and followed the course of the Euphrates. As far as the eye could see there were date palm groves. Next we saw a small town which was the ruins of ancient Babylon. Its hanging gardens were once one of the Seven Wonders of the Ancient World. This is where Hammurabi, King of Babylon ruled and gave us the famous law-code. He ruled 2,100 years before Christ. We know more about Nebuchadnezzar, fifteen centuries later, who bedeviled the Hebrews as described in the Book of Daniel. It is said that Nebuchadnezzar ate grass.

Through this area passed Cyrus, Darius, Xerxes, and Alexander of Macedonia; then the Romans, the Moslems, the Mongols and the Tartars, led by Genghis Khan, and later the Turks. Next on the route we passed Shatt-el-Arab, where the Tigris and the Euphrates unite in a swampy delta. This area is said to be the site of the Garden of Eden. Word was that the Tree of Life was missing. There was not much to see and it is said that it is the hottest, driest spot in the Fertile Crescent. We passed over Basra, Bassorah, in the Arabian Nights, on our letdown and we landed on the delta island of Abadan, where everything is new. Across from the airfield were the tall stacks and towers of the Anglo-Iranian refineries, largest in the Middle East at that time. Our flight time was 06:15 hours.

This area is one of the hottest spots on the face of the earth. During WWII there were thousands of U.S. military stationed at Khuramshahr, which was a huge port next to Abadan AAF. The GI's there off-loaded huge quantities of supplies being sent to Russia. At Khuramshahr the GI's re-assembled American fighters and bombers and the Russian pilots test-flew them locally before they were ferried to Russia. It was said that there was more volume at the bustling wharves in 1944 than in all the foreign trade in Persia in one hundred years preceding the war. We learned that there were 200,000 GI's there and they had the highest suicide rate in the armed services. It was a totally dull and dead spot to be stationed and there was absolutely no commingling of the Muslim population and the American servicemen. However, like many places where American servicemen served during the war, there was little or no chance of an attack by the enemy. Few Americans have ever heard of the place and in all the years since WWII, I have never seen any mention of Khuramshahr in publications or seen any video or television coverage. The U. S. Army also built several highways through Iran (Persia) and to the Russian line where the transfer was made to them. We became very aware, for the first time, that this very dull and far-away spot was an extremely crucial site for the Russian Red Army and Air Force.

The food in the combined AAF mess hall was outstanding. The cooks were mostly Polish refugee women. How they came to be way off in such a remote part of the world is not recalled, but all one had to do was dine in the mess hall and he was most happy the women were there. After the meal a movie was shown in the large mess hall. I recall we saw Olivia De Havilland in *The Snake Pit*, a very uplifting movie if there ever was one. But in those days we watched almost anything, even the depressing, and some in the most depressing locations.

Early the next morning we departed for Karachi, India, proceeding down the center of the Persian Gulf to Sharjah (Oman), across the Gulf of Oman, abeam Baluchistan (India's westernmost state), by Jiwani, another ATC refueling base, and on to our destination,

Karachi. I learned that oysters thrive on the shallow sea bottom of the Persian Gulf, and one of the great pearl gathering centers of the world was Bahrain Island, which passed under our right wing prior to crossing over Sharjah.

There were two or three airports at Karachi, but the USAAF base was the one with the huge dirigible hanger, the world's largest. It was built by the Germans when they believed that that type of aircraft had great promise in the future. The airbase was on a par with the AAF facility in Cairo, with many permanent buildings. It was considered one of the great aerodromes of the world. The terminal building was built before the war by the Dutch and the Indian National Airlines. Near the airfield was Malir, a British Army Post where Monty trained his Eighth Army before his North African battles with Rommel. If Rommel had captured Egypt, Monty was to fall back to Malir and regroup. Karachi was also the terminus for the 2,000 mile Indus River that flowed down from Tibet and was also famous for a fine natural harbor.

For a transient crew, tent city was our domicile, and it was fine at that time of the year. The tents were a British style tent, far superior to the Yank tents. They were a tent within a tent, allowing a layer of air to flow through and moderate the smothering summer heat.

We stayed two days in Karachi for reasons unknown. I would guess that it was because we were now in the China- Burma-India Theater which, some might say, was a whole new scene. We went to town for one day and acquired a feel for the place, and it was a different feel to be sure. The streets were loaded with beggars and the word *Baksheesh-Sahib* (meaning they wanted a tip or hand-out, Sir!) followed us everywhere we went. Some of the beggars were as young as three and they tugged at your pant-leg not letting go until they had received something. Some were so crippled and deformed they could scarcely say the words. Bit by bit you grow accustomed to this wretched scene, as it was so prevalent and overwhelming.

Sacred cows loitered in the streets. Cow worship- "a poem of pity" Mahatma Gandhi called it. Cow worship was believed to have grown out of ancient superstitions to prevent cattle from being killed in time of famine. The caste system prevailed and the only women we saw on the streets were Pariahs, or untouchables, crouched down

127

sweeping up horse manure. You can rest-assured that what the women swept up was not wasted, but probably used at home as fuel. Another caste was the stone carriers. At our airbase where ramps and taxi-ways were being expanded, all the crushed stone was carried to the construction site by women with large flat pans on their heads; they were beasts of burden and probably most happy to have a job earning rupees Many little shops, no bigger than ten by ten feet, were all over the city. In these shops they made anything you might wish, such as mosquito boots, a favorite for the U.S. GI's in the CBI. Also silver Zippo cigarette lighters with any type of emblem on the face were popular. Ivory carvings were a favorite as were jade carvings and all types of precious and semi-precious stones, mounted or un-mounted. A favorite with pilots were leather name patches with the pilot wings for the A-2 leather flight jackets. I got a nice set of silver wings soldered on a large silver identification bracelet. Silver, brass and bronze items, such as trays or bowls, were very inexpensive. They did a beautiful job for a buyer in a matter of two or three hours, if necessary. If you were not pleased, no problem; they gladly did it over again. Their workmanship was excellent and they wanted the Yanks to be pleased. It was a most fascinating day and another totally new scene for us.

On 19 December we flew from Karachi, southeast to Bangalore, which is on the southern tip of India. Our flight time was 6:40 hours. There was a large modification plant there that re-worked the newly arrived B-24s to fit the needs of a particular Bomb Group or convert them to C-109s for hauling fuel over the Hump. We had no idea what would become of our B-24, but we imagined that it would go to a bomb group, since we had hauled all the turrets and armament half-way around the world, the long way. I vividly remember the runway we landed on at Bangalore. It had a 90-foot rise half-way down the runway. Thus, when landing, one saw only the first half, and it was an anxious moment until the pilot went over the crest of the rise and happily saw that he still had another 3,000 feet remaining.

Somewhere along the route we had lost our radio operator due to illness, so of our original crew of five from Romulus AAF there were only three to dead-head half-way around the globe to Michigan. Would we get home by Christmas?

We said good-bye to Captain Rae and caught the first available AAF transport to New Delhi. It was at this stop that we learned about the Battle of the Bulge- the Ardennes Break- out. The news sounded terrible for the Allies. There were many rumors and the picture painted in the newspapers was troublesome and very discouraging indeed.

We pressed on from New Delhi to Karachi to Abadan to Cairo, all without a rest, and riding in a big twin-engine C-46, affectionately called Dumbo. Without pause in Cairo we boarded another C-46 but had an engine problem and landed at Tobruk for about six hours for maintenance. From Tobruk we flew to Tripoli and then to Casablanca. On this flight from Tobruk, Lt. Lawrence got out his sheets of paper for composing music and worked at that for several hours. I asked him how he could write all those different scores for the various instruments in the orchestra without a piano or a pitch pipe, or something. He told me that he was blessed with perfect pitch, a very unusual and rare ability and he could hear the music as he put it down on paper. I would not have believed this had I not heard him play dual piano duets with the other navigator in Tunis. I sat beside him for hours on end watching him compose music from the brain (or ear) down his arm through his hand and out the end of the pencil and on to the paper. I never composed anything in my life, but I could read music, so was very interested in the phenomena I was witnessing. It also passed the time.

As a ferry crew we had top priority for transport to our home base. We could bump almost anyone; that's just the way it was. At Casablanca we thought we might get to spend six or eight hours for rest. Not so; there was a C-54 leaving for NYC very soon and we were manifested for that flight. We flew to Lages (Azores Islands) and then a very lengthy flight to Bermuda. By then we thought that we would be back at our base by the 24th of December, but dense fog in the New York City area, where our flight was destined, was awaiting our arrival.

The crew flying the aircraft was a civilian contract crew. The pilot elected to make a try for LaGuardia. He made his letdown on solid instruments. The tension mounted amongst the passengers. Many were crewmembers, so were aware of what was taking place. It seemed that the pilot was kicking the rudders excessively and was very rough with the control wheel. Suddenly there was a tremendous surge of power on the engines and he jerked back on the wheel to climb and just at that moment I saw that our wing tip had missed a hanger by maybe ten or twenty feet. I'm sure that one of my nine lives went down the tubes at that instant. He pulled up into a missed approach and as I recall we went to Norfolk, Virginia. Several hours later we were back over NYC, with much better weather, and we landed at La Guardia Airport without incident (or accident).

We went to the military transportation office and were told by an officer there that if we hurried we could get on the Twentieth Century Limited and we would have first class tickets and a compartment. That was indeed music to our ears as we were dead tired. We caught the train successfully from the Grand Central Station and headed west. It was Christmas Eve afternoon and we were so happy to be on the homestretch and still in one piece, despite that "feather-merchant" pilot who almost wiped us out...and just before Christmas.

On this magnificent train, one of the finest in the country, John and I went walking about to look things over. We were immediately "latched onto" by a couple who wanted our company. They were New Yorkers. Now, if you were not in the service during World War II, it is rather difficult to understand how it worked. Let's just put it in simple terms. People just loved to latch on to you, whether or not you wanted to be latched onto. Sometimes they were attractive, genuinely cordial and sincere, patriotic Americans who felt they should brighten up a serviceman's life. Sometimes they were total bores. Sometimes you were not quite sure of their motives, and so one tended to act a bit guarded and maybe even aloof. We learned to accept this and most times it was a nice person who had a close relative in the service and they simply felt they should treat a serviceman like they hoped someone would treat their brother or son. Flyers, some thought, were the most exciting guys in the world to visit with.

We were dead tired, having flown half-way round the globe with only short breaks on the ground between hops. We sat in bucket seats the entire distance and we had just had our pants scared off of us by a stupid-jerk of a pilot who had violated regulation by going below his minimum descent altitude looking for some ground. Our "self-anointed hosts" persisted. We must go to the club car and have a drink and then they would spring for our dinner and the sky was the limit. We went. There was a piano in the club car and quite naturally John sat down and commenced playing in his truly magnificent style. Since he was doing such a great job, a crowd gathered around the piano, and we all sang Christmas carols as we rocketed westward. We had a good time even though tired, but the one thing I remember about this couple was their attitude. They acted as though they owned us, and we both resented it. But, anyway, "Thanks for the drinks and the shrimp cocktail and the big steak dinner, who's complaining?" I woke up in Detroit, looked out the window and there was a huge blizzard in progress. It was going to be a White Christmas at Romulus AAF, if we could just get out to the base.

It was not home, but it was my own little Spartan room in the BOQ (bachelor officers' quarters) The most uplifting part of the day was that the Allies had turned the tide in the Ardennes Forest, which was great news and such a relief. The snow was deep and beautiful. I called my folks in Illinois and sorted my laundry for turn-in. The previous Christmas, Larry Maniex and I were having Christmas dinner in a Congressman's home in Nashville, Tennessee. Larry was now in India, flying the Hump. This Christmas I would go to the club, have dinner and be waited on by German POW's, who, incidentally, were very good waiters. Where would next Christmas find me?

I was back to the grind at instrument school. We now worked seven days a week. I longed for the nine months to pass so that I could get underway and go overseas. I had logged nearly 60 hours of four-engine time on the trip to India and my total four-engine time was building up nicely. Every opportunity I had I would go with my students to Willow Run Ford Plant, buy a new B-24 and spend four hours giving them instrument flying instructions. Every chance I got, I would pick up a B-24 for delivery to wherever it was scheduled to go- Great Falls, Cheyenne, Salt Lake City, St Paul, Louisville, Newark, Tucson or Montreal. Invariably, we would be back the next day, as we always flew on the airlines or on the AAF Fubar Airlines (Fouled Up Beyond All Recognition).

In February I flew with Captain Breithaupt, a supervisor in the instrument school, and we went to Orchard Place, also known as

ORD, or O'Hare Field, northwest of Chicago. It was located in the country, very much a rural area. Douglas Aircraft was building the C-54s there and turning them out at maximum speed. We bought a C-54 and delivered it to Oklahoma City. The Captain gave me several landings at some airports enroute. After delivery he signed me off as "checked out." He knew, confidentially, that I would be going to Homestead, the big C-54 Training School very soon. This was exciting as the C-54 was the jewel of the fleet in the Air Transport Command. It was the aircraft Presidents Roosevelt and Truman used, and was the only really long range transport of the day. Most pilots would give their right arm to fly it. After my check-out, I, then and there, set my cap on going overseas in that airplane. It had leather seats in the cockpit, a crew biffy and two nice bunk beds for crew rest.

Bob Harris, my side-kick, had the same plans. He also decided it was time to get married. I was best man at the wedding which was in Bay City, Michigan. He married a real fine girl, his sweetheart of college days. It was a lovely wedding and all of us who could get away for the day were there.

In February some of our replacement instructors arrived. Each was scanned during his instrument training or refresher training, for those returning from overseas. One at a time the crème de la crème of the crop was called in, as we had been, and told that he was one of the anointed. Most of them were very happy to be selected. We then had to train them as instructors and check them out in three or four different airplanes. About the first of March, Russ Polan went to St Joseph, Missouri, for C-47 school and then overseas. I started to add more instrument training time in the Link Trainer as I heard that Homestead AAF started students off with 20-30 hours in the Link Trainer. It wasn't fun, but it was always good for a pilot, like improving the eye scan rate.

The staff of supervisors we worked for was very good to us. They greatly appreciated our very long hours and hard work. We trained and checked a very sizeable number of pilots, including some WASPS (Women Army Service Pilots) and all WASPS I flew with were fine pilots. I do not recall any major accidents or incidents in our training school. We also delivered a lot of aircraft in addition to our regular hours, just to make sure we were earning our pay checks. As a group we got along extremely well, and, yes, I won my promotion to first lieutenant in December, the day we landed in Marrakech, but I didn't know about it until mid-January.

The last seven days at Romulus I flew daily and delivered B-24s. I flew through or to: Lincoln, Nebraska, Cheyenne, Wyoming, Ogden, Utah, Denver, Colorado, St Joseph, Missouri, Louisville, Kentucky, and Montreal, Quebec. To round things out I flew six hours giving instrument checks rides in the instrument school. I loved the flying and I learned a tremendous amount of very valuable information about the techniques of instrument flying. It all would assist me greatly in years to come, working in the aviation career field. I would learn that later, by comparison, I'd never have another assignment where I would get such varied experiences, and in such large doses. I was very happy, though, to be winding up my nine months, just as the Major said, and shoving off for the big C-54 training school at Homestead FL. Major Bieberbach, without a doubt greased the skids for me to get that very fine training assignment. I was a very junior officer, but would train in the capacity of Pilot in Command. I think each of us received his assignment of choice, a rarity at that time.

CHAPTER X
SINGIN SAM'S COLLEGE OF FLYING WISDOM
AND KNOWLEDGE

As rumored, the first three week period at Homestead was a deep immersion in instrument training in Link trainers. This was coupled with five to six hours daily of classroom lectures. The subjects included all there was to know about the Douglas C-54 Skymaster aircraft and survival training: tropics, jungle, ocean, desert, and in the Arctic. As always we had a heavy dose of meteorology, communications and navigation, including celestial navigation.

The Link Training Department was like no other. All trainers were tied together communication-wise. While on the ground one talked to the tower. When in the air one talked to approach or departure control. It was very much like the real world as far as air traffic control was concerned. One could hear other pilots making radio calls for let-down clearances, crossing the low cone, beacon or outer marker, getting landing clearance and transfers to the tower. A clearance was given before take-off with a readback. All flights were one-hundred percent instrument, and landings were made to near minimums on the ILS (Instrument Landing System.) It was very challenging at first, but after one gained familiarity with the total system, it made flying the Link Trainer much more enjoyable and realistic, while still being demanding. The instructors were top-notch and very sharp in traffic control and instrument flying techniques. All of them were non-commissioned officers.

The ground school training department was first-rate. I have never gone through one that was as thorough and as professionally managed. Most instructors were officers or noncoms; a few were civilians. Some of the civilians had been employees of Pan American World Airways, which up until World War II was one of the very few airlines in the world that flew the Atlantic and the Pacific with "Clipper" flying boats. The school was commanded by Colonel "Singing Sam" Dunlap, the Third. I do not know what prompted that title, although he was a Colonel, USAAF, and his name was Sam Dunlap. One might gather that the title implied some disrespect; it did not. He was held in high regard, and word had it that he was a very gifted and skilled pilot.

My roommate, during the ground-school phase was Bobby Joe Cavnar. Bobby Joe was from Oklahoma, very young, was married with two children and had been an instructor in my flight in our instrument school at Romulus AAF. He was proud of the fact that his father had pleaded a case before the U.S. Supreme Court and had won the case, though not a lawyer.

School progressed and each subject had a very comprehensive final. As I recall 85 % or maybe even 90 % was needed to pass each subject. One of Singing Sam's rules: "When we pickum to fly the oceans, we won't take less than the best." The courses, though hard, were very enjoyable, but it was nice when we had the ground-school and most of our link training behind us.

Just as we were finishing the first half of our training, mid-April '45, President Franklin D. Roosevelt, died unexpectedly in Warm Springs, Ga. In the many years since that fateful day, when I recall FDR's death, I think of Bobby Joe making a tirade about having Harry Truman as president. He ranted and raved saying, "Even that fruitcake, Henry Wallace would be far better than Harry!" I had never been enamored with FDR and his New Deal, as the depression went on for eight years after his election. But I felt a sense of insecurity and sadness at his passing. He was in every sense of the word "The President" without a doubt. FDR had come to power when I was but a sprig of a lad, and guys my age had known only one president. We were all very aware of the fact that FDR had a large number of admirers, almost worshippers, and also a great number of other citizens who believed he was far too ambitious and perhaps a threat to the republic. My Dad, a staunch Democrat, revered FDR. My Mother, a Republican, said long before Pearl Harbor that FDR would somehow get us into the war. She was, at least partially correct. They both remembered WW I vividly, and at that time, my father, a first generation German was often shunned and cursed at. He had four children and a large farm to operate and cared nothing at all about Kaiser Bill and Germany. I had never voted in an election, as the mandatory age for voting was twenty-one. I was some two years shy of that age in the presidential election of 1940, and totally apolitical in 1944.

The base commander, Colonel Dunlap, had an impressive ceremony, befitting the fallen president, with all the troops on parade. It was solemn and proper and as I recall, a very moving formation.

We moved to the other side of the field and started our flight training. We flew both B-24s, with all turrets removed (C-87), and the C-54. Since I had three hundred hours in the B-24 by then, I preferred it of the two aircraft. We would get 60 hours total pilot flight training time; a very hefty flying course.

My roommate was now Major Vernon Elmore. He and his wife had an apartment in town, and he usually stayed off-base at night, except when he had a very early training flight. It was a lucky break that I got to know him well. He would be the Chief Pilot and my immediate superior in Cairo several months later.

The flight training went very well, and much of what was taught to us was from the same book we had taught from at Romulus AAF: the Colonel Duckworth Method from Bryan AAF. Though the Duckworth concept taught the "full instrument panel method" as opposed to the "needle, ball and air-speed method," we often found ourselves flying a plane with cardboard pasted over the gyro instruments so that we had to go back to the basics and prove that we could do as well with the limitations of partial panel flying. Worthy of note, civil aviation, most notably the CAA (later the FAA), moved very cautiously and very slowly into the "full panel" concept after the war ended.

Our problems consisted of orientation on the radio range, using several methods. One could always find where he was on the four-legged radio range with one of the methods. We spent countless hours practicing these procedures and making approaches to a landing. We also made beacon let-downs using the radio compass needle. However, one could never be sure that the automatic loop would not ice up, so there was the manual loop backup method, and we were trained to make manual loop let-downs to a landing, something I was never forced to actually use in years of flying. In addition, I never, in real life, had to find my location on a radio range by doing the laborious orientation problems. One might say, "What a waste of time and fuel!" Not so; it was great training toward becoming a smoother and savvier pilot, particularly with regard to relative bearings and procedures. The AAF pilots flying the Hump, by and large, had only beacons to navigate with, and often during the monsoons season, thunderstorms and accompanying lightning and static often forced them to revert to the manual loop.

The final check-ride came and I felt very confident in my ability to jump through all the hoops the check pilot held up. In fact, we were rather cocky, and Bobby Joe and I said to one another, "What can they give us that we can't handle? We've been teaching and checking pilots on this stuff for nine months."

Well, on the ride, because of heavy local traffic, my check pilot, Capt G. Britton had us at 11,000 feet. I was working a manual loop orientation problem. A piece o'cake, I thought to myself. As I maneuvered the big C-54 around, manipulating the manual loop with the switch on the radio compass control box, attempting to determine whether the station was to the fore or aft of the wing, I began to worry as it seemed I was not moving. I figured that maybe the check pilot was playing some kind of a trick, or else the wind had to be blowing well over 100 knots. I assumed that the latter was highly unlikely, so I declared to the check pilot that I must have done some miscalculations and I wanted to start the problem over again. He sat there in silence watching me get more and more stressed. We were running out of our allotted time. Finally he told me to turn to a heading and descend, which I did. Of course as we descended the wind slackened and we went in and landed as the time for our flight had expired. We taxied to the ramp and parked. He turned to me and said, "What did you learn in the last three hours, Lieutenant?" I was not absolutely sure, as I had not proven it to myself, but I replied, "Sir, we had one bodacious wind up there. I could not believe it, and it almost fooled me." He said, "Right you are Lieutenant, and why did you not believe what you were slowly proving to yourself?" I did not have a good answer. He complimented me on my smooth flying and overall ability, but then dropped the bomb. "I could easily pass you, but you let Mother Nature throw you a curve ball. Yes, I know, you have never seen a wind like that as you worked an aural null orientation problem, and I guess I have not either. But that's exactly what we had, and you may see it again someday, and if you don't believe what you see and know, you can be in very serious trouble. TOMORROW YOU WILL FLY AGAIN!" (OUCH!)

Captain Mistrot who had been my instructor earlier in the course took me aloft and gave me much of the check ride over again. He was very demanding and not his jovial self. At the end of the ride he said, "Congratulations Jacobs, you have passed the check. Now tell me, how did you manage to let that strong wind get you to doubt your abilities? You are as good as any of the students I've flown with here; maybe just a bit too good." I probably shrugged my shoulders, squirmed a bit and probably said little. He then elaborated, saying that the check was lengthy and though much of it not called for, he wanted to assure himself that I was not getting too cocky. I did not enjoy hearing that. Perhaps some of that fighter pilot spirit was still surging through my veins and lingering in the marrow of my bones. Sure, that was it!

Bobby Joe who had worked for me in Romulus thought it all quite hilarious. Technically I had not busted the check; I had simply taken too much time to solve the problem so had not completed the check ride. This re-flying a check taught me a lesson. It was my first-ever redo and I remember it vividly. More important, later, in my overseas flying, I was to encounter a similar situation with unbelievable winds, and the experience proved to be priceless.

7 MAY 1945—THE WAR ENDS IN EUROPE...V. E. DAY
****

Singing Sam Dunlap the Third gave us our graduation speech in the base theater. He was a terrific speaker, an older gentleman, about 50, with considerable wisdom. I remember he had words of wisdom about navigators. He cautioned, "Watch how your navigator handles his sextant. You don't want to spend weeks on the ocean in a dinghy like Eddie Rickenbacker did because your navigator carelessly packed his sextant around in his A-3 bag." I listened and filed it all away in my memory drum. Later I put it in play. He also advised, "If you are flying across the Atlantic and all of a sudden the navigator tells you to turn ten degrees to the right, question him, and question him thoroughly. You've been taught enough about navigation to know whether or not he's giving you a bum steer." Again, into my memory drum it went. "Always question and examine everything; people make mistakes every day, and when you are flying the ocean you just cannot tolerate errors. In a few days you will be overseas and you will be flying more than you ever imagined. We have hundreds of thousands of GI's that want to get home in the worst way, and you will play a big part in that. God put a head on your shoulders and in most cases filled it with good common sense. Be sure and use it. Good luck and God Speed." Singing Sam received a standing ovation, though such was not customarily given. He had our respect and admiration. He was the perfect man for the job he held, and we all agreed that his school at Homestead AAF was truly outstanding.

And so I left Homestead; back to Nashville to pick up a crew and head overseas. Hitler knew I was coming. That's why he went to his bunker and put a gun to his head. I'd see his demolished Reich's Chancellery soon. Bobby Joe got his wish and stayed at Homestead as an instructor. I could not fathom that, but I was not married with wife and kids. I heard many years later, that Bobby Joe was a motivational speaker in Texas. Bobby could handle that with ease!

And wasn't there a bit of serendipity in how all this fantastic flight training came about? Or was it my little guardian angel perched on my shoulder, plus a dash of karma dust?

CHAPTER XI
WIND, SAND AND STARS

Berry AAF, at Nashville hadn't changed a bit since December 1943. Now it was a staging area for overseas deployment. I was anxious to get my crew, my orders and be on my way. The formation for handing out orders was held outside on a beautiful day. An officer was standing on a wooden platform reading off names and orders were being handed out by administrative clerks. When the names of my crewmembers were called, I went forward to the stand to receive my orders. As I did, I noticed a young blond Second Looie with an athletic build and a very "crushed" Flighter cap come bounding down a slope to my right. As we walked together the last few feet he asked, "Are you Lt. Jacobs?" I said "Yes, and are you Lt. Considine?" "Sure am!" We shook hands, sized up each other rather carefully, and privately agreed that we could get along comfortably well for at least a week. We quickly learned that we were both, at least in our minds, natural born fighter pilots, shafted into transports and such was our lot. We had that in common. We hit it off very well right from the start, and I felt good about having a guy like John to fly with, to "wherever."

Without a minute's hesitation I opened our orders. They read: "that we would proceed at the proper time from Nashville, Tennessee, to Casablanca, Morocco, via Presque Isle, Maine for the purpose of delivering aircraft, #42-72602 and at the final comp, the Navigator and Engineer will return to their proper stations and other crewmembers will comply with the Special Orders in their possession." Because of all the hype we had heard at Homestead about flying the Atlantic, we were not at all surprised by our destination. Our navigator was 1/Lt Charles E. Hurst, our flight engineer was Pfc. Melvin L Zimmerman, and our radio operator was Pvt. Virgil E. Schultz. We wondered somewhat about a radio operator who had gone through specialized training and was assigned to Trans-Atlantic operations and had not yet been promoted to at least PFC.

We met the other three crew members and prepared to depart. We would ferry a new, right-off-the assemblyline, plush C-54 to

Casablanca via the Central Atlantic routes; Newfoundland, The Azores, direct to Casa. This C-54 had just been delivered to Nashville from the plant at Orchard Place (ORD), Illinois. It had an airline-type interior, 44 nice, comfortable passenger seats, a crew compartment that included a private biffy, sink, and upper and lower bunks. We also had two lovely heaters. My previous crossing in a B-24 from Goose Bay Labrador to the U.K. at 15,000 feet was truly a frosty experience. This crossing was in the top- of-the-line transport of the day; there was none better and this bird had class. The two pilots sat in very nice, cushy leather seats. The navigator and radio operator each had a nice roomy compartment and the flight engineer sat on a fold-down seat between the two pilots. The stop at Presque Isle, Maine, was routine for aircraft bound for overseas delivery. An inventory was made, small cargo put aboard, then the aircraft released for it's foreign destination. From Presque Isle we flew a relatively short hop to Stephensville, Newfoundland and remained over-night (RON, in military lingo.) The next leg to Lages in the Azores was the most crucial leg of the journey. A flight from a continent to a small group of islands in the mid-North Atlantic was one calling for careful and meticulous preparation. Once again the Air Transport Command briefing staff and weather personnel provided us with top-notch assistance. Our take-off was late at night so that our arrival would be in daylight. Our navigator brought us straight in to the island without any last minute corrections. It was a thrill seeing the peak of a mountain sticking out through the clouds, right on schedule, in the early morning hours, assuring us that we had, in fact, found the Azores Islands. Of course someone called out "Land Ho!"

We remained over night, and the next day flew on to Casablanca which was relatively routine and a piece-o-cake. It would have been pretty difficult to miss the continent of Africa. We sold our aircraft, received a receipt for the delivery and found the bachelor officers' quarters. We were overseas to stay. Casa would be our new home-base for several months.

My very good friend and flying school classmate, Bob Harris had arrived at the base two or three weeks before we flew in. He and his copilot had a room together, so John and I requested a room together; no one had a private room. We then got squared away by signing-in on the base. This procedure consisted of going around to all of the various sections or departments on the base and making our presence known. There was a like procedure before one departed one base for another. The most important office to a pilot was the operations section of the squadron of assignment. I was informed that I would be required to fly in the capacity of co-pilot over the various routes of the North African Division before I would be assigned as pilot in command. This policy did not surprise me, but in looking at the network of routes for our area of responsibility I reckoned that I would be "jerking gear" (raising the landing gear, one of copilot's chief jobs) for several weeks. Though a very junior first lieutenant, I had already grown accustomed to being "in charge," so naturally I wanted an early upgrade. It did not happen quickly.

The airbase was large. The buildings were made of masonry, so were not the typical WW II "seven year" buildings. The rooms in our quarters had cement walls, but the walls were about seven feet high and the roof peeked at about twelve feet; so the open space above allowed for ample noise to reverberate from room to room with ease. It was, however, better than open bays, such as we had in flying school. One field phone hung in its leather pouch on the wall in the common hallway. It had that field phone jangle. The phone was always answered, as our operations called us on that line to alert us for our flights. It seemed that several pilots were always on standby, awaiting their alert call.

The system used by the scheduling office was a simple "first-in, first-out" rotation. When one returned from a flight he went to the bottom of the pilot or copilot list. The crews were madeup from the various crew positions by those at the top of the list. This procedure did not allow for crew integrity, so one usually flew with different crew members on each trip. I was in the C-54 section; I would normally be crewed-up on only the C-54. We had fifty-two C-54's assigned to the base and most were new and the "plushed-up" airline version.

The big push was on for flying troops home via our far South Atlantic route. There were four or five other routes across the Atlantic and ours was the most "far-out." Our operation was called by the code name THE GREEN PROJECT. We flew the troops of

General Mark Clark's Fifth Army, of Italy, to Natal, Brazil, via Dakar, French West Africa. Our passengers were then flown by AAF Troop Carrier pilots from Natal, Brazil, to Florida. We usually flew north to nearby Port Lyautey to pick up our load of passengers. Most of our passengers had arrived there via surface vessels; however, some were flown down from Italy by bomber crews in B-24s and B-17s, and some flown to North Africa by the pilots of the North African Division of the AAF Air Transport Command in Curtiss Wright C-46s and Douglas C-47s, the stalwart "Gooney Bird."

After we had picked up our load of passengers, we flew down the west coast of Africa, some eight to nine hours to Dakar, French West Africa, today called Senegal. Dakar was an Atlantic seaport on the tip of the bulge of west Africa. It was also the closest African airfield to the continent of South America. When in high school I had read one of Charles Lindbergh's books about a flight he and his wife, Ann, made in a single-engine float plane, a Lockheed Serius, on this same, somewhat shorter Atlantic-crossing route. At that time, I never, in my wildest dreams, imagined that someday I would be flying the exact same route, but in a big beautiful four-engine transport. And doing so repeatedly, for weeks on end.

Upon arrival in Dakar we would RON. The passengers would proceed on in the same aircraft, for the over-water segment, but with a rested crew. After about eight to twelve hours crew-rest, we would depart on a newly arrived aircraft with a load of tired troops. With a navigator who was permanently stationed in Dakar, surely not the garden spot of the world, we would fly south by south-west crossing the equator and the Atlantic.

Our Cazes Airbase newspaper informed us that our C-54 wing at Casablanca had 20 C-54s crossing the Atlantic daily. Half would be westbound, fully loaded, and half eastbound, quite empty. That meant, also, that on any given day we had twenty aircraft between Casa and Dakar. We flew all hours of the day and every day of the week. Though this may sound impressive, we were moving only 440 troops per day or 3,080, a week. Compared to today, two DC-10s could easily accomplish the same, much faster, and much cheaper, particularly when considering the manpower involved. My memories of Dakar are:

1. FOOD: No matter what time of day or night we landed, we were invariably fed somewhat fresh eggs in the mess hall. This was not all that bad except for the heavy grease. In Casa we had powdered eggs. After sleeping seven or eight hours, we were awakened and fed some more eggs. We always wondered if the permanent party at the base ate only eggs. The cooks and waiters were all natives, and I think they surmised eggs to be a quick and easy fix.

2. THE BEACH: If it were midday we might go to a nearby beach for a quick swim before sleeping. The water was infested with small sharks. Base personnel told us that the surrounding water was only 60% water; the other 40% was shark. We would only go out waist deep, and we would keep our eyes on the native kids. When they screamed and hollered and headed for the shore we knew it was time to move fast in the same direction. Most of the native kids swam in the buff; in fact their uniform of the day and/or night was 100% nude. Their language was reported to be ultra-simplistic. A very short alphabet and a very brief dictionary. I recall that "Yamarick" meant, "how are you?" and "Yamagon" meant "I am good." 'Thought perhaps you'd like to know that!

3. TRINKETS: The natives had all kinds of hand-made trinkets to sell. One I remember best was the Giddy-Giddy. It was to be worn around the neck and it was about the size of a silver dollar, made from some kind of hide and had nondescript etching or colored markings. It was to ward off evil spirits and at the very same time was to bring good fortune to the wearer. We, of course, had to buy a few to send to our friends and relatives who were trying to shed a curse or two. Other things for sale were figurines of various types, mostly depicting black African culture. We failed to appreciate the unusual work at that time. In recent years I've seen very similar African artwork and the price would indicate that we, long ago, failed to purchase a real bargain or two.

   4. THE HEAT: Equatorial in latitude, approximately
seven degrees north, Dakar was always hot. The humidity
was also very high, and trying to get crew rest was a real
problem. Needless to say there were no fans or air
conditioning, or anything resembling a cooling system. A
night lay-over was somewhat better but still hot.

   I could continue and tell of the downtown section of Dakar,
French West Africa, but most would have an unpleasant tone, as it
was really seedy. I will say that the average American serviceman
who saw a little bit of the area, felt as I did, regarding the French as
colonists. There was considerable evidence that they were oppressive
and very little evidence that the lot of the natives had improved
significantly, under their regime.

   A nine to ten-hour flight across the Atlantic and the equator put us
at the most northeasterly point on the South American continent, at
Natal, Brazil. The city was a very pleasant upgrade from Dakar, in
more ways than one. Though also hot, the air was not as oppressive,
and the food was fantastic in comparison. In the mess we had lots of
green leafy lettuce, fresh vegetables and fruit; abundant bananas were
a real treat and always in our outbound flight lunches. That is what I
remember most fifty-five years later; the lovely flight lunches we ate
as we flew north-northeast, back to Dakar, and more eggs.

   The town of Natal was very pleasant and the stores sold many
things that were not easily obtained in the States. As I recall I sent
some nylon stockings home to my mother and sisters. I also splurged
on a very impressive Swiss Breitling navigator watch, which would
reveal more information than even a navigator could comprehend, and
do it with Swiss precision.

   The time we spent on the ground at Natal was no more or no less
than we spent at Dakar, or even at Casa, where we were often
southbound again in about 12 to 14 hours. I recall one day at Casa I
had been in bed for only four or five hours and the hall-way phone
jangled, giving me a two-hour alert call for my next flight south to
Dakar. Did we complain, or run to a union boss and file a protest?
Not on your tin-type; we just went down to Ops, strapped on the C-54
and headed for Dakar one more time.

While I was still 23 years old I had made many Atlantic Ocean crossings. I thought that remarkable, but thousands of young American youth were engaged in far more awesome and dangerous exercises. THE GREEN PROJECT was one small part of the Transport Command's outstanding accomplishments during WWII, and few people ever heard of it. However, the boys who rode home on our far south route, I'm sure, will never ever forget it as long as they live. It was that long-awaited trip they had dreamed of.

5. THE FLIGHT: Some detailed aspects of the trip from French Morocco to Natal, Brazil are worthy of mention. The flight from Casa or Port Lyautey to Dakar went from fix to fix, usually using non-directional beacons, and on an airway, The route was usually close to or within sight of the Atlantic. Surely the AAF had considered the stories that had been spread through the years regarding the rough Bedouin tribesmen, who, when coming upon a downed or lost airmen, had a ritual which was, shall we say, a bit distasteful. The tribesmen would pluck out their victim's eye balls, castrate them, and put all four objects in their mouth, sew it up and bury them up to their lower lip on an ant hill in the sand. We often made sure that a new man on the crew was aware of this ghastly detail on this stretch of the trip, just to make sure that he could cogitate and fantasize about it all if he became bored.

From north to south, signs of inhabitants became more and more sparse. At eight to ten- thousand feet one would not see much detail such as a camel caravans. Seldom did we see vehicles.

An hour south of Casa we were beyond the Atlas Mountain ranges. I recall Agadir, Mogador, and Villa Cisneros. We felt we knew Ifni, a tiny country, since there appeared to be few signs of life in the few square miles; so we all joked that we'd seen all of Ifni. We flew abeam Timbuktu, which has long been referred to as the most desolate place on the planet. There was a weak non-directional beacon there, so, no doubt, there also were two or three very unlucky and lonely GI's maintaining the site.

The famous French author and poet, Antoine de Saint-Exupery flew this same route which the French had established from Toulouse to Casablanca to Dakar in the 1930's. He wrote eloquently of it in his very popular book, *Wind, Sand, and Stars. Here* is a fascinating quote.

"A pilot's business is with the wind, with the stars, with night, with sand, with sea. He strives to outwit the forces of nature. He stares with expectancy for the coming of dawn the way a gardener awaits the coming of spring. He looks forward to the port as to a promised land, and truth for him is what lives in the stars."

The weather over the entire route was generally quite good, except in the mid-Atlantic. While the weather crossing the Atlantic was generally favorable and sometimes unbelievably beautiful, there were three or four of our crossings that were extremely rough. The reason for the disturbance was the ITC (Inter-tropical Zone of Convergence). The ITC was the result of the large North Atlantic high pressure area, which rotates clock-wise, converging with the South Atlantic high pressure area, which rotates counter clockwise. When the characteristics of the two air masses were dissimilar, presto, there was great rivalry between the air masses as a result and anything but smooth flying. This was especially true a few hours after sunset.

On a leg such as from Dakar to Natal, there is a point of no return, which simply means that you do not have sufficient fuel to turn around and go back. Hence when you hit a line of vicious thunderstorms, with towering cumulus to 60,000 feet and with flashing lightning like you'd never seen before, you were confronted with a dilemma: how best to sneak through the wrath of gods, like Zeus, before he knew you were coming through. In all my years of flying, I have never experienced such extreme turbulence, along with St Elmo's Fire, which, while harmless, is more spectacular than any I have witnessed. Hail also had its way with us, sounding like numerous machine guns hammering our aluminum frame.

The unstable conditions were usually at their worst at night, due to the cooling aloft at the tops of the building cumulonimbus. This sharp cooling at the tops of the cumulonimbus coupled with the warm temperatures at the base (from relative warm water), created a super-adiabatic lapse rate. No matter what you called it, Mother Nature took exception to this out-of-kilter situation and wanted to rectify things, and doing so with a vengeance. The combination of the warm air rising above the cooler air, and the cooler air trying to get below the warm air created vertical drafts that were indescribable. We did not have radar so could not pick our way through the vast thunderstorms. (Radar was not on transports until after the war). We usually flew where the lightning "wasn't." However, sometimes when you were in heavy build-ups you found that you had not guessed well and the lightning that surrounded you was indescribably fierce, as was the accompanying turbulence. A static discharge, which some pilots misinterpreted as a lightning-strike was really an equalizing process by mother nature that occurred when a large aircraft flew through clouds with a varying and different electrical charge. It usually presented itself on the C-54 nose as a massive ball of fire, and was gone in a few seconds. Prior to the static discharge the four props looked like Fourth of July pinwheels and the airflow over the wing looked like a river of fire. We could, after some experience, sense the approach of the discharge and would turn the cockpit lights up full bright, so that we would not be momentarily blinded.

The C-54 was a very well-built aircraft, but it had certain characteristics to be carefully heeded. Paramount of these was flying within prescribed speed limits, both maximum and minimum, when in heavy turbulence. All manufacturers of aircraft issue the same sage advice: Avoid heavy turbulence; do not hesitate to make a one-eighty (a one-hundred and eighty degree turn) and leave the area.

I was flying as copilot on a trip westbound to Natal and we were beyond the point of no-return. It was night and as we approached a line of thunderstorms across our path, we attempted to avoid the area of heaviest lightning. As we got closer to the activity it became apparent that we were in for a very rough ride and there would not be an easy way through. The pilot must have been asleep in school when the subject of flying in turbulence was taught. He did not slow to 150 miles-per-hour as prescribed for our gross weight, by the aircraft manual. I was absolutely stunned when he lowered both the landing gear and then one-quarter wing flaps. Both actions were contrary to the operations manual in almost all large high-performance aircraft. It was *verboten*, as in prohibited. I'm sure I became a soprano on the spot. I tried to tell him, without screaming, that we should slow down and retract the landing gear and the flaps. As we pitched about the sky, I told him in a loud voice that the wing is much stronger in a clean configuration, but he wanted no talk about aerodynamics from a young co-jockey. He was wrestling with the controls something fierce. The instrument panel was shaking so violently for a while we couldn't read the instruments. Without a doubt it was the wildest ride in my entire flying career and I had very serious doubts whether or not we would come out the other side in one piece. I'm sure my guardian angel at that point was racing around beefing up the weakest points of the airframe. The plane's fuselage creaked and groaned as it twisted and bowed. The props and the wings were awash with St Elmo's fire. We got a terrific static discharge on the nose, blinding us temporarily. Of far greater concern was the sound emanating from the wings. They were vibrating like a tuning fork, a sound I had never heard before in any aircraft. I had read about the danger of a harmonic vibration that exists in certain aircraft under severe turbulence, resulting in the wing snapping off like a match stick. But our karma held up and we made it through. My respect for the aircraft soared, and for the dim clod in the left seat, I vowed I would never fly with him again if I could possibly avoid it; it was called self-preservation.

In July I was once again blanketed with serendipity; I landed a beautiful "special trip." I recall it vividly; a sharp rap on the big wooden door of my room in the BOQ. Although it was forenoon, I was zonked, and out like a light. I had landed at our Cazes Airport in the early morning hours after a flight from Natal, Brazil, with a very short crew rest in Dakar. "Lt Jacobs, have you ever flown a B-17?" "No, Sir," I replied, "But I have quite a bit of B-24 and C-54 time." There was a pause. "Report to Major Zieger, Chief Pilot, at 1400 hours today. He is in the Headquarters Building downtown. He wants to talk to you."

I got up and showered. Luckily they had not turned off the water, as they often did for six to eight hours every day or two. I walked across the street to the Mess and had a light Spam lunch. It could have been Vienna sausage, but it was one or the other. I found some wheels into Casablanca and the Headquarters Building. Major Zieger was a very personable, congenial man, twice my age. He explained our mission and the more I learned the details the more exciting it appeared to be. Major General Stowell, our CG, had a somewhat plushed-up B-17. He was making it available to General Desre, the

CG of all French troops in North Africa. General Desre, I learned, was going to Paris to participate in the preliminary conference being held there prior to the Potsdam Conference in Berlin. I was to be co-pilot for Major Zieger. I took the B-17 Tech Order (Dash-1), plus a questionnaire back to my billets to complete; it was cram time on the B-17.

Two days later we headed north with the General on board, across the Mediterranean to make landfall in southwest France. The General's hometown was Niort, France, just to the north of Bordeaux. We circled to land there on the grass field, which accommodated the Flying Fortress, but roughly. As we taxied to what appeared to be a small hanger, we noted a sizeable crowd. We parked the big bird and the General stepped out to a roaring welcome from hundreds of greeters. Obviously, the hometown boy had a fine reputation. He made a short speech and re-boarded, and we were off for Paris. We flew fairly low as we wanted to view the countryside which was new to us. Though a war-torn country, to be sure, all appeared so beautiful, green and lush from the air. A marked change after weeks of flying back and forth over the western Sahara Desert and the South Atlantic.

My flight log reveals that we landed at Orly in Paris. My recollection of Orly at that time is foggy, but I do remember our Paris hotel, vividly. It was the Ritz Hotel on Place Vendome, and it was for general officers only. Apparently, someone in Casablanca had the pull to get a lowly airplane crew into the Ritz, which is still today, THE RITZ, and world-famous. There was one small catch; at that time, so soon after VE-Day, one was required to eat all meals in the hotel where billeted. This meant that when I went to the dining room for meals, I would be seated at a table with only general officers, mostly, infantry, airborne and armored. Major Zieger was never around for me to accompany. Sometimes I was at a table with five high ranking generals. Some "stars" asked me how I came to be staying at The Ritz. I had the feeling they were always puzzled by my reply. A first lieutenant staying at the Ritz ...HMM? And a fly-boy!! HMM? Who are you flying, lieutenant? A French General? HMMMMM??

Major Zieger was an operator of the first order. His family, so he related to me, was an original partner with the Heinz family, like in ketchup. His family was from Germany and he spoke German

150

fluently. He claimed that in the late thirties, through a cousin who was a high ranking officer in the Lufftwaffe, he had attempted to acquire an ME-109 to enter in the Bendix Air Races. The war had snarled his plan.

The Major was an Eastern Airline pilot before he entered the AAF. He wanted to go to Berlin in the worst way. Our orders did not specify Berlin, but he somehow made our B-17, and us, indispensable to those going to Big B for the Potsdam Conference. Someone cut some orders to lay on the mission for us. We were officially covered. We took off with some passengers and considerable baggage a day or two later. We flew over Frankfurt and the sight of the destruction was absolutely incredible. The same scene was repeated over each large city along the route, all the way to Berlin. The city of Berlin, of course, was in total rubble and in many areas you could not even detect where the streets had been. We landed at Templehof Airport, which was simply a large grass field with no runways, but with a massive terminal building. Fortunately the bomb craters had been filled and packed well, though we lurched heavily when going over some of them. There were so many we could not miss them all. Some AAF bombardiers had done a fine job.

We had fulfilled our mission, but the Major had to see some of the remains of the city. We acquired a jeep and driver and set off for the Unter Den Linden (Strasse) and the Brandenberg Tor area. His German helped immensely, but others on the strasse sensed that we were unique. We were packing no arms, and we wore AAF class A's and wings. There were very few if any Yanks to be seen in Berlin and we saw no AAF types at all. The Russians, who were in combat gear and fatigues, were everywhere and found us most interesting. All officers carried a sub-machine gun, automatic rifles or side arms. Most had a bottle of vodka. It became a potential problem almost immediately as they gathered around us and wanted our rank, our wrist watches, our wings and even the buttons on our blouses. They had plenty of script. Worse yet, they insisted we sit down on a pile of rubble and have a drink of vodka with them. It was a bit dicey, as many were half tanked and some got surly when we declined. The whole scene was unreal and bizarre, to say the least. Major Zieger warned, "Keep a smile on your face at all times!"

The Major was speaking with a German lady who had a dish of home made butter that she had brought to the street to barter. Her young son, perhaps ten years old, was with her. He had made a great mistake of bringing his bicycle with him. As she and the Major were speaking German, a couple of inebriated, very young Russian soldiers came by and decided that they wanted the boy's bike. When they attempted to jerk it away from the youngster, he resisted. His mother screamed for him to release the bike and let them have it, but he held on a moment too long. One of the soldiers took his rifle and slammed it against the boys head severely and repeatedly 'till he crumpled. Blood gushed all over. The other soldier hailed down a huge truck filled with soldier, some of whom were females. The two soldiers dragged the boy out into the street and pitched him, like a rag doll into the truck, which drove off with a roar, the mother screaming.

My better judgment said, "This place isn't for us. To these troops from the East, this war's not really over. It's at the height of get-even time." It was not uncommon to hear sporadic gunfire. Many of the subways were still flooded and the stench of still-entombed bodies was prevalent everywhere.

Major Zieger was bent on seeing the Reich's Chancellery before it got too dark. I agreed. In Berlin in summer the sun sets very late. The Chancellery was not far at all, but by jeep it took many stops, turns back-tracking to get there. With a small bribe of one of my lieutenant's bars, the Russian lieutenant let us go inside, though a large sign outside said "No Entry" in four languages. Fortunately the officer of the guard spoke some German and he accompanied us part of the time. We went through several large rooms and in the large room, which the lieutenant said was Hitler's office, I managed to dislodge a large brass coat-hanger from the wall. It was a real struggle. I still have it today, but no one believes that the little paper-hanger hung his coat on it, so it is only a show-and-tell item for family and close friends. The office had been ransacked, I'm sure, by many before us, but we went through some filing cabinets and large drawers and gathered some nice portraits and photographs. I picked up two copies of Mein Kampf from a huge wall library.

As we made our way out of the huge, generally demolished, building, it was getting dark. While climbing in our jeep with our loot, a major general drove up with another individual who had a GI uniform, but with no insignia, somewhat like a war correspondent. They were hoping to enter as we had. We advised them that we thought it was too dark for them to see well to get around, and advised against it. The general, looking at the loot we were holding in our arms, suggested that perhaps we might just wish to share some with him and his friend, Alexander D Seversky. Because two stars are considerably more potent than an oak leaf cluster and a little silver bar, and since we recognized the civilian's celebrity status, we of course obliged. The sergeant who was with us felt that he could quickly find his way back inside to replenish his and our losses, including the Mein Kampf (who needs one, let alone two?) With very little daylight remaining, he did re-enter and successfully retrieved another armload. We left, satisfied with our bounty, as did the general and his celebrated comrade.

We then drove to Templehof Airfield, fired up our B-17, and flew over to nearby Gatow Airport and stayed overnight. While eating breakfast the next morning, in a small mess hall, a brigadier general approached and addressed Major Zieger. His mood was testy. "Is that your B-17 out there Major?" "Yes, sir." "Where are you from and what are you doing here?" "We are from Casablanca and we flew some passengers and baggage up from Paris for the conference, Sir." "Casablanca, did you say Casablanca? We have no information whatsoever on a B-17 from Casablanca. You have somehow finagled a deal to get a flight in here. No AAF people are to RON in Berlin. NONE! If you brought passengers up here, you were to turn around within the hour. I will give you 20 minutes to get that B-17 in the air." I was standing with my half-finished breakfast tray before he had finished the last part of his command. I could tell by the veins in his neck that he was dead serious. We had our wheels in the well before the specified 20 minutes had passed, and our big bird pointed toward Paris-back to a much more peaceful scene and back to the Ritz.

Three days later we left with General Desre for his home-town of Niort again, and then on to Casablanca. One comment on Paris: you could, at that time, stand at the Arc de Triumph and look down the Champs Elysses to the Place de la Concorde and maybe see only a half-dozen vehicles in the total two-mile distance. It is impossible to imagine today.

I logged 25 hours flight time in the B-17, had a relatively clean German helmet, some pictures and papers from Der Fuhrer's office, and of course my (formerly his) coat hanger and also his "wild ideas." I saw more rubble and revengeful hate than I ever dreamed of. I never learned how I got that lucky trip, but chalked it up, as usual, to good looks and clean living, plus a dash of Karma. Oh, yes, I also learned how to dine with general officers in a more relaxed manner. Most "felt" my situation. For sure, all had been lieutenants at one time. Some may have even enjoyed my presence as it may have cut down on the sometimes excited conversations (arguments) they had about certain aspects of the very recent battles of the war.

Did we affect the outcome of the Potsdam Conference? Hardly! We left all that to Harry Truman, Winston Churchill (and Clement Atlee) and of course Joe Stalin, who made out like a bandit, gaining tighter control of Europe east of the Elbe River.

A couple of days after my return to Casa, I was again flying a C-54 toward Dakar, with another load of happy homeward-bound warriors, most wearing purple hearts, many with clusters.

To us they were heroes one and all, and so overjoyed to be going back to the Good Old USA After my return from the Natal trip I was informed that I would go to Marrakech and upgrade to aircraft commander. At last I would get back in the left seat where I felt I belonged.

The training at Marrakech was similar to that in Homestead, Florida, though much shorter in duration. It seemed to be the practice of the powers that be, that even though Homestead was recognized as the gold standard of transport flight training schools, "We must prove to ourselves that this pilot deserves to be upgraded in Our Command." My instructor expressed the opinion that he thought we were wasting fuel going through all of the same exercises that I had been trained and checked on less than three months previous. I probably got some "fine tuning" on the program, but it was very expensive training. During my stay there I was billeted in the famous Moumonia Hotel, which had been requisitioned by the Army Air Forces, but without all the luxurious furnishings. It was Winston Churchill's domicile when he wintered in French Morocco prior to the war. Situated between two ranges of the Atlas Mountains, it had a climate similar to Palm Springs, California. The exotic Arabic city was, and still is, one of the most interesting in Africa and is still a great tourist attraction for Europeans. I passed my check rides in Marrakech and returned to Casablanca, a one hour flight, within a week.

My roommate John (Cons), had been flying the line as copilot, as I had, and on identical routes. We didn't see much of each other as our schedules were so heavy. When our time in Casa merged, and I was now a first pilot, we went to operations and asked to be crewed together and they were happy to grant our request. I recall that we flew together as a team from that day forward, with a few exceptions. It was a real pleasure flying with John, a light-hearted, gregarious Irish lad from Newton Center, Massachusetts. John was brought up in a strict Catholic home. His father never drank alcohol and encouraged his son John to abstain, which he did. He did smoke cigarettes, while I did not. He could put a wicked spin on a ping-pong ball and ran me ragged in that game. I finally gave up trying to beat him. Our friendship has endured through 50+ years and our wives are also good friends. We have visited through the years in each other's homes and have taken vacations together. When we visit, we quite naturally relish talking about the good old days. In our dotage it is interesting how we always converse in the "Hot World War II Pilot Lingo" and find it all so natural. Yes, we have sharp, vivid memories, and no, we never, ever embellish, or nudge any of the facts to our benefit.

Singing Sam Dunlap III, in his graduation address at Homestead AAF, had cautioned us about monitoring a navigator and the attention the navigator gave to his sextant. The moment of reckoning came for me at Natal, as we were preparing for our return flight to Dakar. A weapons carrier came to our transient quarters to drive us to operation. Our navigator came out of the quarters lugging a B-4 bag for his clothing, and an A-3 bag, which we referred to as a parachute bag. He first heaved the B-4 bag into the carrier and then swung the A-3 bag up and when it hit the floor of the carrier I heard this sharp clunk. Singing Sam's words flashed through my mind. I asked the navigator if his sextant was in the A-3 bag and he replied in the affirmative. I asked him with a bit of sarcasm in my voice if he had ever read about the experiences of Eddie Rickenbacker and his weeks on a rubber dinghy in the Pacific, dying from lack of water and food and trying feverishly to knock down a sea gull. He knew exactly what I was talking about. I told him to check out his sextant thoroughly before we left and he said he'd do so.

We departed on schedule; it was an early morning departure. Our flight was on a northeasterly heading and, of course, into a westerly moving sun; the daylight hours would pass quickly. The nav took a noon day fix and told me to turn right fifteen degrees. More of Singing Sam's good words crossed my mind: "If you are out in mid-ocean and a navigator gives you a big correction in heading, question him thoroughly, and have him show you how he justifies the new heading." I did just that, and in the reasoning he presented, I had some concern, as I felt that he seemed rather unsure in his reckoning. I advised, "let's stick with our flight plan, since we know that has to be pretty solid, and without a big shift in winds aloft, we will come very close to Dakar, and, also, be sure you use that drift meter when you can." The weather on the first half of the trip was good, everything looked great.

Every dog has his day, and every pilot has a doggy day, when, bit by bit, and step by step everything turns to a can of worms. Next, our fair weather gave way to high clouds, and then lower clouds obscured the ocean. Soon the daylight turned to darkness. The nav could not get a fix as he could not see the stars, and though his sextant was suspect, he had not let-up on his desire for me to correct to the right. I suspected the requests were no more than hunches, harking back to that original large correction he had requested. I acquiesced a bit and gave him a few small corrections.

As the ETA (estimated time of arrival) approached for making land-fall with Africa, we could not pick up the signal for the Dakar radio range or beacon. Due to distant thunderstorms there was too much static and I slowly came to the realization that we were too far from our destination to receive the signals, even weakly. Eddie Rickenbacker and also Amelia Earhart's episodes crossed my mind with a loud twang. Singing Sam told us that we had been taught enough about navigation to interrogate a navigator and do it thoroughly. I got out of my seat and went back and asked the navigator to show me his computations and air plot. I detected some alarm in his demeanor. He revealed that his sextant was, in fact, totally unreliable and had given him all kinds of weird inconsistent readings.

We were not totally lost, but in all honesty, we didn't know where we were. We could still be over the Atlantic or we could be over the desert north of Dakar or over the jungle down in the vicinity of Liberia. Once again that guardian angle was perched on one of our shoulders. The high clouds above us gave way and there was a big, absolutely gorgeous, moon. Soon the clouds below also gave way and we could visually make out from the orientation of the coastline that we were well south of our intended course and we were headed for dense tropical growth. We quickly reverted to very basic navigation and began map reading. We turned north and after about an hour, with not a lot of fuel to spare, we finally heard the signals from Dakar, through the static. Soon thereafter we saw the lights of the city, homed in on the fix and airport and landed without further incident.

Thank God for the wise advice of Colonel Dunlap. He had told us that "each trip across the ocean must be planned like it was the most important trip of your life, and if you get complacent, little errors would grow and become big ones, and soon you'll realize that you are receiving all kinds of bad breaks, and all on the very same day." He was so right! We were all highly irked at the navigator, realizing that he had never really checked out his sextant with enough care to assure its accuracy. That very ordinary routine Atlantic crossing could very well have been our swan song. I, officiously asked him, "Tell me, Lt. Doaxs, what did you learn today?" He showed considerable remorse, contrition and was very embarrassed. I was happy to be safely on the tarmac and did not report him. I doubt if he ever mishandled his sextant again.

THE ATOMIC BOMB IS DROPPED FROM THE ENOLA GAY ON HIROSHIMA, JAPAN

ANOTHER ATOM BOMB IS DROPPED FROM BOCK'S CAR ON NAGASAKI, JAPAN

V-J DAY—THE JAPS SUE FOR PEACE—WORLD WAR TWO IS OVER

****

157

This news was absolutely fantastic, and everyone breathed a great sigh of relief. But our project to move troops from overseas back to their much-loved native soil continued unabated for several more weeks.

On one flight we were visiting with a soldier who had "liberated," among other things, a gun factory in southern Germany. He had requisitioned (or confiscated) several pistols. He wanted to sell some at $45.00 each. I told him I'd be glad to buy one, but his bags were in the belly, and we'd have to be pretty lucky to be able to find it. Our flight engineer thought with a bit of luck we might be able to retrieve his bag through what we called the "hell hole," an access door in the floor on the flight deck. We were in luck; we had only to remove a few duffel bags before we came to his. He opened his bag, and somewhere at ten thousand feet, over the Sahara Desert, he parlayed his stash into big bucks by selling about a dozen or more. I still have mine; it is a very nice piece, and has yet to be fired for the first time. I hope to get around to doing that someday.

One of the most interesting features about flying the 5th Army to Dakar and Natal was talking with the combat troops about various aspects of the war and their personal experiences. Most were seasoned veterans. We always invited the men to come up to the cockpit for a visit, and the vast majority accepted. Many were highly elated to hear all about our magnificent airplane and some, very willingly talked of their war-time experiences. The majority had seen very heavy and extensive combat, and some had had some very harrowing experience. The men we were transporting had to take a back seat to no other wartime group. Though most were hardened veterans, and perhaps had many reasons to not be particularly light-hearted, we had the pleasure of visiting with these guys when they were probably at their peak elation. Many, though "old" in experience, and in appearance, were still very young in years. You could see their young age when their face lit up, while revealing something about their boyhood or schooldays. All were so very happy to be alive and headed home. It was great to assist in one of the happiest moments of their lives, a day they had long dreamed of, WAR'S OVER-WE'RE GOING HOME!!

With the news of victory in the Pacific came a flurry of rumors. Russ Polan, my good friend from flying school days, had transferred over to Casablanca from Oran, and was flying C-47's. Their mission was winding down rapidly. His wife, June, had given birth to a baby girl some months earlier and Russ was most anxious to get home to see her. We C-54 pilots knew we would not be going home, as there were many months of long-range flying yet to be done. We suspected a transfer to Cairo or to India. The rumors soon became fact. Twenty-five crews and about 15 C-54s would be transferred to John Payne Field, Cairo in late September. John and I, along with my good friend, Bob Harris, ran down to operations and volunteered. We were happy with this news, as we all knew there was a huge mission of transporting troops west from the China-Burma-India (CBI) theatre and also from the Persian Gulf area. We would be flying the Fertile Crescent between Cairo, Abadan, Iran, and to and from Karachi, New Delhi, Agra and Calcutta.

The duty in Casablanca for us was finished and we looked eastward to a new adventure, with more ports of call to add to our ever-growing geographic list. Casablanca had been extraordinary duty. We were now seasoned trans-Atlantic pilots. We also could readily find our way down the west coast of Africa, and sometimes tell exactly where we were just by looking at an ever-so-small village or bay. We had not injured a passenger or bent an airplane, but most importantly we had made thousands of homeward-bound GIs so very, very happy. The expressions on their faces, when they tried to pass on a very genuine "thanks," said it all, loud and clear. I had turned twenty-four during this six months. I was no longer a young punk that GIs (jokingly) chased away from airplanes, saying, "Hey kid, get away from that aircraft- that's not to play with!" as depicted by Bill Mauldin in his famous WWII cartoons. And I was still tall and slim, just like Lindbergh, and of course we all had more Atlantic crossings than did Lucky Lindy, but who could ever come close to that very famous reputation and legacy? No one ever would or could. He was still every pilot's genuine boyhood hero.

CHAPTER XII
FLYING INSIDE A GLOBE OF STARS

The mention of Cairo brings back fascinating memories: Sun and Sand, The Nile, The Pyramids and The Sphinx (mathematics and engineering) and the Muslims.

The Sun: One does not have to spend many weeks in Cairo to realize that the sun is all-pervasive and almighty. Of course there are many places on the earth that combine sand, clear skies and supreme sunlight, but it seems that in the Lower Delta region of the Nile, the sun is there in all its glory for those who worship it as the Ancient Egyptians did. We tend to accept the sun daily and adjust accordingly to its strength.

The Sand: How could you ignore it? The entire airbase was built on pure, hard-packed sand. Only the ribbons of blacktop laid down as main thoroughfares provided any change. When a dust devil or twister came across the area, the sand they bore would give you a nasty sting. At night, during a heavy sandstorm, the halo we saw around our single light bulb hanging down from the ceiling, was made up of sand. So was the brown coloring on our dampened handkerchief we placed over our nostrils when we slept. Once, while returning from the city on the back seat of a motor-cycle, the engine froze at 40 mph. The shear pin on the drive shaft of our former Wehrmacht BMW two-wheeler failed to shear because it was a steel nail. Sand blowing across the blacktop highway provided us with a much easier landing in our very nasty spill. That day the sand was a real blessing for John and me, although we were badly skinned and scraped from the fall.

The Nile River: An amazing phenomenon. Imagine a river with sufficient year-round resources that allows it to flow through some nearly two thousand miles of sun-scorched sand. It flows along unimpeded by anything except a great man-made dam. The Nile is supplied by two Niles in the upper regions. One is the Blue Nile that flows out of Lake Tana in Ethiopia. It has a confluence with the White Nile from Lake Victoria in the south, and they converge at Khartoum in the Sudan. The Nile is the longest river on earth and surely one of the most fascinating. The Sudan is the largest country on the African continent. The joining of the two Niles, with alternating sources of rainfall, flows unabated, as if by a computer program, with unbelievable consistency and constant levels. It is truly an amazing story. I encourage the reader to find a book, authored by Emil Ludwig, a German author, entitled, *The Nile.* It was written many years ago, so it may not be too easy to find. I read it as a youth and it was as exciting as *Tarzan, the Ape Man.*

The Pyramids and Sphinx: When flying into Payne Field, whether from the east or the west, the Pyramids were a constant reference point. We knew very well where things were in relationship to the Pyramids. Through centuries man has wrestled with the question, "How did the early Egyptians manage to build those monstrous edifices and tombs?" I have read many theories, but I am not sure that I can fathom any one theory. As amazing as the Pyramids are, the structure of the corridors or chambers around the base of the Sphinx are unbelievably complex. They make the Pyramids seem like a relatively simple engineering accomplishment. The interlocking of massive pieces of stone with right angle couplings seemed to me to have been next to impossible to put into place without huge machinery with very heavy lifting capabilities. Even then it would appear to be a Rubric Cube.

Mathematics and Engineering: Very little can be built today without using the geometric measurement developed by the mathematicians of ancient Egypt. Egyptian *heiratic,* pen on papyrus, dates back to about 2,000 BC. They were looking into algebra, beyond arithmetic in 1700 BC. The plummet (a plumb-bob) was used by Egyptian builders to find the vertical in cutting and fitting bricks or stones. With such tools they performed engineering marvels. The stones of the great pyramids have a mean vertical variation from a straight line of only $1/100^{th}$ inch and they were brought together as close as 1/500th of an inch. Few of the ancients left a more impressive record of practical achievements than did the Egyptians. Their massive Pyramids are great engineering achievements and also masterpieces of mathematical sophistication. Using simple instruments like the plummet they constructed the Great Pyramid of Cheops so that it faces directly north, south, east and west and with an accuracy of an astounding one-twelfth of a degree.

Computing the length of a day from the earth's rotation was quite simple; figuring the number of days in a year was more complex. Yet in 3,000 BC the Babylonians had divided the year into 360 days- a rather advanced mathematical feat. Egyptian calendars were, however, even more accurate, with a 365-day year, which they then refined to include a quadrennial leap year. No one knows when man first discovered that a stick's shadow could measure the sun's movement across the sky, but it was before 1,500 BC, the date of the oldest known sundial.

An Aside: Rameses II was an ancient Egyptian ruler left approximately 200 wives and fathered 160 children. Centuries later, a U.S. company named one of its prize condoms, Rameses. We do not get the connection between a father of 160 children and a condom, but we do not yet have all the facts. Hello, Rameses!

The Muslims: Is the Pope Catholic? Are the Egyptians Moslem? You win a small portable prayer rug if you answered yes to both questions. As a general rule, at least from my observation, the Muslims were far more beholden to the Koran than is the average Christian to his Bible. They usually carried a prayer rug to work. They faced Mecca and fell to their knees five times each day to pray. On the airbase we saw them praying everywhere. Of course we were briefed not to act curious regarding their solemn ritual. During Ramadan, the holiest of seasons, which lasted, as I recall, about 30 days, the strict Muslim did not eat or drink anything from sunup to sunset. Ramadan occurred in July, the hottest month of the year, while I was stationed in Cairo. The holy period progresses through the months of the year.

Each day we noticed how various workers got weaker and weaker as the day wore on. By quitting time, some seemed hardly capable of mounting the stairs of their shuttle buses to go home, and sunset was still some hours away. Many Americans, particularly in recent years, associate Arabs, including Egyptians, with terrorism. I do not equate the average Arab or Egyptian with terrorism at all. They are somewhat like the American Indian, much maligned in the press, where the political factors are poorly understood. I spent three years of my life in Casablanca, Cairo and Tripoli; not once did I have money or items stolen. And, as I recall, we never locked our room doors, even if lucky enough to have a lock on the door.

Much of the hostility against Americans in these towns had political connections. In Egypt, the populace wanted the British to "Go Home," and fast. In Tripoli, Libya, the rock-throwing at the GI busses, usually by teenagers, was caused by the recognition of the state of Israel in 1948. Our president, Harry Truman, was a strong proponent of that United Nations action, which displeased much of the Arab world, particularly the Palestinians, many of whom ended up behind barbed wire for decades. It seemed to those of us who lived in the thick of this that there was a great ineptness in the whole process. However, when it comes down to deciphering the real truth of anything involving the Jews and Arabs, the situation is very curious, involved and complicated. Each group will no doubt continue to stick by their religious precepts and peace between the two will be elusive. Cairo was, and is, the center of the Arab World, but not the center of the Moslem world.

Throughout the Second World War, and long before, Cairo was always one of the most important global way-points. Field Marshall Rommel and his Afrika Corps fought mightily to reach Cairo, but only got as far as the western outskirts of the city. The USAAF Air Transport Command played a role in the Rommel's repulse by flying in very high priority supplies to Cairo for the Brit's Montgomery.

The city was a veritable melting pot in the Near and Middle East, and though the British were the chief occupiers, beginning with the 1880's, the city had also been influenced through the years by the French, who built the Suez Canal. In 1884 German Chancellor Otto Von Bismarck called a meeting of 14 powerful European nations and included the United States. The purpose of the conference was to divide Africa among the power nations, to establish borders and to enact barriers to trade, to avoid conflict. My sources do not divulge what the citizens in Africa thought of this scheme, but it was done. It appears that early-on the British Lion and the French got the pick of the litter, so to speak. Belgium got the Congo, The Netherlands got the south and the Spanish and Portuguese got various and sundry territories. The Germans had very significant countries under their government for many years and it is noteworthy that they had a great many Christian missionaries on the continent for many years. Ironically the Germans ended up with nothing after the First World War. Then after World War II nearly 100% of the colonies were transferred out of the hands of so-called powerful nations. It was called "De-colonization."

It was not at all uncommon to hear French spoken in the business district of Cairo, and most of the local male and female workers employed at the base spoke French fluently. Most well- educated folks spoke three or four languages, with Arabic being the predominate tongue.

Our new assignment to Egypt was viewed by us with considerable anticipation and excitement. With the cessation of hostilities, the overall world tension had been reduced, and day by day we would notice that things were done with a bit less urgency. With our move to Cairo our mission was oriented not just to the movement of troops, mail and supplies, but, when west-bound, we very often operated as Medical Evacuation flights (Med-Evac), sometimes having a full load of litter patients. We enjoyed the privilege of being part of a medical mission and became well acquainted with the nurses, doctors and medical technicians in their very important mission.

I had arrived at my new duty station at Cairo in September 1945 after ferrying a C-54 from Casablanca. Flying from Morocco to Egypt, across the breadth of North Africa was about the same mileage as flying across the USA. The scars of the WWII tank battles east of Tripoli and Benghazi and around Mursa Matru, Tobruk and El Alamein were just as prominent as they had been when I flew a B-24 from Tunis to Cairo in 1944. My new assignment orders to join a squadron at John Payne Army Air Field in Cairo were dated 1 Oct 1945. A large number of those reassigned from Casablanca arrived on the same date.

My good friend from cadet days, Bob Harris, as well as John Considine, my copilot, were also transferred to Payne Field in Cairo and we decided to try to room together. It was quite infrequent that we were all at our home base at the same time. We somehow arranged to have an adjoining room remain vacant so that we could set it up as our dark room for photography work. We gave others access to our prized possession, providing they knew a bit about photography. While at Casablanca we had learned something about developing, printing and enlarging black and white prints.

The John Payne Airfield was a gigantic airport. It had two long blacktop runways. Everything else was sand. The large area that encompassed all the housing and administration buildings was also solid sand, with the streets merely strips of blacktop. All the buildings were what we called "permanent" and brick was widely used in all structures. I recall nice plantings, both flowers and shrubs, around the headquarters building. That was about the extent of the landscaping on the base. Thus, when we had a "schmall" or heavy wind, the sand blew and flew; fortunately these storms were infrequent. Our officers' barracks were one notch higher than those at Casablanca, but the rooms were larger.

Cairo had been a huge Curtiss C-46 and C-47 base. The big twin-engine C-46 "Dumbo" transport could haul the same load as the four-engine C-54, but without the range. Until our arrival, to the best of my knowledge, Cairo had few if any C-54s in its mission. There were too few C-54s available AAF-wide and they were needed in transoceanic transport. We changed the picture considerably. One hundred and thirteen C-46s were parked at the far end of the base and "retired." (Each day, during his 24 hour duty, the Aerodrome Officer was obliged to drive his jeep out to the C-46's and count them…Ha!) We would, in the course of a few short months be a part of the European Air Transport Command while the North African Air Transport Command would shrink and become history.

The command in the China-Burma-India Theater, always referred to as the CBI, was a far larger command than the North African Division. Our efforts were focused in moving troops out of the CBI, westward to Cairo. Other transport squadrons, based in the U.S., also flying C-54s, flew them home to the U.S., mostly across North Africa to Casablanca, then to the Azores and Newfoundland. The passenger movement by the Air Transport Command was small compared to the tens of thousands who were sent home via surface vessel. Few people realized that there was a huge number of Americans in the CBI. Through the war years there were some two and one-half million American GI's who served in the theater, both Army Air Corps and

Army, and also a few Navy personnel here and there. Millions of the home front folks, unfortunately, were hardly aware that there had also been tremendous heroics in that part of the world.

The draw down was in progress, and once again we would play a part in the huge exodus. Our mission would continue for some nine or ten months, unabated, before we would lower the flag at John Payne AAF and turn the very fine airfield over to King Farouk, who would hang his name at the main entrance (but not for long).

To put our new mission of flying troops from Central Asia to North Africa in perspective, a brief review of histories of the area might be in order. Prior to World War II England was at the helm in Egypt and the Anglo Egyptian Sudan. Italy had commandeered Libya, Ethiopia and Eritrea, though the latter two fought and won their independence in the 1930s. The French ruled over Morocco, Algeria, Tunisia and lesser developed countries in Central Africa. The Germans, also coveting territories in Africa, like the others, had retained little of their territories after WW I. To the victor goes the spoils, and when they were soundly defeated in WW I, they were shut down in every sense of the word.

World War II changed Africa tremendously, the United Nations having great influence. After the war the British were invited to make their exit, *post haste.* Italy was totally toothless as a loser, and the French, slowly and reluctantly allowed the king of Morocco, who had been in exile in Madagascar, to return to the throne. Tunisia seemed to return to independent rule without violence or hostilities. (On a visit to Tunis in 1998, we found a thriving, huge metropolis, obviously prospering, and hardly recognizable). There was much blood shed in Algeria, and Charles De Gaulle finally called it quits there and withdrew.

So, in October of 1945, with World War II ended, the foment surfaced amongst the masses and the Egyptians rioted repeatedly to show their desire for immediate withdrawal of the Brits. Also, the many fractured local Arabic groups in Egypt jockeyed for turf and position. As American military, we did not understand all the ramifications of the hostility evident in the city. We were very aware that the city was often off-limits to the U.S. troops, and sometimes, when going to or from town on a GI bus, rocks would be thrown by boys, breaking windows in the bus. If we were in town enjoying interesting sights, and riots broke out, we were under standing orders to board the first bus available and return to the airbase.

Keep in mind that we were in Cairo only about half of the time we were stationed there. I figured that I spent more time in India than in Egypt. As in our flying from Casablanca to Dakar and Natal, Brazil, we were often back at our home base only two or three days before heading again to Barrackpore Air Base in Calcutta, now in Bangladesh.

We started our flying to Calcutta almost immediately after our arrival in Cairo. We would fly east, cross the Suez Canal, then turn northeast and fly almost over Jerusalem, continuing to Habbanyia, Iraq. We then turned southeast toward Abadan, Iran, which is at the mouth of the Tigris and Euphrates Rivers where they empty into the Persian Gulf. Kuwait, very close by, was an alternate airport, though they did not want us to go there except in an emergency. We would have a 10-12 hour crew rest at Abadan and then proceed on the next leg to Karachi, India.

Karachi was not the cleanest town in the world, but when we landed the Indians would board the aircraft before we got off and spray heavily with their aerosol bombs. We gasped for fresh air as we headed for the doorway and went down the steps. We were allegedly loaded with germs that could possibly contaminate the folks of India! We thought the whole procedure a bit extreme, but you could say they were at least trying to improve things. But why pick on such clean cut USA flyers and passengers.

After a crew rest in Karachi, usually in tents, we would then proceed to Barrackpore Air Field, which was well out of the city of Calcutta. There, in the early months we stayed in bashas, a simple thatched roof and wall cabin affair. It is hard to explain a basha as it had its own aroma and ambiance. Each basha had a bearer or "boy" who was there to make up the cots, do our laundry, sweep the floor with his brush, made of small branches, and run errands. Most of them were friendly, pleasant and were ready to do extra tasks for a rupee or less. They spoke limited GI English. Transient bashas accommodated four to eight crew-members. Rooms at the Hilton, they were not, but they did keep us dry in torrential downpours. We

167

always checked our shoes in the morning to make certain that some creature was not nesting or sleeping within. It was not at all un-common to have a mongoose cavorting around in the basha. They seemed to become very sexually aroused around a soiled laundry bag or maybe a pair of dirty sox. Anyone who served in the CBI will attest to that. They multiply like mink, and are therefore banned from U.S. soil. You get the picture!

Often, our crew rest in Calcutta was a bit longer than at Abadan or Karachi. During the first few flights into Calcutta we'd go into town. There was a Red Cross Club in town and there were a variety of tours for a very minimal fee. We took these tours to satisfy our curiosity, but then, bit by bit, we dispensed with the visits. It was more relaxing to go visit with the flight nurses, if any were there. Like us, they were all over "the line" flying a heavy schedule.

Calcutta is indescribable. Ten thousand Mother Theresas probably would make only a token improvement. It was overcrowded, the people impoverished, disease-ridden and starving. It was not at all uncommon to see bodies of adults and children along the road, or even on the sidewalk, apparently having succumbed in the night. I believe that then and perhaps now, it is the city of the world that epitomizes poverty, disease and hopelessness. One redeeming feature is/was that the dead were burned in funeral pyres called the burning Ghats and their ashes then thrown in the Hoogley River, a tributary of the holy Ganges River.

I had purchased a second-hand Bell & Howell 8 MM movie camera in downtown Cairo shortly after I arrived there and I took a lengthy bit of movies in the burning Ghats. Some years later when I showed the movies to family and friends, they really did not appreciate all the fine detail that I worked so hard to include in my Cecil B. DeMille production. The burning of human remains has long been the custom in India. A family of means could afford expensive, sweet-smelling wood for the pyre as well as the floral arrangements and baskets of rose petals which the children sprinkled around their grandfather's body. It made for a very solemn and pleasant service. We saw only the higher caste funerals, and I'm certain there was a big difference between the higher caste and those of the untouchables. Before lighting, the eldest son walked around the pyre and chanted a sing-song sort of melody. He would then light the fire while the family wept quietly. After the body was burned, the navel, which is never consumed by fire, is withdrawn from the pyre and taken to the nearby Hoogley River and placed there with further ceremony. We did not understand the meaning of all this, or perhaps it just slips my mind, which isn't all bad.

Our homeward-bound flight usually departed at about 0800 hours. In the first three or four months our loads were usually medical air-evac. Who were the patients on these flights? Early-on some of the air-evac patients were from POW camps in SE Asia. The present-day International Airport at Singapore had a huge POW camp, called *Changi,* for Allied military. The book, *King Rat*, by James Clavell, author of both *Shogun* and *Noble House*, tells most vividly the story of life in that camp, and about a gutsy American GI who made out quite well by raising rats and selling them to other prisoners for food. The book is fictional, but the POW camp did exist and it can be seen today. Its POWs suffered severely. Though it sounds revolting, when faced with starvation rat meat was really quite tasty and could keep a man going for a week, according to the story.

Many of the litter patients had tuberculosis. Some were other than U.S. servicemen, basically very sick Canadians or English litter and ambulatory patients. We usually had two flight nurses aboard, and if we were carrying more serious cases, we also had a Flight Surgeon, an MD. After the first few trips, the flights carried evac patients who were less ill or injured. Calcutta was the gathering point for all infirm troops who were to go air-evac out of the CBI. The large hospital there would group and manifest them and medical crew. We, the flight crew simply showed up on schedule at base operations and flew the plane to Karachi. As we got more and more acquainted with the system and the medical personnel, we knew what type of patients we had aboard. We would make a serious attempt to pick the smoothest altitudes for the patients' comfort.

On one flight we had a civilian "tech rep" who I think worked for the AAF but was from the Pratt & Whitney engine company. He had decided that he wanted to kill a Bengal Tiger before going stateside. As luck would have it, he and his native guide did locate a tiger. He, unfortunately, had a single-shot rifle. (Dumb!) He shot and only wounded the tiger. His guide dropped his gun and took off. The tiger tore the so-called hunter apart but did not choose to devour him. The guide returned with help and rescued the remnants of the man. The medics patched him up as best they could, but he needed far more expert surgery than was available in India. He was aboard our flight. He had to lie on the floor of the plane, because he could not be placed in a litter with so many splints and straps. A doctor and a nurse watched over him very closely. We stopped for a crew rest in Karachi, but the patient, doctor and nurses went on to Abadan and Cairo. For some reason, not understood by us, medical people seemed to thrive on working twenty to thirty hours without rest. Flying for that length of time and being on duty takes tremendous stamina and lots of will power. They made it to Cairo OK, but I don't think we ever heard the final outcome of the badly wounded patient. I saw the man when they changed some of the dressings and it seemed a miracle to me that he could still be alive.

As the weeks went by we gradually reverted to a passenger-carrying transport unit and each flight was filled with a full load of happy homeward-bound passengers. Our eastbound flights carried fewer passengers, but we seemed to always have a load of mail, small cargo, packages and the like. In December I flew a C-54 loaded with frozen turkeys which gradually thawed enroute. They were off-loaded at Abadan and rushed to refrigeration. They smelled pretty gamey to us and the smell competed with the noxious odor that always prevailed from the huge oil refineries at Abadan and nearby Kuwait. Maybe the troops in Karachi and points east went without turkey that Christmas. Our military was not completely out of India until June of 1946, ten months after V-J day. Closing down the dozens of bases was a time-consuming process.

After the summit conference at Yalta in February 1945, FDR met with King Ibn Saud of Saudi Arabia on a U.S. Navy cruiser, in the Great Bitter Sea. FDR agreed to build an airport for Saudi Arabia at Dhahran. The huge ARAMCO (Arabian/Ameican Oil Co.) was located there. Army Engineers based in Koramsha, Iran, close by Abadan Air Base, were chosen to do the job. The men at this base had had a most miserable tour in one of the hottest spots on earth. When they were told they had to go down the Persian Gulf to Dhahran S.A.

and build a new air base they nearly rioted, we heard. The war was over, many were draftees who felt that another six months in that God-forsaken part of the globe was more than they could stomach. But, of course, they went and built the airstrip, taxi-ways and a small group of buildings for a very small contingent of USAAF personnel to operate the base. We immediately started using it as our first way-point and place to RON when flying from Cairo to Karachi and Calcutta. I had the honor of landing the first four-engine aircraft ever to land at the base, and probably in Saudi Arabia, near the end of January of 1946. The base exists today and is a huge international airport. Desert Storm troops of the Gulf War know it very well. Though very few people realize it, American AF personnel have been stationed there ever since our 1946 flights, up to this day.

Week by week Barrackpore Air Base grew smaller. As it downsized, our RON quarters improved, as permanent party person-nel were leaving. It was easy to see things change. The attitude of the natives who worked on the base became a bit more independent, though not aggressive. The Indians did not care for the British, who had been there for decades. We were not held with the same disfavor; we were well liked in comparison, but there were things brewing in the minds of the people and it all had to do with independence and freedom, very noble motives.

There was also a very complex mixture of religious contests, far above our comprehension. As a base downsized some elements become almost ineffective, simply because there were fewer and fewer people to hold the infrastructure together. Security was noticeably lessened and thievery increased. However, many of the Indians who had worked on base for quite some time were very trustworthy and honest. The stealing was being done by outsiders, or off-base gangs. They came in the night as regularly as the jackals' screams.

I had some career "happenings" while at Cairo. The most pleasant was a promotion to the rank of captain. It was a wonderful upgrade and one I had dreamed of from the day I got promoted to first lieutenant. That is a common mind-set of one in the military. I was rather surprised about the promotion as we all felt that the promotions had dried up since the war was over.

Fortunately they allowed a very short list and then all promotions virtually ceased until the Korean War started. The fact that our Operations Officer, Major Vernon Elmore (Whispering Vern), was my roommate back at Homestead may have improved my chances.

We also met an Army/ AAF board in downtown Cairo to see if we could obtain a regular commission. All aviation cadets were given rank only in the reserves (actually AUS) at the time of graduation from flying school. One who could obtain a regular commission would improve his career opportunities and his chances for advanced education in military schools. A Brigadier General Vernon Walters headed the board interviewing all who applied. When I went before the board, I had already heard that General Walters, who was an Army man and not an Army Air Corps officer, had a very dim view of Air Corps pilots for good reason. They had tragically and mistakenly dropped bombs on his troops in the battle at Anzio, Italy. When I entered the room I noticed immediately that all the colonels on the board were Army men (non-pilots) with the exception of one AAF Colonel; he was a Flight Surgeon. He was the only officer who asked a question that was not a bit edgy, or so it seemed to me. The questions were along the line: "Why do you deserve flight pay, Captain? I probably fly as much as you do, and I get nothing." "What do you do besides fly an airplane, Captain?" When I replied that my primary MOS (military occupational specialty) was flying and I was flying almost the maximum number of hours permitted per month, I was told that if I wanted to go anywhere in the Air Corps I'd best learn how to do something beside drive an airplane about the sky, or, "Captain, get yourself into a specialty." I thought I was doing a pretty darn good job at what I was assigned to do. I did not get the regular commission I desired, but felt no deep regrets, as only one flying officer in all of North Africa won one. I would try again later and I would consider their admonition in the months to come.

General Walters, a man of exceptional ability, later worked for seven U.S. presidents and I have seen him many times on TV. He was fluent in several languages and I believe one of his most recent assignments was as U.S. Ambassador to Germany. We felt he could have lightened up for our interview. I felt like a dead-beat when I walked out of the room, but I learned some things and stored them away for a later day. The interview may have had a very significant effect on my Air Force career.

In early April, as I recall, I had sufficient total time in overseas flying to be awarded an Air Medal. I believe it was 1,000 hours of accident-free line flying in our theater. Major Elmore had transferred to Paris and he was replaced by an operations officer who had the reputation of taking to the air very infrequently. One day he saw me as I was preparing to fly. "To get your Air Medal, Jake, all you have to do is write-up the justification, with supporting documents, type it in final form, without error, and submit it in three copies, and you may get it." I said, "Ernie (his name was Pyle), you can take that Air Medal and shove it. I suppose you'd have us call our own formation and present it to ourselves. Don't look for an application from me." And that is how I never received that particular ribbon, though I departed the Air Force with twice the number of hours that the average pilot had. All of the others who were eligible to receive it, gave somewhat similar responses to "I hardly ever leave the ground" Ernie.

Another encounter new to me was a threat of courts-martial. Three of us were billeted in one room. We had one "tin" chair. We felt we deserved more, and asked at the billeting office if we could have one or two more. The indigenous employee said, "Sure, go around to some of the empty barracks and pick up one." He was thinking of "tin" chairs and we were thinking of something more sumptuous. We went to a barracks which we later learned was a barracks for transient field grade officers. We picked out a real nice wooden easy chair with nice upholstered cushions. On mulling it over, we thought we deserved two, so got another. When the loss of the chairs was noticed by the billeting officer he went into orbit and started a search. In short order he located the chairs and went to the legal officer and filed charges. He was Captain Cohen and he was a ground-pounder (non-flying type). He came across to us as having an intense dislike for fly-boys. Bob Harris was in India when we were ordered to the Commanding Officer's office, so he missed the fun. The Lt. Col. read us the riot act, making the whole thing much more serious than it actually was. One would think we'd stolen a Pyramid. He advised us to seek legal counsel and decide whether we wanted to go for a court-martial or accept an Article 104. We talked to an attorney in the legal office and he could not keep a straight face. He advised that we demand a court-martial, as he knew it would be thrown out without any action. We took the risk and did so, but were called back into the commander's office and dressed down again. While talking to us the C.O. addressed us as 2nd Lt. John M. Considine and First Lt. Harold A. Jacobs. Suddenly he noticed I was a Captain and John was a First Looey. He became somewhat disorganized in his chastisement and dismissed us. Later we learned that we had a softly worded reprimand in our files and nothing further would take place. Something did take place. We were back to one "tin" folding chair, but we had loads of laughs out of that fiasco. That was my one and only "brush with the law" during my career.

As our base at Cairo also downsized, some of our flights were shared with crews based in the states. Many of the planes we flew were their airplanes which they flew from the U.S. to Cairo. We'd fly the passengers and mail/cargo on to Calcutta, then return to Cairo with a load of passengers and they would then continue the flight back to the U.S. Soon some of them would start flying on to Calcutta. At that time it was our job to ride with them on their initial flight east of Cairo and check them out on the route. I rode with one crew whose navigator wanted to get rich. His scheme was to import tea from India to Cairo and make a huge profit. He established a contact in downtown Cairo who agreed to buy all the tea he brought back. This navigator knew very little about Egyptians or Indians. I was not in a position to countermand his scheme, though I thought it all smacked of contraband or smuggling. When we arrived in Barrackpore, he gave an Indian bearer (houseboy) about $200-300 to buy tea and asked him to deliver it to our aircraft which was scheduled for an early morning departure. The bearer disappeared in the trees and the darkness. The next morning we finished the flight plan and our passengers were on board. No bearer had yet shown with the sacks of tea. We were just ready to crank engines, when we spotted a long line of little brown skinned Indians from a couple of blocks away coming through the trees (always full of monkeys) toward the aircraft with huge bales of tea wrapped in hemp atop their heads. It took me back to the *Gunga Din* movie. The pilot delayed the departure somewhat while far more tea than we could easily handle was loaded aboard. Also far more than desired ended up in the cockpit bunk room; the aroma was almost over-whelming. I did not say anything as my job was only to acquaint the crew with the route between Cairo and Calcutta, and the pilot was in charge of his personnel. But I thought the people in traffic or operations would surely stop it. They must have not seen it as they did not, and we flew to Karachi with the tea. The nav had a friend who was to take the flight on west and he was to watch out for the priceless commodity (read contraband). We were involved in smuggling.

The tea arrived in Cairo, followed by the navigator a couple of days later and he somehow transported it to his contact in Cairo, who, of course, was in a most enviable position. The navigator could not take the tea farther, and he was forced to accept the price the Egyptian merchant offered, which was no more than what he had paid for it. The merchant knew tea and the nav did not. So the nav had to settle for the statement that the tea was of an inferior quality and all of his risk-taking and effort failed to pay off. The navigator was also very lucky that he was not in deep trouble with higher authorities for hauling, not *"Tea For Two,"* but *"Tea for Two Thousand"* across several borders. At least it was a legal commodity. It was a long time before I enjoyed a glass of iced tea.

Cairo had its highs. On one occasion Bob Harris, John Considine and I were out at the Pyramids. The routine entourage of dragomen with their long white robes and red fez were there to sell a camel ride or a climb into the interior tomb room. We had done that already. I do not know what got into us, but Bob Harris and I decided to climb to the top of one of the largest nearby Pyramids. The cap (top section) had been removed by conquerors so there was a flat plateau perhaps 25 feet square at the top, on which one could stand. John wanted no part of it. Bob was a very conservative type, although he held a pole vault record in the Big Ten. I enjoyed living on the edge-sometimes. This was one of those times. I had a small Brownie camera and up we went, slowly and carefully with each step, which took almost a max leg lift. In places the stones were broken and we had to climb around the pieces of stone. At the top, we, of the young and restless, looked across the sand laden horizons and felt like we were Christopher

Columbus, or more fittingly, Napoleon. When we started down, the impact of the stupidity of it all came over us. The 450 feet of altitude and the sixty degree angle seemed very treacherous. One misstep or a stumble and a body would bounce like a ball down the very steep incline and become one sad sack of remains. There were, of course, no ropes or any semblance of support or security. Gravity awaited a misstep. We descended in absolute silence, except to caution each other to "watch-it." The camel man had told us not to do it, but why should young, cocky AAF pilots listen to a smelly camel owner; he had only thrown down the gauntlet. We reached the bottom safely and we forthwith asked the camel man if anyone had ever fallen coming down. He said, "Yes, of course; a Canadian soldier was killed a day or two before." He was only a camel man selling rides on his aromatic camel, but with pyramid advice he was dead-on. Today I have solid proof; pictures of Bob and me atop one of the Seven Wonders of the Ancient World.

King Farouk, who was the heir to the Egyptian throne, if the British would only get out of town, was a playboy extraordinaire. He liked women and reportedly had vacation spots well supplied with women of varying pulchritude. One evening, and it was a rare event, about six or eight of us were downtown in a very nice restaurant. I believe it was Maxim's. Two or three flight nurses were in our group. It was just a group of officers from the airbase out for an evening at a nice restaurant. Unfortunately, King Farouk and his party were also in the same room with us. One or two of the nurses caught Farouk's eye and he decided to have fun throwing spitballs at our table. He'd take part of a paper napkin and dip it in his water glass, roll it up and throw it. His aim was pretty good, and he and his gang were having lots of laughs. What do you do when a King who is about to get his throne back, throws spitballs at you, for no other reason than he is a childish oaf, spoiled rotten and probably half-smashed. We would have left but we had ordered nice steak dinners and we'd never get out without paying, steak or no steak.

We ignored the King and he finally turned to other childish pursuits. When the steaks arrived, we ate them and then made our exit without further trouble. King Farouk, did, some time later, get the British out and ascended to his throne. However, the local folks were on to his follies and his incompetence, and he fled to a hideout in Europe, where "fired kings" tend to hole-up. His life span was quite short. He went the way of indulgent playboys and his name was obliterated from the entry way at "our" Air Base. He reminded me of the Pillsbury Doughboy, but with a fez.

I experienced one of the most eerie sights I have ever seen, while flying across the Persian Gulf one night. The flight west from Karachi to Abadan is over water 95% of the time. Apparently the Gulf waters were absolutely smooth, like a mirror. The sky was clear as a bell and there was no moon. The stars and planets reflected in the water giving the illusion to one flying at about ten thousand feet that he was inside a globe of stars. It was an amazing sight and one I shall never forget. Look down and see the heavenly bodies! Of course most folks when hearing my tale chuckle and politely change the subject. They also doubt my word when I tell them about the beautiful rainbow I saw with my wife while walking on a beach in Maui- at night. More recently I received substantial support for my saga, from a rescue crew that flew to pick up crewmembers who had ejected from an aircraft out of the island of Diego Garcia, in the Indian Ocean. They saw the same phenomenon and expounded on it profusely, saying, "It was an absolutely unbelievable sight!"

In about April of 1946 Joe Stalin made a big rumpus over a country called Azerbaijan, above the far northwest corner of Iran. He thought that he might as well grab it since American troops were still in Abadan, Iran and not pulling out. The threat to do so seemed very real to the U.S. government. Thus Washington told him we were pulling out of Abadan within a month and forced him to lay down his sabers regarding Azerbaijan. As you can imagine, it is not all that simple to close an airbase in a very short time, but we did it and much of it with our C-54s. One of the last flights John and I had from Abadan was with a load of female passengers who had worked in the various mess halls making that delicious Polish potato soup. The weather forecast on departure from Abadan to Cairo, was for very bad weather, like a *"schmall"*, a desert wind/sand storm at Cairo. Our two alternate airports barely qualified as alternates; not too great. When we arrived in the vicinity of our airport in Cairo, we were advised by the controller to proceed to our alternate, and he gave us their weather conditions. The runways at the two airports were not as good as our base, nor were the approaches comparable. I asked to speak to the operations officer and asked for permission to make one try. He was lukewarm, but said, "Go ahead, for one try only; be advised the wind is terrific, but almost directly down the runway." We started our approach on the old radio range. All four pair of eyes: the co-pilot, John, the flight engineer in between us and the navigator, Lt. Barkentine looking over his shoulder, peered ahead for the sight of the runway. At about 1,500 feet and descending I was "on the beam" but with a fifty degree correction for the cross-wind. John said, "Hey Jake, do you really believe that beam? Look at our heading!" He had the voice of a soprano. We continued the approach and the wind veered. At about 300 feet we got a dim view of the runway and the wind continued to swing around to nearly square on our nose. We touched down at about 20 miles per hour groundspeed and rolled out. When I made an attempt to turn ninety degrees off the runway, the plane, due to the wind, simply weather-cocked back into the wind, like a weather vane. The nose wheel moved sideways easily because of the blowing sand on the blacktop. After about thirty minutes of struggle we parked in front of the terminal with all those "wonderful cooks" totally airsick. They had run out of barf bags as well. Later John and the navigator asked how I could proceed on the approach with such an unbelievable cross-wind. I told them about my check ride at Homestead where I failed to believe such a strong cross wind even though everything indicated that it existed. Shades of Colonel Singing Sam Dunlap III and his sage advice. That was the second encounter with his words of wisdom that I had stored in my memory drum many months before.

C-47s, the trusty and dependable Gooney Birds, flew the shorter missions out of Cairo, to Beirut, Turkey, Greece, Asmara, Eritrea, Khartoum, Anglo-Egyptian Sudan and Luxor. Most of us who flew the C-54 had the urge to fly to some of the nearby exotic airports, if for nothing more than getting another piece of paper currency to add to our Shortsnorter. Because we were not familiar with the airports or routings, it was necessary to fly as copilot on the first flight. I had precious few opportunities to make these flights as we were gone on the India run much of the time. I did get on a few and the opportunities came about as my year in Cairo was winding down.

One flight was to Asmara, Eritrea. Why were Yanks at this remote mountainous town that the Italians had built up when Mussolini had his fist on the small country? Well, at Asmara, the Army Signal Corps, early in the war, had built giant radio transmission towers for long distant transmissions. I heard that they had only four or five such installations in the world; two others were in New Delhi and Hawaii. The airport was on a plateau at about seven or eight thousand feet and the approach to landing was tricky. One had to fly high above the forest until just before the threshold to the runway, and then suddenly the runway rose up to meet the landing gear, so to speak. The runway was very short, which added to the thrill. I remember vividly my one night there. I was asleep on my GI cot in the transient quarters. I awoke with a start as I felt something or someone licking my ear. I pulled a chain above the bed that turned on the light. A huge swamp rat jumped to the floor and trundled away like a small pregnant dachshund. He was one big and ugly rat, and he ruined my night's sleep.

Next we flew to Jeddah, Saudi Arabia. Jeddah is very near Mecca, a forbidden city for the non-Moslems. The airport at that time was nothing but hard-packed sand. There really was no airport. The Gooney Bird could handle the conditions easily. We were obliged to RON there as we had to fly some of the royal family to Riyadh the next day. I was flying with Hoot Gibson, a Flight Officer, who knew Saudi Arabia quite well. He told me that when we landed, two men from the American Consulate would meet us and ask us to come to their house for dinner. He said, "We do not want to have anything to do with them as they are homosexuals, so prepare your excuses." Sure enough, the two were there, and as Hoot had predicted, made the invitation. We declined and they left without further adieu. We then had to find a decent place in the town, which was the saddest place I'd seen on the face of the earth. The town was on the Red Sea, but even the Red Sea at that point was unsavory and ugly. Our hotel was likewise the saddest. The next morning we went to the airplane, ate some rations. Thank God for K rations! We watched the native boys gas our C-47 out of five gallon tins, which they slashed open with a machete. I have movies of that episode. The royal family members arrived and were seen off by the American consulate fellows. The passenger list included some males, females, children and two kids (goats). It was a very bumpy ride. I don't recall if the goats got airsick, but most of the passengers did. We never located Riyadh as it had no radio beacon, and there was simply too much haze and blowing sand, so we went on to the Gulf and landed at Dhahran. While there we saw the great King Ibn Saud, who had united all the tribes of the peninsula under his one kingdom. He was very tall, close to seven feet, big and impressive. He was, of course, decked out in his fine array. I was close enough to him to see large scars on his face, no doubt from the days of saber battles subduing his opponents. He was not at all a youthful man, probably in his seventies. I never learned how that trip was laid on; it was somewhat unusual, but those were unusual years right after the war. On this trip I also met Tex Haneke, the US geologist who reportedly was credited with having made the huge oil discoveries in 1936 in various parts of Saudi Arabia. He and Hoot, the pilot I was flying with, had become friends in the past two years and he invited us to his house at ARAMCO for a beer.

Next, a nice trip to Luxor and the Valley of the Kings. The base flew R & R trips to Luxor on occasion. I got myself scheduled on one of those flights as copilot, as the route and destination were new to me. It was one of the most fascinating excursions I've ever been on. Several of the military passengers aboard were good friends, including three or four flight nurses. All in all it was a marvelous three days and a great break.

The next new destination was the Holy Land. This was another base R & R trip, conducted by the Red Cross. Jerusalem is a short flight from Cairo, even in the somewhat slow Gooney Bird. We rode the distance from the airport on the coast to Jerusalem in a 6 x 6 GI truck and spent the full day in Bethlehem and Jerusalem and returned to Cairo that night. It was a great experience at very little cost. John Considine was the pilot on that trip and I recall that we had lunch and took pictures at the King David Hotel. Our tour guide was a Palestinian who claimed he was a Catholic. Since you could count, as the saying goes, all the Moslems who had become Christians on your ten fingers, we rather doubted his claim. We bought some bottled water, supposedly from the Jordan River, to have our kids baptized in the future. My bottle is in the bottom drawer of my dresser today, 5o+ years later. We joked that the water no doubt came out of a local tap.

A few months before this trip to the Holy Land, John and I had planned to ride on the motorcycle to the Holy Land. The trip came to naught, as the motor had seized and had to again be rebuilt. That was a lucky break for us, as we were far too ignorant and not well enough informed of all the pitfalls that we could have encountered on such a trip. The territory looked so peaceful and benign from 10,000 feet. We had viewed it countless times, but later we learned of the many problems we might have had.

Next, were Athens and Rome. Though Greece is not far from Cairo, I had not been there, as we who flew the C-54 four-engine transport were always busy on the long hauls. One day when I had the duty as Airdrome Officer, I went out to meet a C-47 coming in from the Holy Land. I met the plane because I saw there was a VIP aboard. The VIP was one rather inebriated Justice of the US Supreme Court. We helped this elderly gent with wobbly legs negotiate his way down to the tarmac from the C-47. The base commander wheeled up with a staff car and zipped him off to the VIP quarters. I checked to see where he was going to go from Cairo and found that base flight would fly him to Athens and Rome in two days. I checked the crew compliment and since there was no copilot assigned, crew scheduling put me on the trip. Two days later we were off to Athens. The AAF folks there took the Justice to see the Acropolis and to get some lunch. You guessed it; on their return, the man appeared to be in cups again and almost unable to climb the four steps into the Gooney Bird. His aid put down about six or eight blankets on the floor and he slept off his "spirits." When we landed at Ciampino Airport in Rome, he was in fair shape again. We all went into town and were billeted at the grand Excelsior Hotel. We bid him adieu and thought we had seen the last of him. The pilot knew the town and suggested we eat at Alfredo's and have some of his famous fettuccini. We went in a cab to the restaurant and there sat the Justice with two or three others. He appeared to be feeling no pain and insisted we join him at a larger table. He seemed to be taken with pilots. He drank too much wine and did not add to the ambiance. We were glad when the meal was finished and we could take leave. His relying on the bottle may have been because of fear of flying, or maybe his medication and alcohol and altitude produced some of this manifestation or perhaps he was too elderly to be imbibing, but I doubt it. So much for my first flight to Athens and Rome, two cities I would see a lot of in the next four years.

Bob Harris, who I had been with from cadet days, felt that he should go home and leave the AAF. He had married just prior to going overseas and was anxious to get home. He needed one more year of college for his degree. So, in March, 1946, John and I, plus many others, said farewell to Bob, one of my closest friends in the Air Force. (After getting his degree, Bob re-entered the AAF with a regular commission, went into B-47 training and was killed in that aircraft in a mid-air collision in 1955. He left a wife and three children. The pilot of the other aircraft was at fault.) While in Cairo, we three had discussed at great lengths all the pros and cons of life in the AAF, and I was the most positive of the three about making it a career. John was also anxious to finish his two years at Notre Dame. He, too, had elected to leave the AAF and departed in May for Westover AAF, Mass. He and I had flown hundreds of hours together and were great friends. I was the last of the three Musketeers left in Cairo and was very lonely, as many other friends were also leaving.

In June of 1946 I flew one of the very last flights to India. Facilities were shutting down now at a rapid pace. We hauled only high priority stuff out. The mayhem wrought on the many new beautiful USA aircraft shipped to Karachi started. It made me absolutely sick. There were acres of new planes, including P-51s. I had longed to fly one, but they were all smashed by bulldozers. It seemed so senseless that I could not take a P-51 for an hour's flight. We were not even allowed to remove a clock from the instrument panels before the big earthmover rolled over them and flattened them. They all must be completely destroyed in accordance with the stupid legal agreements drawn up by lawyers when the war was young. Today a P-51 would easily fetch one million dollars or more.

So the days of flying across the Arabian Peninsula, the Indian Ocean and wrestling with a C-54 in a monsoon-laden India drew to a close. (No more monkeys to dodge on take off or landing. No more jackals screaming in the sticky, humid Indian night.) The military was leaving Cairo at an ever-increasing pace. I moved into a nice private room with a shared bath; I even had a telephone in my room. Our C-54s were being transferred to other bases. Since I had signed the "indefinite" block indicating my wish to stay in the AAF, I was fair game for a personnel officer to send me to "wherever." I heard things that sent chills down my spine. I was a pilot; I loved flying and did not strive for any ground-pounding job. The personnel officer was talking about my going to Dhahran, Saudi Arabia. He said they needed a morale and recreation officer down there. Was he crazy? There were just a handful of military there, perhaps 15 or 20, and while I had to admit their morale was rock bottom, there was little I would be able to do except join them in their misery and depression. Fortunately, Major Vernon Elmore, who by now was Operations Officer at Orly Field in Paris, came down to pick up one of our C-54s. When he saw me he said, "What are you doing here, Jake? I heard that you had rotated to the States." (How's that for serendipity?) I quickly told him, "I'm looking for an escape hatch, Major; there have been noises about my joining those poor souls in Dhahran, S. A. I, hereby, on the spot, volunteer to sacrifice myself and my talents on the alter and serve with you in Paris!" He assured me that I would join him at Orly, as he needed experienced C-54 pilots badly, and no one was going to send me to Dhahran. It was an anxious two weeks before I received my orders, but he was true to his word. I could not believe that things had turned out so well.

During one of my last trips through Dhahran S.A., I was approached by a man in Base Operations. He was from Aramco Oil Company. He asked if I would be interested in a job flying for Aramco. I knew very little about the job, but I did know they were just starting to buy DC-6s. I told him that my plans were to remain with the AAF and the most generous salary he offered, though tempting, did not alter my plans; I had seen enough of that part of the world for awhile. I then inquired, "How did you happen to be here and offer me a job? You don't really know anything about me, do you?" He said, "Oh we've been on the look-out and making inquiries for quite some time. You are one of the chosen few." It is so nice to be wanted! Little did I realize that I would frequently see a great deal more of that corner of the globe, but, not once did I regret turning down his offer.

The eleven months in the Cairo assignment was a fabulous tour. I had made many new friends, built up great flying experiences, and had seen a great deal of new and exotic real estate. I was also a year older, Yipes, I was twenty five. But then I had a decent rank and was very comfortable with conditions, with myself and with the outlook for the future. Who wouldn't be thrilled; going to Paris to continue to fly the big four-motored bird, from the City of Light?

======================

CHAPTER XIII
TOUCH AND GO'S – PARIS

During the simmering heat of August, 1946, I flew away from my desert home at John Payne AAF in Cairo and was ecstatic with the whole scene on arrival at Orly Field, just outside Paris. It was such a great feeling to be in the northern climes again with cooler temperatures, green grass, shrubs, flowers and trees. The sudden change and the realization that I was actually going to be based not only in Europe, but in Paris, was great. What a fabulous and exciting change.

No friends would accompany me to Orly. That was a new experience. Always before at least a couple—maybe three or four good friends—made changes of station with me. I soon learned that most of the pilots assigned at Orly were somewhat new to the European Theater of Operations (ETO), and for some it was their first tour overseas. There were about 50 pilots and 15 navigators in our transport group. A few of the married officers lived off base on the local economy.

The pilots on base were housed in an old mansion-like home, appropriately called the Pilots' Palace. It was different, but very comfortable. It was near the officers' mess and only a few blocks from base operations. As always, a shuttle bus (truck) ran around the base and we used it to get to our pilots' ready-room. I was amused at how, in the morning when the indigenous workers hopped on the bus, each had a little sack lunch. And always, under the arm, they carried their loaf of freshly-baked French bread. The aroma of all those loaves of fresh bread was enough to drive one crazy. Of course when they got on the shuttle bus, they'd shake hands with all their fellow French men or women and it seemed they all talked at the same time. My two years of high school French did little in helping to translate their conversation. This scene, for some reason, is one that remains fresh in my memory from my early days at Orly Field. I think it was because of that wonderful aroma of French bread.

Our flying mission from Paris was to provide air transportation througho6ut Europe, and also to Casablanca, Tripoli, Cairo and to Dhahran, Saudi Arabia. We also flew some high priority supplies out of Roberts Field in Liberia in Central Africa. Roberts Field was a base used heavily during the war years. It was on the ferry and transport route across Central Africa to India, and was in the process of being closed down. At Orly we had C-54s and C-47s to carry out the missions. I was perhaps the pilot with the highest number of flight hours in the C-54 aircraft, but I also enjoyed flying the Gooney Bird (C-47). It was the aircraft used on many of the shorter flights which went to "new and exotic" destinations. Both aircraft were used for trips to Germany. Fortunately, I was designated an instructor pilot in both aircraft.

Very soon after my arrival at Orly, I learned that our entire group would move to Rhein Main Air Base at Frankfurt Germany in six or eight months. The French wanted us off their field as they had the big task of turning it into a huge international airport. During the seven months I was at Orly, each week I saw many changes. A new passenger terminal was being started and also a new air traffic control tower. The French controllers gradually took over from the AAF controllers who were prevalent when I first arrived. We soon learned that French traffic controllers liked to have sick-outs or mini-strikes which were most disconcerting, and unsafe, to say the least. Air France, the national French airline, slowly built up their small fleet of aircraft and increasingly became a factor in the airport's daily traffic.

Two of my earliest flights were to Erding Air Base, Munich, West Germany and then to Bremen, up on the North Sea. At Bremen I saw a number of F-80 jet fighters parked on the dock, apparently having just arrived by boat. It was the first time I had seen this new jet fighter, which I would later fly. Within a few days I was on my way south to Rome, Tripoli and Cairo. On return I flew to Oberpfaffenhoffen Air Base, 40 Km to the southwest of Munich. Little did I realize at that time that my wife and I would later live for several months in a small village of Wessling, just to the east side of this airbase. Our home there would be a "confiscated" Nazi party member's house, and very nice. On return from the flight to Oberpfaffenhoffen, I flew with a U.S. - based crew and gave them a route familiarization check to Dhahran, Saudi Arabia.

Upon return from that long trip I had several quick trips to Germany. On one flight to Munich we stayed downtown in a hotel right next to the bahnhof (railway station). The hotel had been bombed heavily and half of it was gone. The remaining structure was several floors high, but pencil thin. It gave all the appearances of being ready to topple if a slight breeze came along. Not much sleep was had that night.

Another trip to Bavaria was to Furth Field at Nuremberg. We had a prominent U.S. judge as passenger. The judge would be participating in the wrap-up of the Nuremberg trials, as depicted years later in the movie, *Judgment at Nuremberg*. No, it was not Spencer Tracy. The judge spent a great deal of time standing between us in the cockpit. He wanted to see the countryside. To accommodate him we dropped down to a lower altitude before reaching Nuremberg. I remember his comment, "What an absolutely beautiful country." And it was. I recall reading that General Eisenhower also said that Bavaria and Southern Germany, including the foothills of the Alps, were, in his opinion, the most beautiful and scenic spots on earth. At the time we flew the judge to Nuremberg we did not fully appreciate the historic event that was to take place; judgments were made that would be debated for years to come.

And then came another one of my lucky breaks; almost a routine dose of serendipity. I was called into the Chief Pilot's office and asked if I would like to fly to Washington D.C. Major Elmore said, "You are going to have a rather prominent person on board." "I can handle that Major, who is it?" "Jimmy Doolittle and his wife." "G-R-E-A-T!" What AAF pilot would not be thrilled with such an opportunity? "When do we leave?" "Soon," he said. "There will be three pilots and two navigators, and you will fly straight through with only fuel stops at the Azores and Newfoundland. Jake, get yourself prepared for a short alert and maybe a speedy departure."

I was thrilled out of my skivvies and when I told some of my newfound buddies back at the Pilots' Palace about the trip they turned green with envy. "How the hell did you pull that one off, Jake?" My usual reply, "Clean living and good looks. Oh, and maybe, also, that guardian angel perched on my shoulder."

We departed Orly with General and Mrs. Doolittle on the afternoon of 28 September and headed southwest to the Azores Islands, a nine-hour flight. The aircraft was not a plushed-up model, though they had installed a few nice, comfortable airline-type seats for the comfort of VIP passengers. Brigadier General William F. McKee, the ATC Commander in Europe was also a passenger. General McKee was somewhat of a rarity. He had an Observer rating, and, as I recall, he had flown balloons in the First World War.

We three pilots flipped coins to see who would fly the three legs. I was unlucky and got the second leg, the one from the Azores to Newfoundland; it was the red-eye segment. Upon landing at Lajes, General DooLittle was met by the base commander and some of his staff. We all ended up in the officers' club where we ate breakfast, an occasion that was always a pleasure in the Azores. They were famous for serving the best breakfast "on the line" and they served it 24 hours a day. I remember I had hot cakes and scrambled eggs, with blueberry syrup. "Oh, come on, how could you remember that?" It is easy, as that is what I had every time I touched down on that island. Very soon after we had eaten we were in the air and headed for Harmon Field in Newfoundland. I was in the left seat and looking at a long night ahead. General Doolittle from time to time came to the cockpit to stretch his legs and visit with us. Our conversation was not about the war or even airplanes which we'd loved to have had him talk about: such as *"Thirty Seconds Over Tokyo"* or flying the Gee Bee, or a hundred other great exploits he could relate. It was a very casual and mundane conversation, but interesting. He spent some time with the navigators also, watching them plot their Loran lines and taking celestial shots for three star fixes. He was interested in all aspects of the flight though I'm sure none of the basics were at all new to him.

Upon arrival at Harmon after ten hours of flying, we learned that we'd be landing to the southwest with a non-precision approach that would be unusually steep due to the terrain. I had not landed on that runway before, which was not a big deal. But due to fatigue factor and very turbulent air, I came in a bit fast and high on the final approach. When I saw that it was going to be a questionable situation, though I hated to do it, I advanced the power, raised the gear and flaps and went around for a second approach and landing. All went fine on the second approach, but I was unhappy with the whole scene. It was simply that in all my days flying big aircraft, I had never had occasion to do that, and certainly not with one of the greatest heroes of World War II aboard.

My next contact with General Doolittle was in about 1992 or 1993. I attended a celebration at the San Diego Aerospace Museum where Jimmy Doolittle was a guest of honor. The museum sold pictures of several celebrities who were being honored that evening. One could buy a picture (the proceeds going to the museum) and the celebrity guest would autograph his picture. Before going to the event, I looked up the date I had flown Jimmy Doolittle to Washington D.C. When I took my picture to him for an autograph, I mentioned that I had flown him and his wife from Paris to Washington D.C. in September 1946. I had to repeat the comment again. Like all older pilots, his hearing was shot. His reply was brief. "That is ancient history. I'd just as soon not talk about ancient history." So I did not get to personally apologize to him for coming in hot and high at Harmon Field, Newfoundland, way back in nineteen hundred and forty-six.

I had written my old buddy from our Casa and Cairo days, Jack Considine, and told him of my trip. On arrival in Washington, D.C. I called him and he flew down from Westover AAF. Mass. His uncle, of World War I vintage, was a Colonel and Chief of Staff for General Harold L. George, Commanding General of the Air Transport Command. Jack wanted me to meet his Uncle Tommy. So we went to ATC Headquarters and marched into the CG's office like we were colonels or higher. Of course Uncle Tommy welcomed his nephew and friend (me) cordially and took us in to meet Lt. General Harold L.George. Who else was in the general's office but General McKee, who had flown over from Paris with us. General McKee looked at me with a dumbfounded expression as if to say, "What in hell's name are you doing here Captain?" It was explained quickly, but for a moment, there was one very surprised brigadier general. After a few days in the capitol we returned to Paris. It was a fine trip.

After the return flight to Paris I made a flight to Roberts Field, Liberia. I do not remember specifics about the flight itself, but I recall that it was one of the last flights into that airfield before the AAF pulled out. We, as always, were hauling out essentials and leaving the non-essentials and the heavy stuff behind. A captain and four or five enlisted men stationed at Roberts were to be flown out on the last flight out. I had become fairly well acquainted with the captain, simply as one of the pilots he saw every week or ten days. He was a fine young man, very efficient, personable and willing to oblige. He seemed to be doing a fine job in closing things down. He was looking forward to flying out soon for a permanent change of station. As in all such places there are many indigenous personnel who do a lot of the grunt work, like working on the grounds, in the mess hall, and in the quarters. We were also aware that there was considerable unrest between civilians of various political factions who were vying for more turf and more power.

We said goodbye to the captain at base ops, departed Roberts and flew back to Orly. A couple of days after our return, another pilot asked if I had just come back from Roberts Field in Liberia. I replied in the affirmative. He said, "You were lucky Jake; right after you left, the blacks killed the captain and the enlisted troops—hacked them to death with machetes." I was stunned and saddened. I had no idea that there was that much tension. Firestone Rubber had a huge plantation nearby and we assumed that that was a very stabilizing factor, as they had been there long before the war started.

"Didn't you have any fun-times in Paris?" you ask. Well, sure, we had good times. We went into the City of Light, saw shows like The Follies Bergere and The Casino De Paree, went to a few night spots around Pigalle, did some sight-seeing, shopped, and bought watercolor artwork along the Left Bank. We even attended the Opera a night or two—perched in about the 5th balcony looking almost vertically at one-half of the stage; the result of buying a cheap walk-in, last minute ticket.

However, because we flew the C-54, we spent a lot of time in Rome, Tripoli, and Cairo, on Dhahran S.A. turn-around trips. Many days each month were spent away from Paris.

There was a lady in town, somewhat associated with the USO or the Red Cross, who often brought a busload of young damsels to the officers' club for Saturday night dances. The young ladies were nice girls, but we all knew that they, plus their chaperone, just may be (not for sure, but just maybe) looking for future husbands. *C,est la vie*. I don't recall a single acquaintance who married a French girl at that time. I have no idea why things happened that way. But later, in Germany, wedding vows with frauleins were much more prevalent, once the non-fraternization rules were lifted. What does this prove? Absolutely nothing at all.

One rather rainy day I was called into Major Bailey's office and told that a Colonel from the American Embassy was coming out to Orly and Major Bailey wanted me to fly with him. The Colonel wanted to have a look at some French airfields out on the Cherbourg Peninsula and to the south. He wanted to fly visual flight rules (VFR). When he arrived, he and I went into the weather station and were briefed. It looked a bit doubtful as to whether we could fly VFR. He wanted to fly in the C-47 and he decided we would proceed VFR and if we could not maintain VFR we would turn around and head back to Orly.

We departed and headed west. We had to steadily lower our altitude to stay visual. I suggested we call ATC and get an instrument clearance to Cherbourg and when we got there, simply make an instrument approach and see if we could carry on with what he wanted to see in that area. I could tell from his actions that he really didn't want to fly instruments. He admitted that instrument flying was not his *forte* and jokingly told me that instrument flying came just below bailing out. As a ten-month instrument instructor and having flown with pilots with varying rank and ability, I had developed a technique for easing a nervous pilot into doing his best and keeping him at ease. The Colonel was nervous, but did quite well. In my mind he was learning more about instrument flying, which was more important than seeing those small airports on the coast. It also was obvious from weather reports that we would not get to do what we had set out to accomplish anyway. I called traffic control and filed a flight plan back to Paris using a triangular course so we'd get a bit more flying time. The Colonel flew on, doing well at the controls, all the way back to Orly. At Orly he made a GCA (ground controlled instrument approach). He did a fine job in the approach and made one of the softest and smoothest C-47 landings I have ever seen. He was pleased as punch and was so hopped-up about how well he'd done. He stood and talked with me when we got back to operations for quite some time. He then dropped the bomb. "Captain, I'm going to get you transferred to the U.S. Embassy where you will be my Assistant Air Attaché." WHOA! I think the Colonel thought that I'd be very happy with such an opportunity. I tried to break it to him as smoothly as possible that I was not sure about working at the Embassy and that I was a short-timer and due to go stateside. He said, "I can circumvent any of those problems. I want you to think this over very seriously. I will call you in a day or two, or maybe I'll come out and we can try this trip again."

Well, he did call and I, with respect and as politely as I could, told him that after considering everything, I'd like him to consider one of the other pilots. He was displeased with my answer and told me to think about it some more. He said it would be a career-enhancing move. He showed he was not happy by saying, "Captain, I guess you realize that I can have you transferred whether you want the transfer or not." I said, "Yes, Sir, I fully realize that, and I will give it more thought." He was a very decent man and I might have been very pleased with such a job, but not at that time. I talked with Major Bailey and he said he would talk again with the colonel. The offer was dropped and I heard nothing more about it. Later I wondered if the major and the colonel knew more about this from the very start than was told to me. That was one of the opportunities I had, that would have made a drastic swing in my career.

In early December, another officer and I flew to Fuerstenfeldbruck Air Base southwest of Munich. We were to meet a board and attempt to convince them that we should be given regular commissions. Again we took a written test and met a board. This board was composed of about eight AAF colonels. Once again came the question, "What do you do Captain?" "I fly. My primary job is a pilot, and I fly C-54s throughout Europe, to North Africa and to Saudi Arabia. It is a full time job." Once again came the comment, "Pilots are a dime-a-dozen. What else can you do?" I could tell by the way things were going, that if I were not a PX Officer or perhaps a Billeting Officer, I just wasn't in the competition. One nice colonel, who actually had an effect on my Air Force career, said, "Captain, I very strongly recommend that you go to a specialty school when you return to the states. Without a specialty of some kind, you will be very lucky to stay in the Air Force for 20 years. Do you have any preference?" I told him that I had considered training to become an aircraft maintenance officer. I was dismissed. Later, I got a form letter saying I did not make the cut. I was not a bit surprised, but certainly disappointed. (Seven years later, I would be stationed at Fuerstenfeldbruck Air Base for two years.)

In December '46 a new navigator checked in. His name was Jerry Post and, along with flying as a nav, he also worked in the scheduling section. He put himself on a flight with me and I think from that time forward he was almost the permanent navigator on my crew. We hit it off very well. He was a very meticulous navigator and one of the very best, though younger and not as experienced as some of the older hands. We became very good friends and remain so today, fifty-plus years later. Jerry retired from the Air Force with the rank of Lieutenant General. Three stars.

One of the more harrowing flight experiences in all my years of flying is worth relating. It is not a saga of heroics but rather one that harkens back to the sage advice of Singing Sam Dunlop III, the Colonel at Homestead Florida who seemed to possess an abundance of sound advice. One such proverb was, "Every once in a while when things are going pretty well, and even though your plans are well laid, things can start to go wrong. For some strange reason, little bad things turn into major problems that accumulate, and before you realize it, you can be in very serious trouble. It is part of this profession. You must be prepared to cope when bad things start to accumulate and build up."

We were on a routine flight from Paris to Casablanca, again, for another base closure. The weather forecaster said that there was a very good chance of wing and propeller icing at our flight altitude and that the westerly winds aloft would be very strong. As always, we had two alternate airports listed in our flight clearance and we knew that, though neither had real good weather, they met the minimum requirements. We proceeded en-route, and, as forecast, we had wing and propeller ice about as heavy as I had ever seen. We lowered our altitude and got rid of most of the ice. But the winds proved to be even stronger than forecast. Abeam Lisbon (to the west of us) we checked their weather and it was borderline as an alternate; but, by regulation, it was still acceptable. Casablanca was near minimums and

Port Lyautey, our nearby first alternate was still adequate. We flew on, but our gas consumption was higher than normal because of the earlier icing, the lower altitude and the prolonged flight time caused by stronger winds. We arrived in the vicinity of Casa and were informed that the field had just gone below minimums for landing. We asked for the Port Lyautey and Lisbon weather. "Lisbon had just gone below minimums also," the controller said. We had only one field available and that was Port Lyautey, a U.S. Navy airfield only 80 miles north of Casablanca.

We proceeded to Port Lyautey and started our instrument ap—proach using the non-directional beacon. We were inbound to the field and down to about 1,000 feet over the Atlantic. It was pitch black; the beacon that we were homing on went off the air; dead. The controller called immediately and excitedly informed us that there was a failure light on the beacon equipment in the tower and asked, "What are your intentions?" We executed a missed approach procedure and climbed. Our options were very few. We asked if he could get a technician to make a repair. He discouraged that because of constraints of time; a man would have to be located, and that was not a sure thing. "Sir, I'd suggest you go to your other alternate." Our destination and the other alternate airport were closed by weather. We were down to near-zero options.

Having flown a training course at Marrakech, Morocco, in early '45, I knew of their beautiful weather, just like Palm Springs, California. I asked Jerry, the navigator, to give me a heading for Marrakech, and to the radio operator, a request for the latest weather and to find out if the airfield was operational. I also asked the flight engineer to closely re-compute our fuel reserve. We got a report on the weather and it was clear at Marrakech. Our fuel remaining was minimal for the flight, and no one could tell us whether or not the French operated the field after sunset. It was very late at night. We climbed on course to about ten thousand feet. There are menacing mountains around Marrakech. About half-way to Marrakech, about an hour flight, we broke into clear weather, with a beautiful full moon. We came in over the city and saw no lights at the airfield. We could not contact anyone on their radio frequencies. All of our fuel tanks were nearly empty. I ordered all to fit parachutes, just in case the engines started failing from fuel exhaustion. We circled the airport and Jerry kept calling on the radio's emergency frequency. *"Bonsoir, Monsieur, Lamp Electrique s'il vous plait...Bonsoir, Lamp Electrique, s'il vous plait."* I directed those that wanted to bail, to get prepared; I was going to try to land by moon-light. Nobody made a move. They'd go with me and the moonlight, even if it were dead-stick and very silent or coughing engines. If I'd not been so pre-occupied with the whole scene, I would have been flattered.

Lindy had arrived over Paris after a 33 and one-half hour solo-flight. Before departure from the U.S. he could not find any information on the exact location of Le Bourget Airport relative to the city center. It was dark, he was fatigued, but he eventually located the airport as there were thousands of car lights on the highway - Parisians driving to Le Bourget to welcome him. Flood lights were laid out to assist, after some side-slips to lose altitude in the lightened aircraft, he touched down amidst the throng, and into the history books.

Eureka! The Marrakech Airfield runway lights came on and the aerodrome lit up. We made a quick turn, diving into a very short final approach, and landed. We parked and I asked the engineer to stick the tanks, (with the measuring stick we had for such purposes) so we would know how accurate the gauges were. He did so, and said nothing. I said, "Sgt Patton, how did the remaining fuel look?" He said, "Captain, you really don't want to know...but, if you must, two of the four we were using fuel from, were dry. We must have used the fumes or the last teaspoonful pulling into our parking spot." Not profound, no heroics, not historical, but we all felt just about as good as guy should be allowed to feel after a full blown "pucker flight," and a very long day of flying."

I have not commented on the physical condition of the cities we flew into. As is known, Paris was not bombed or harmed during the war. I have read that Hitler ordered the city to be sacked as the Allies approached in their advance across Europe. The German generals simply ignored his orders. Everyone loved Paris. Prague was a very favorite city of Adolph Hitler and it was also spared during the war. Isolated areas of Rome were damaged, but not from air raids, mostly from rifle fire or machine gun bullets as the Yanks came into town.

All German cities were greatly damaged, beyond comprehension, and mostly from air raids. Wiesbaden, Germany was an exception, as the Army Air Force wanted it in top shape for their occupation headquarters of the country. Likewise, the northern part of Frankfurt, where the large I.G. Farben complex was located, was spared, and that is where General Eisenhower had his headquarters. The main building was a magnificent structure and compareable in the states to General Electric or General Motors Headuarters. The large I.G.Farben dining room building became the officers' mess. In the evenings a German Big Band played for dinner and dances. The band was very large- perhaps 25 to 30 musicians- and they were as good as Miller, James or Dorsey. It was a very popular spot and the food was exceptionally good. We went there when we had the opportunity. Most of the couples dancing were officers and their wives. German girls were not allowed in the club because of the non-fraternization rules that held firm until the Berlin Airlift started in the summer of 1948. On flights to Germany, we'd usually fly over and return to Orly the same day. It was always a full day, but billeting space for RON was still in rather short supply in Deutschland.

On the eighth of February I made another round trip to Casa. On the tenth of February, which was my fourth anniversary of entering on active duty with the AAF, we departed Casa with a full load of base-closing cargo. Very soon after take off we lost the #2 engine; the weather was not good; the sea gulls were walking. We returned and landed at Casa OK, and operations gave us another C-54 with another max gross take-off weight. Take-off was at 2330 hours. We lost #1 engine immediately after take-off and again we returned and landed with only minimum ceiling and visibility at Casa. It had been a bad day. Four years of flying without an engine failure and then I had two on the same day. My Karma did seem to poop-out, at times, in Morocco. The following afternoon we successfully departed again and were back at Orly at 2015 hours. I said to Jerry, "By now you must conclude that you are crewed with one totally snake-bit pilot." He just laughed and continued to assign himself to my crew.

Although I have told of many episodes herein about flights to Germany and Casablanca, the majority of my flying hours while at Orly were logged on the Paris-Rome-Tripoli-Dhahran S.A. run. On one flight to Dhahran we went to Teheran, Iran and then back to Dhahran before heading for Cairo. On the flight south out of Teheran one of Teddy Roosevelt's sons or grandsons was aboard. I believe he was with the State Department. He spent a lot of time in the cockpit. He took lots of pictures of our handsome crew and mailed pictures to me when he got back to Washington D.C. He also sent his home address and telephone number and invited us to come visit with him if ever in Washington D.C. Though quite hospitable, we thought that was a little bit odd.

On this flight J.K. Schnapp was the navigator. J.K. was Jewish and we were a bit curious as to why he was put on the orders to Dhahran S.A. as things were gradually heating up between the Jews and the Arabs. And policies were changing accordingly. Once we left Rome we were in the Arab World. J.K. laughed about it and said he felt safe, being in the AAF uniform. A couple of months later, when he flew with another crew in a C-47 over the very high mountains of Iran, en-route to Teheran, the airplane had engine problems and the crew had to bail out. J.K. walked out of the rugged mountains and made it back to a safe haven. He was greatly assisted all the way by the rural Iranians. Iranians are not Arab, but most are Moslems.

In late February and early March we flew a heavy schedule carrying supplies and passengers of our unit as we moved from Orly to Rhein-Main Airfield. Finally the move was complete and we were ready to declare Rhein-Main our new home. Orly had been one fine base for an overseas tour and I felt fortunate to have had that experience. My French-speaking ability, however, had improved only slightly. We would miss "April In Paris" but there would be other years to see if that month held any particular charms.

And what did I think of the French? Well, that is a difficult question to answer, as I had very mixed feelings. My maternal ancestry, though Scandinavian originally (read Viking), lived in France for generations, so I no doubt feel just a dab of kinship. France, I believe, at the end of World War I and World War II, was drained of much of its strength—morally, physically and to some extent mentally and spiritually. The cream of their youth had been killed in the stupidity of World War I and to a lesser degree in World War II. There were very harsh feelings between all factions after

197

World War II, i.e., the Free French, the Underground, the Informers and the Vichy French. In Paris things were more complex. Many young French mademoiselles had freely fraternized with German officers and soldiers. After De Gaulle entered Paris with the American forces in August 1944, these young ladies repeatedly had their heads shaved. I saw evidence of that when I was there in July of 1945.

To me, the average Parisian seemed somewhat distant and outwardly not particularly fond of the American military. But then again, a friend of ours who was a Parisian said, "Well, the French were not particularly fond of their fellow Frenchmen after the war." She was a political science professor at Sorbonne University who felt a deep sense of gratitude toward the Americans. She apologized for some of her fellow citizens for not being more appreciative. However, she had traveled widely, and was over seventy, so had picked up wisdom and understanding along the way. My wife and I spent 4 days in her home in 1983, and she enlightened us considerably on many facets of the "French History and Enigma." One must also keep in mind that the average Parisian is a very different breed of cat than the folks in the hinterland. It is somewhat like comparing a New York City dweller with the rest of the citizenry across the heartland of the United States.

And so we bid *adieu* and a*u revoir* to the French and a *Guten Tag* to the Deutchers in *Franfurt-am-Main*.

CHAPTER XIV
WHAT A RIDE!

Rhein-Main was a newly-opened base with monumental growing pains. We knew, of course, what things would be like as we had been flying in there from time to time from Orly. Being based there was a horse of a different color. First we learned that Germany can be bitter cold in winter and in early spring. Our officers' quarters were manufactured modular units grouped together with modular hallways and bathrooms. Though everything was new and clean, it all seemed so flimsy and temporary. The little pot-bellied oil heater never seemed to put out sufficient heat and the cold seeped in through the flimsy walls. But we were in tall clover compared to the Germans The people of Germany were in dire straits. There was a shortage of everything, and the civilian population was desperate and suffered greatly. It was most depressing to us as well, though we were only seeing it when we left the base. It was easy to simply say, "They started the war and we were the victors, and to the victors go the spoils." But it is not quite so easy to "flip it off" when you are in the midst of their degradation, poverty, humiliation and suffering. When we went to town, it was usually to go to the large PX north of the center of town. The bus from the base would drop us off near the *bahnhof*, and we would catch a streetcar to the PX, a fifteen-minute ride. All along the route the Germans would be picking up and stacking the bricks from bombed buildings. They chipped the brick clean of old mortar so they would be used again. Many of the people were elderly, or seemed so to us in our twenties. We saw very few youthful workers. The Germans appeared to be worn-out, cold and hungry. One had to wonder what kept them going; like robots they worked away at such a fruitless task, and with such an indomitable spirit.

There were tens of thousands of bombed buildings which needed to be put back together again. We would speculate among ourselves, "Will they finish in twenty years, forty years or perhaps one hundred years." They paid little attention to us in our warm, attractive uniforms, complete with coats and gloves. We really did not pay a great deal of attention to them as individuals, in their misery. The sight on every trip was the same as the previous trip; though they worked steadily, little headway seemed to be made and the agonizing picture never seemed to change. Little did we realize that this tenacity, stubborn determination and drive would, brick by brick, put the country back on its feet in a very few years. The compassionate and benevolent USA Marshall Plan aided enormously in the turn-around for the Germans.

After our purchases at the PX we'd hop on the streetcar and return to the bahnhof to catch the bus. We had all the chocolate, cigarettes, cookies and tidbits we wanted, and I always had a smidgen of guilt as the street car rocked and lurched over the patched streets past the folks with their wheelbarrows and shovels and their frozen dogged determination. I really did not enjoy the trip, but I made it several times. I often wondered how many of those workers lived to see the miracle of the new Germany; maybe not too many. However, a year later things would change dramatically due largely to the Berlin Blockade and the subsequent Berlin Airlift.

In my home town and in the surrounding rural area there were several farm families of German descent. My paternal grandfather and grandmother had emigrated to the U.S. from Germany just before the Civil War. Another family was the Klingelhoffers. We knew the family quite well as their two children went to our high school and also to our Methodist church. Mr. Klingelhoffer had two sisters who lived in the Frankfurt area. He passed one of his sister's name and address to my mother who forwarded it to me, and I contacted her. The sister's name was Gustil Brill. She was married to a physician. They invited me to come for a visit. Both spoke English well enough for slow conversation.

Gustil was a very attractive lady about 55 years of age. I would guess that her husband was ten or twelve years older. He had served as a doctor in the German Navy during World War I. Their temporary home was, like most, in a bombed-out structure. Their quarters were in a substantial structure, though it was about fifty-percent destroyed. The neighborhood was about seventy or eighty-percent destroyed. I found the address and rapped on the door. Gustil came and unlocked the door and then removed a wrapped chain that provided additional security. She told me that they had been robbed several times as the doctor had drugs that were targeted. But more often they were robbed of their food. They had the luxury of a refrigerator, but it, too, had a padlock on it. Their quarters were quite small, but adequate. In comparison to others, no doubt their quarters were considered well above average in thoroughly bombed-out Frankfurt. The doctor's medical services were most often paid for with bartered food or services. Money was almost a non-commodity to the German people.

Gustil prepared a simple snack of cheese, rolls and tea. I felt quite guilty eating the food. The doctor brought out a bottle of Armagnac, a brandy-like liqueur, which he'd received in payment for services. He said it was fine stuff. We had a small glass of that. It had a real kick, to be sure. The good doctor, after a couple of glasses, wanted to talk about the war. I was most uncomfortable discussing the subject as his views were far afield from mine. His wife sensed my discomfort and would change the subject. But he'd go right back to the war, expressing his views about the huge errors Hitler made. Much of his philosophy went back to the mistakes made after the First World War, a period that I knew little about. I did gain some insight on the current German thinking and it was a very interesting evening; however, I learned perhaps more than I wanted to know about the plight of the average German in their neighborhood. Gustil was an avid skier and she lamented that she would probably not ever get to ski again. I promised to return, and did so about a year later, when I returned for the Berlin Airlift.

Our prime flight route was from Frankfurt to Rome, to Tripoli, to Cairo and to Dhahran, Saudi Arabia. The powers that be decided that it would be more efficient to place a crew on detached service in Tripoli. The positioned crew could fly the Dhahran, S.A. portion; down one day and back to Tripoli the next. The flight schedule was very long and heavy, but only for those two days, as there was just one round trip a week. I volunteered to go to Tripoli for 90 days temporary duty. Back to the desert, which seemed to be in my blood, and yes, it truly had a way of calling me back.

I took a crew to Tripoli, which included Jerry Post and the best radio operator, flight engineer and flight clerk of our group, and for about six or seven weeks flew the two-day-a-week turn-around. The rest of the time we spent on the lovely Mediterranean beach at the base. To add to the pleasure, the consolidated mess hall was about as fine as we'd seen. Most of the cooks were Italian and they delighted in turning the food-stuff they received from supply into five star meals. At the beach we played volley ball at great length and started to get pretty good at the game. We also acquired fine sun tans. Every week one of the C-54 crews would come down from Frankfurt with the plane that we would fly east, and they would vent their envy at our fortunate schedule and recreation. We were actually flying almost 100 hours per month, more than the crews in Frankfurt. The so-called good deal came to an end when a different plan was set-up and we returned to Rhein-Main, where our tans quickly faded. But spring was in the air and we even went out and played a game of golf, on a very nice course, though I was new at it and had little talent at the sport.

I made application for maintenance officers training, as I was due to rotate to the ZI (Zone of Interior) (USA) in June. When my out-bound application hit the desk of Colonel Birchard, my commanding officer, he called me in to his office. He said, "Jake, we have you scheduled to go to the VIP Squadron in Washington, D.C. I realize that you did not know that yet, but you don't really want to turn down an opportunity like that do you?" I believe at that time it was the 89th Special Mission Squadron, the unit that flew the president, cabinet members and congressional members to various parts of the world. I explained to the good Colonel that I thought it was necessary to specialize if I were to continue with my AF career. He looked a bit dumbfounded at my reply, and told me that I was an extremely fortunate pilot to be one of the very few selected for that outfit, and I was being selected without ever having made an application. I was, of course, somewhat flattered, knowing I must have an impeccable reputation to be encouraged to cancel the application for school and go to Washington.

Perhaps I made a grave mistake, but I told the colonel that I had given it a lot of thought and would appreciate it if he would forward my application for the school. He just shook his head, and said, "If that is what you want to do, I certainly will not stand in your way, but I'm sorry to see you pass up this wonderful opportunity." When my application got to headquarters in Washington D.C., I was forthrightly put on a list for meteorology school since I had college math and physics. I learned later that the weather forecasting needs were much higher than were the needs of the maintenance field at that time. There are those "exigencies of the service" again. I had no desire whatsoever to become a meteorologist and about that time wished in the worst way that I had done as Colonel Birchard recommended and gone to the VIP Squadron.

And that, my friend, is how I became a "weather prognosticator." Or, as a friend and fellow forecaster referred to himself and me: "Weather Weenies."

A few days later, I received my orders to return home, or at least to Camp Kilmer, New Jersey where I would receive further orders. My orders read "surface travel" and when one has to cross the ocean that meant a boat ride home and not an aircraft ride. Very few people at that time were privileged to fly home, so it had nothing to do with status or standing. I had never been on a large ship, so I actually thought of it as a holiday or an adventure. I sadly bid *auf viedersehen* to my friends, and particularly Jerry Post, as we had become fast friends. But I was off on a whole new quest.

I took an overnight sleeper train to Bremerhaven and checked in with the boat travel office. There was a day or two wait before sailing, but time passed quickly and then came the time to climb the gangway. The ship was crowded, loaded to the gunwales. Though a captain, I was assigned to "F Deck" and had a choice of bunks; the top canvas hammock or the bottom canvas hammock or any of the three lovely canvas hammocks in between. Yep, we were one deck above the bilge compartment. I made my selection, as did a tall, skinny, youthful-looking blond captain about two feet across the way. He looked familiar and I felt that I had seen him before. We chatted as we stashed our "stuff" in various places, which were few. He then left, and another Army lieutenant from very nearby approached me and asked, "Do you know who you have been talking to?" I said, "No, but he looks familiar; who is he?" "That's General Eisenhower's son, and yes, there is a very strong resemblance. I have been stationed with him for several months and he's a real regular guy, a real straight arrow."

When John Eisenhower returned he was approached by an Army major who asked him to bring his stuff and follow him. John did as instructed. A few minutes later he was back claiming his old spot. I asked him what that was all about. He told me that they were simply trying to show him favoritism and have him sleep in a field-grade compartment where the bunks were only two deep and had box spring mattresses. He wanted no part of it, which was a display of character. I'm sure that he had to cope with that all the time. His steady girl friend was also on board the ship. She was traveling with her parents and her father was an Army colonel. I saw the couple often together, walking around the deck and he introduced her to me. As I recall she was an attractive brunette. I believe they later married and had three or four children, one being David Eisenhower who married Julie Nixon, daughter of President Richard Nixon.

In a later connection with the Eisenhower family, I met Julie Eisenhower who spoke at a fundraiser in Escondido, California. Julie Eisenhower was autographing her latest book. I went to the table where she was signing books and asked her if I could have a minute of her time. She said, "Sure, and gave me a very friendly smile. I told her hurriedly of what I have just related about meeting John Eisenhower on the ship, and asked her how her in-laws were doing. She said, "Fine. You mean to tell me you are 76 years old?" I told her "Thanks, but add a couple of years. The conversation quickly became boring as she wanted to talk about how young I looked. The light was not particularly good in the hallway where she had her signing table. She gave a tremendous speech to a packed Hilton dining room audience - riveting!

Everyone aboard ship was given a duty to pull, at least those with my rank or lower. An officer had to be in or close by each enlisted men's compartment. As I recall the shift was about four hours perhaps every day or two. I was assigned the colored men's compartment. At that time the armed forces were not integrated and a black group of service men on board was segregated in their billeting space. There was always a black NCO supervisor, as well as the officer, on duty. The bad part of the duty was the location of the compartment. What location do you think the black troops would draw for their quarters? If you guessed the bow of the ship you are correct. It was the worst place on board when it came to pitching and rolling motion. I often came close to becoming seasick, and would have to go out on the deck and feast my eyes on the horizon to stabilize my sense of balance. We had heavy seas almost the entire distance to New Jersey. No balmy summer breezes at all on this trip.

When we approach New Jersey I had duty in the bow, and, like all others, was enjoying the excitement of coming into our home country port. All of a sudden there was a stir, and the Negro sergeant began calling out names and instructing those whose names were called to report immediately to sick bay. I thought that very strange and asked the sergeant why 20 or 30 men were going to sick bay, when we were so close to disembarking. He said, "They are going to see the Doc and get circumcised." What a time for a communal circumcision ceremony. Another black sergeant who overheard the remark laughed, and said, "Captain, you know he's pulling your leg, of course; they all reported to the sick bay during the voyage and tested positive for VD. They will be traveling to Camp Kilmer in a separate bus." And that is what I remember as we sailed past our beloved Statue of Liberty, and into our USA harbor.

I was home again. Behind me were two years at Monmouth College and approximately five years in the Army Air Forces. I was still only 25 years old, with a wealth of experience in the air, and I still had a passion and love for flying. Having come to a fork in the road, I decided to "take it," as Yogi Berra would say. I would soon be embarking down a new path, a complete change of working conditions, but would also continue to fly. I felt my move was wise; weather forecasting is a career field that would guarantee more permanency in the Air Force. And it is also a specialty that is critical to, and very much a part of the world of flying.

As a kid I had made many model airplanes from balsa wood and paper kits, and I always picked the sleekest and the fastest aircraft of the day. That is where my interests were, and I never, ever imagined or pictured myself in the cockpit of a bomber or transport plane. Some would say it was a childish dream; perhaps. As a young man in college I continued the dream of becoming a fighter pilot and the flight training in the two Civilian Pilot Training Programs (CPTP) added momentum and thrust to that still, somewhat nebulous, dream. In Preflight School at San Antonio, when I had to make an almost instant decision on going to a RAF flight training school, the fact it would guarantee me single engine advanced training, and supposedly a path to fighters and combat, provided the answer. I said, "Yes, Sir," loud and clear. In AT-6 flight training I excelled in gunnery and formation flying and I loved acrobatics. I just knew down deep that I was destined to be a fighter pilot.

But things do not always work out according to Hoyle or the accepted reckoning or scuttlebutt. Many graduates of my 43-K pilot class from other single engine schools were assigned to the Troop Carrier Command, flying C-47s. We all graduated in early December 1943. The D-Day invasion was in June 1944; thus the timing was perfect for transition training and transfer to England for the big drive in the Normandy Landings and the subsequent push across the continent. Many young shave-tails were very disappointed in this change of direction, from single engine fighters to multi-engine transports.

So we single-engine graduates who blithely assumed we'd roar off into the Wild Blue Yonder in a P-51 or a Jug didn't have the big picture. Bit by bit we slowly learned that the exigencies of the service always came first. We didn't even know what the word meant when we won our wings. But those exigencies set our course, just as they should have, and it all was very hard for us to swallow when the orders were handed out, and the assignment revealed.

As I returned home, the world was at peace, or so we naively thought in June of 1947. One year later Joe Stalin would blockade Berlin and the famous "Showdown at O.K. Coral," the Berlin Airlift, would commence. I would volunteer to return to Germany for that effort, back in the C-54 cockpit again, hauling grain, flour and coal from Rhein-Main to Berlin.

In retrospect, I had to admit that my career, thus far was One High Flight and One Fantastic Ride. Without a doubt there were some assists by my guardian angel along the way. And, oh, yes, a bit of karma dust and maybe, even some black magic from my Dakar Giddy-Giddy. I wonder what ever happened to that Giddy-Giddy?

CREDITS

Alan Thomas, #3 BFTS friend, classmate and school historian. His research at the RAF archives at Kew, England was most helpful.

A.J. "Bert" Allam, secretary of #1 BFTS, Terrell TX for early history on all seven BFTS schools.

The late Harry Berkey, Secretary of Miami, Oklahoma Chamber of Commerce for his rendition of how Miami won over the Spartan School of Aeronautics in Tulsa, Oklahoma to place the school in Miami, OK.

Mrs. Lillian Taylor, #6 BFTS Link Trainer instructor and later president of the #6 BFTS Association for information relating to that training school.

The late George A Mayer, one of the instructors at #3 BFTS who later organized the #3 BFTS Association and set up several reunions in both the UK and USA.

Colonel Harry Witt who has carried on for several years as Wagon Master of the USA Wing of the #3 BFTS and written the newsletter for the western Atlantic (USA) group.

The late Leona Hollman, who compiled a beautiful scrapbook of news-clippings during all the years of the #3 BFTS's existence. In the late 1980s George Mayer had the scrap-book professionally published and gave a copy to all members as a gift. It is a treasure.

The late Richard A Roberts, 43-K graduate from Eagle Pass Texas, a gifted cartoonist who provided fine cartoons for all of his flying school newspapers. His cartoons grace several newsletters even today, some 50 plus years later.

David A Walker, AOPA magazine for early history on the flying schools in Arizona.

The Rocket Run, a booklet prepared by the Historical Section, Hq. North African Division of the Air Transport Command. It was prepared for the passengers flying the "main line" from Casablanca to Cairo to Abadan, Iran to Karachi to Calcutta. It is a fine booklet about a route I flew perhaps 150 times, so my personal observations, recall and knowledge is interwoven with those in the travel guide.

Mrs. Nancy H .Russell who willingly assisted me in many of the intricacies of MS Word.

Lt. Col. J.K. Havener, Director, Public Relations For the B-26 Marauder Historical Society For his Wealth of Knowledge in that aircraft.

Colonel Chuck Watry who was a tremendous help in leading me through the thicket and also editing the book.

And last but not least, my loving wife Madeline, who endured the lengthy experience and read and re-read manuscripts again and again; without complaint.

Printed in the United States
834800002B